Playing Outside the Lines

A Method Book Series for Learning Irish Traditional Music on both Boehm and Simple System Flutes

Leslie Anne Harrison

Volume II

The Primary Color Palette: Single Ornaments for Irish Flute

I0808772

www.melbay.com/30874MEB

WWW. MELBAY.COM

To Bob, Dale, and Kevin, my guiding lights for intellectual curiosity and creative problem solving

Also by Leslie Anne Harrison:

Playing Outside the Lines, Volume I
Tools and Foundations: Fundamentals of Irish Flute

Contents

Preface v

The Primary Color Palette: Single Ornaments 1

Chapter 1: Glottals 2

Chapter 2: Finger Vibrato 18

Chapter 3: Slides 33

Chapter 4: Cuts 49

Chapter 5: Taps 67

Chapter 6: Bounces 83

Chapter 7: BCD' Triplet 98

In Closing: Review and Next Steps 107

Acknowledgements 108

Complete Symbols Key 109

Fingering Chart 110

Accompanying Recordings 112

Suggested Listening 114

Additional Resources 115

Bibliography 116

Index 117

About the Author 120

"The music of Erin…can excite the most tender and refined,
as well as the most powerful emotions of which the human mind is susceptible."
—Francis O'Neill, *Irish Folk Music: A Fascinating Hobby*, 1910

Preface

Welcome to Volume II of the Playing Outside the Lines series! These method books are intended for both Boehm and simple system flutists who are interested in learning Irish traditional music. Volume I contains extensive discussion of Irish flute fundamentals (articulation, posture, tone, fingerings, playing by ear, session etiquette, and tune types, to name a few) and foundational techniques (backbeat and breathing). Volume II begins a close examination of ornamentation, but first, let's review:

A Brief Review: Preparing the Canvas and Sketching the Shape

Backbeat is the use of pulses to accent rhythmically important notes within a tune. It is as elemental to an Irish traditional flute player as canvas preparation is to a painter. Although backbeat is a personal choice and the strength, location, and frequency may change from player to player, it is an important part of giving tunes lift and drive. Its use and placement also *change* from tune type to tune type, with compound meter tunes using a different backbeat pattern than reels. Backbeat is critical to supporting and placing breaths, and it also informs the ornamentation we will discuss in Volumes II and III. As such an essential foundation of Irish traditional flute playing, backbeat cannot be adequately summarized in a single paragraph. If you haven't done so already, I therefore recommend you thoroughly review *Preparing the Canvas: Backbeat* in Volume I.

We also covered *breathing* in Volume I, a basic necessity for any flute player (or anyone, for that matter), but also a critical component of shaping Irish traditional tunes. Often built out of running eighth notes played at a very fast tempo, tunes present a unique breathing challenge to even the most accomplished of flute players. Learning where and how to breathe in these tunes is an art form in itself. The very best players will not only use breaths to shape phrases within a tune, but they will also create a symbiotic relationship between their breath and the music. A truly great player will make you believe a tune is breathing with them. As with backbeat, breathing changes from tune type to tune type. It is also an important consideration for the ornaments that we will cover in Volumes II and III. As such, I recommend reviewing *Sketching the Shape: Breathing* in Volume I.

Volumes II and III: Ornamentation as a Color Palette

In the spirit of continuing our art metaphors, let's review our definition of playing (coloring) outside the lines. First, it is *the interpretation and fleshing out of music beyond its basic written notation or aural version.* And second, it is *the cultivation of a personal voice within the rich and complex framework of a tradition.* Ornamentation in Irish traditional music is a fundamental part of satisfying these two goals and as such, it is a critical part of learning to play Irish traditional music. It is one of the most important parts of making Irish traditional flute *sound* like Irish traditional flute, and it will be one of the most significant parts of making *you* sound like *you.* In short, ornamentation is the individual color palette unique to every artist. It is so extensive and full of possibilities, in fact, that our explorations of the topic will continue throughout both Volume II, *The Primary Color Palette: Single Ornaments for Irish Flute,* and Volume III, *The Advanced Color Palette: Combined Ornaments for Irish Flute.*

So now that you are comfortable with backbeat and breathing, or *preparing the canvas* and *sketching the shape,* you are ready to begin using ornamentation, or *color.* It is said that artist Barbara Cooney yearned to work "in full color" when she was first starting out (Horne 93). Like Ms. Cooney, I clamored to work in full color from the very beginning. Breathing? Forget it, I knew how to do that. (I didn't.) I wanted to use ornaments, immediately. If I had been a painter, I would have been slathering paint everywhere without any basic understanding of color—probably on an unprepared canvas, without sketching in any artistic shape. Odds are my painting wouldn't have turned out the way I wanted it to, and the same was true for the tunes I played. What I didn't fully appreciate in my initial enthusiasm is that artistic endeavors benefit from time, patience, and analytical thought (at least for me). This is especially true if one wants to learn how to create a work of art from scratch, rather than be handed a paint-by-number kit. Volume II therefore covers ornamentation gradually and thoroughly—and will give you the tools to one day create the artwork *you* envision for yourself within the history and practice of Irish traditional music. With this in mind, *The Primary Color Palette: Single Ornaments for Irish Flute* explores ornamentation progressively, one ornament per chapter, with plenty of review and opportunity for practice.

How to Use This Series

You may recall that the system used in these books is one that I created to understand and teach the complicated and evolving ornamentation of Irish traditional flute playing, particularly for flutists who may already have a background in western classical or folk music. These books are not intended to replace listening to recordings, attending concerts and sessions, or studying and playing with great Irish traditional flute players. These books are also not intended to standardize ornamentation and techniques. These books are simply an introduction to a selection of *my interpretation* of Irish traditional music. They are a snapshot of how I understand the tradition today; they are my own version of playing outside the lines.

Volume II contains four different sets of exercises in each chapter: *Preliminary, Contextual, Combined,* and *Tunes.* In *Preliminary Exercises,* you will learn how to play the specific ornament being taught in that chapter. *Contextual Exercises* will place each ornament into a richer melodic context. *Combined Exercises* will then put this new skill next to several others learned in previous chapters. Many of these exercises can—and should—be played up or down an octave from where they are written. *Tunes* includes six tunes which you will follow throughout the entire series, adding one ornament or technique per chapter, in order to fully master and appreciate the complex and multi-layered process of playing outside the lines. Like many other method books, it is suggested that you progress chronologically and do not skip sections.

Throughout the series, you will find tips for negotiating the exercises and techniques, all of which can be played on both Boehm and simple system flutes. To aid in your progress, you will find specific tips that apply to your instrument, as well as general advice that applies to everyone.

Boehm Tip | Look for these boxes if playing a Boehm flute.

Simple System Tip | Look for these boxes if playing a simple system flute (also known as an Irish flute). If you are playing a simple system flute left-handed (right hand at the top of the instrument, left hand at the bottom), you will need to reverse any right and left references in these tips.

Transition Tip | Use these tips if transitioning between Boehm and simple system flutes. If you are transitioning from the tin whistle, use the simple system tips if you've decided on an Irish flute. Use the Boehm tips if you've decided on a classical flute.

General Tip | This advice applies to both flutes.

If you are not sure which flute you want to play, or if you are interested in transitioning from one to the other, see *Which Flute?* in Volume I for more information.

A graduated Symbols Key will aid you in your progress, adding ornaments as you go. Many of the ornaments may look familiar to western classical players and may have very similar interpretations. This is why these symbols were chosen: they are intended to build upon the knowledge and muscle memory that many players may already have. *It is very important to understand, however, that their execution should sound different than the equivalent classical technique.* The difference in execution will be explained in each chapter. Volume II will continue using the symbols from Volume I and will also introduce the following:

SYMBOLS KEY:

Volume I: Backbeat and Breathing	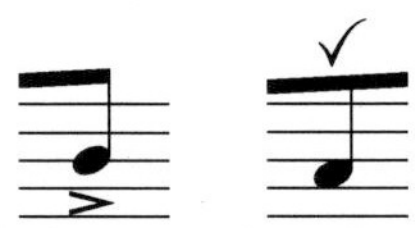 b. beat, breath
Volume II: Single Ornaments	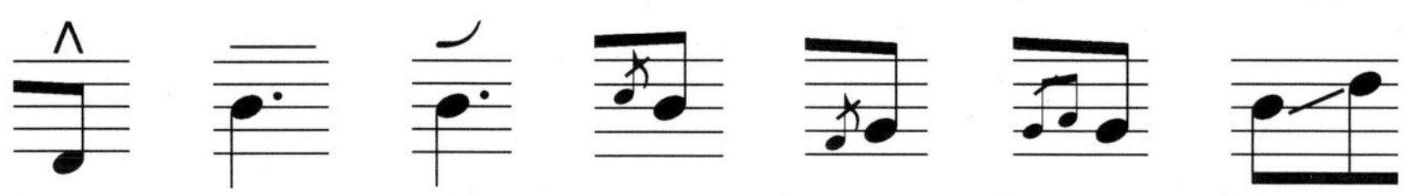 glottal, finger vibrato, slide, cut, tap, bounce, BCD' triplet

As we discussed in *Articulation* in Volume I, the default in Irish traditional flute playing is to slur almost everything together. If you do encounter repeated notes of the same pitch, you can separate them lightly with a tongued attack. However, many of the techniques and ornaments in this book provide an alternative to tonguing, and it is often preferable to use them instead.

There are accompanying recordings throughout Volume II to assist you. In each chapter, you'll find recordings that demonstrate the execution of a single ornament or technique, as well as recordings of *Boiled Goat's Milk* and *My Love is in America.* This will allow you to hear the gradual progression of these tunes, one ornament or technique at a time. In contrast, you will only find recordings of *Dever the Dancer, The Dingle Regatta, The Pretty Blue Seagull,* and *The Congress Reel* in the very first chapter, and then again towards the end of the book; these are intended to provide an accelerated demonstration of the book's ornaments and techniques.

 This icon will let you know when there is a recording of an exercise or tune. There is a complete list of these accompanying recordings at the back of the book on page 112. This list will also tell you which flute I'm playing on each tune. In order to provide a helpful listening experience, some tracks may be played under tempo.

I hope you enjoy Volume II of Playing Outside the Lines! Happy fluting!

The Primary Color Palette: Single Ornaments

"One person cannot ever name the color of an object to the entire satisfaction of another. The nerves of the eye do become more sensitive to color through mere practice of seeing, much as a musician's ear is sharpened through constant practice."

—John F. Carlson, *Carlson's Guide to Landscape Painting*

Ornamentation is one of the most important aspects of playing Irish traditional music. It is the color that brings a painting to life, and just as each artist tends to create their own unique palette, each musician often has a distinctive collection of ornamentation. I classify ornaments into two categories: *single* and *combined*. Single ornaments do not occupy their own rhythmic space. In other words, they do not replace notes within the tune, but simply amend notes that already exist. Many of these ornaments are also the building blocks for more advanced combined ornaments, which is why I think of single ornaments as the primary color palette. We will discuss combined ornaments in Volume III, *The Advanced Color Palette: Combined Ornaments for Irish Flute.*

As you begin exploring ornamentation, it is very important to integrate these techniques into your muscle memory so that they will be at your disposal when playing tunes. Equally important, however, is to make sure that the muscle memories you adopt are exceptional representations of these techniques. I'm not necessarily saying that you must perfect a technique exactly in the way *I* tell you to. Irish traditional music has a rich history of musicians learning on their own or informally with more senior players. As one flute player said to me last year, "I didn't know what a music teacher was." This practice has led to a multitude of players with wonderfully individual styles of playing and execution of technique. Indeed, this diversity is one of the richest facets of the tradition. What these players have in common, however, is a commitment to the *sound* of Irish traditional music, and a desire to play the music well and with historical awareness and integrity.

So when I suggest that you integrate an exceptional representation of an ornament into your muscle memory, I'm simply asking you to experiment, to find something that fits the dual purpose of satisfying your own ears and fingers as well as the *sound* of Irish traditional music. This will involve careful listening and critical thinking, it will demand that you turn your eyes away from the page, and it will require you to absorb and evaluate the playing of other flutists. You can start with the accompanying recordings and *Suggested Listening* in this book. I've included tips and exercises to encourage your progress and provide an entry point moving forward.

As a reflection of the wonderful diversity within the Irish flute playing tradition, many of these ornaments have a myriad of options in terms of which fingers are used. You'll notice this especially beginning in *Cuts* on page 49. You may not settle on exactly how to play an ornament right away and this is perfectly fine. Be willing to let your ornaments develop slowly, evaluating all your options thoughtfully and making your choice with intention. You'll find that if you're perfecting one version of an ornament and then find you like a slightly different version better, your fingers and brain will have already begun to internalize the sound and action of the ornament.

Chapter 1: Glottals

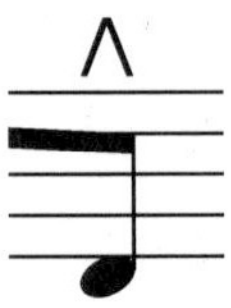

The *glottal*, also known as a *glottal stop* or *throating*, is a fascinating technique, and one that I'd never encountered before playing Irish traditional flute. This sound is created with the *glottis*, which is the space between your vocal chords. Some players use glottals often enough to classify them as an articulation. Others use glottals sparingly (or not at all) and may therefore consider them more of an ornament. For our purposes, we'll call glottals an ornament.

In classical flute technique, the closest thing I can think of to a glottal is the *k* of a double tongue attack. A glottal is deeper however, coming from the back of the throat with an articulation very similar to coughing—or scoffing. The closest approximation is to scoff an *uh* syllable. (Scoff a silently scornful *uh* to yourself; this is exactly what you're looking for.) An *uh* syllable creates a wider, broader attack than the sharp and pointed classical *k*, especially when combined with a strong abdominal pulse. The proportion of the throat attack to abdomen often depends on the player: some combine a softer abdomen with a harsher throat attack, while others use a powerful abdomen and a softer throat. The sounds on either end of this spectrum are slightly different, and you will want to experiment and find the proportion of throat attack to abdomen that you prefer.

When done correctly, glottals bring out the lower harmonics characteristic of a dark Irish traditional flute sound and oftentimes push tone nearly to the breaking point. In short, glottals truly make an Irish flute bark. They are also wonderfully fun to play. Conal Ó Gráda and Kevin Crawford are two players who use glottals to great effect (Ó Gráda's *An Fheadóg Mhór* also has an excellent discussion of the use and execution of glottals). Glottals can be used to separate two notes of the same pitch, to stress a rhythmically important note, or to give emphasis to a melodically *and* rhythmically important note. For now, it may be advisable to avoid placing glottals on melodically strong but rhythmically weak notes, as this will very effectively undermine your backbeat. My own preference is for using glottals to articulate the second note of a repeated pitch, particularly on notes that offer greater resistance by having the majority of the keys or holes closed. Ds, particularly hard low Ds, are my favorite notes to glottal.

Boehm Tip | Glottals, like hard Ds, can also spread and crack on Boehm flutes. Be sure to keep the same firm embouchure you adopted when working with hard Ds in *Tone, Color, and Intonation* in Volume I. The strength of this embouchure should come from the center of your mouth, not the corners. You may need to bear down hard on your airstream to prevent cracks. Don't move your embouchure when you glottal. To review hard Ds, see *Tone, Color, and Intonation* in Volume I.

Simple System Tip | Have fun with seeing how far you can push the tone on your flute before it cracks. With a strong embouchure, this can be pretty far.

Glottals: Preliminary Exercises

Since glottals are powered by the abdomen and articulated by the throat, begin by warming up your abdomen with these next exercises. Do not use your tongue or throat to begin the sound, only your abdomen. Exhaling a strong **ha** articulation will accomplish this nicely.

TRACK 1

1.

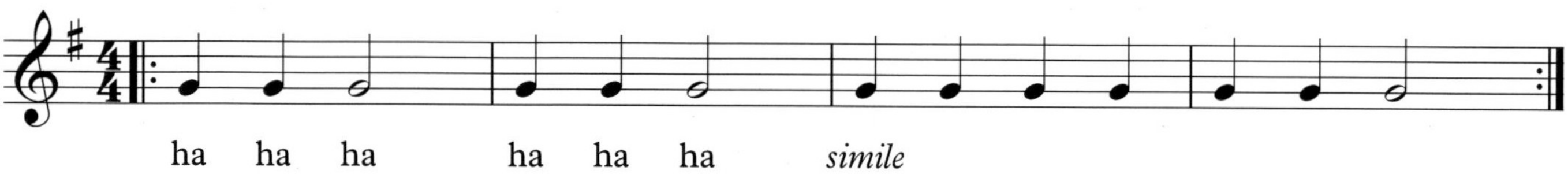

Play these exercises slowly. Every note should start with a new breath and abdominal pulse. Your abdomen should return to its starting position between every note. Do not clench your stomach muscles as this will prevent free movement of your abdomen. This technique will feel familiar since we already practiced it in *Backbeat in Compound Meters* and *Backbeat in Reels* in Volume I. If you skipped directly to Volume II, now is a good time to return to Volume I in order to review backbeat.

> **General Tip** | When working with **ha** attacks, do not get into the habit of re-forming your embouchure between each note. Glottals, particularly glottals at faster speeds, will require a firm and unmoving embouchure. Practice this concept now during these preliminary exercises.

2.

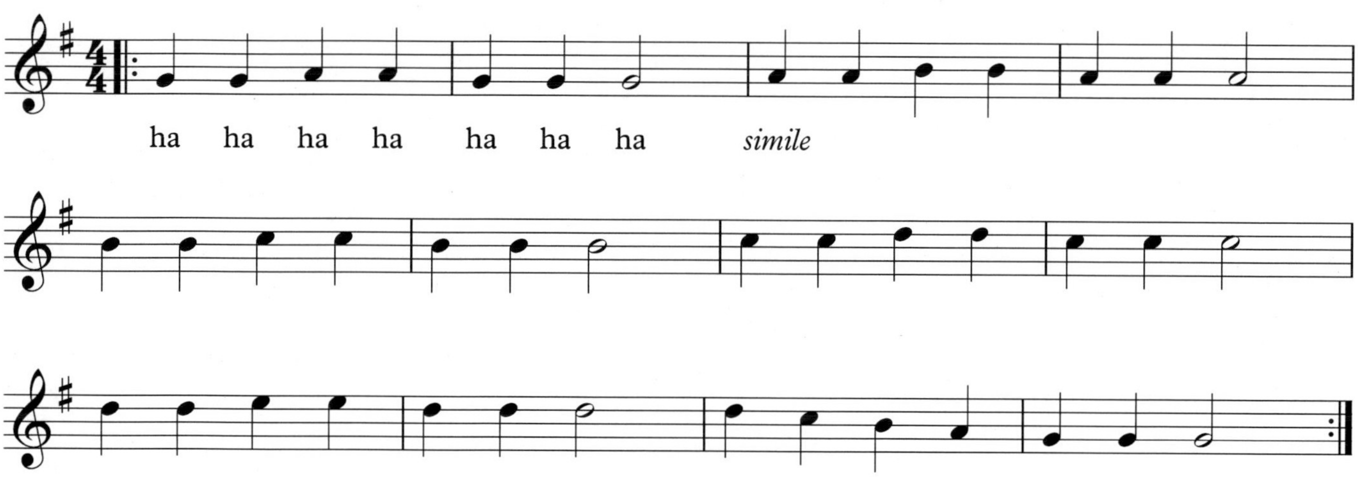

3.

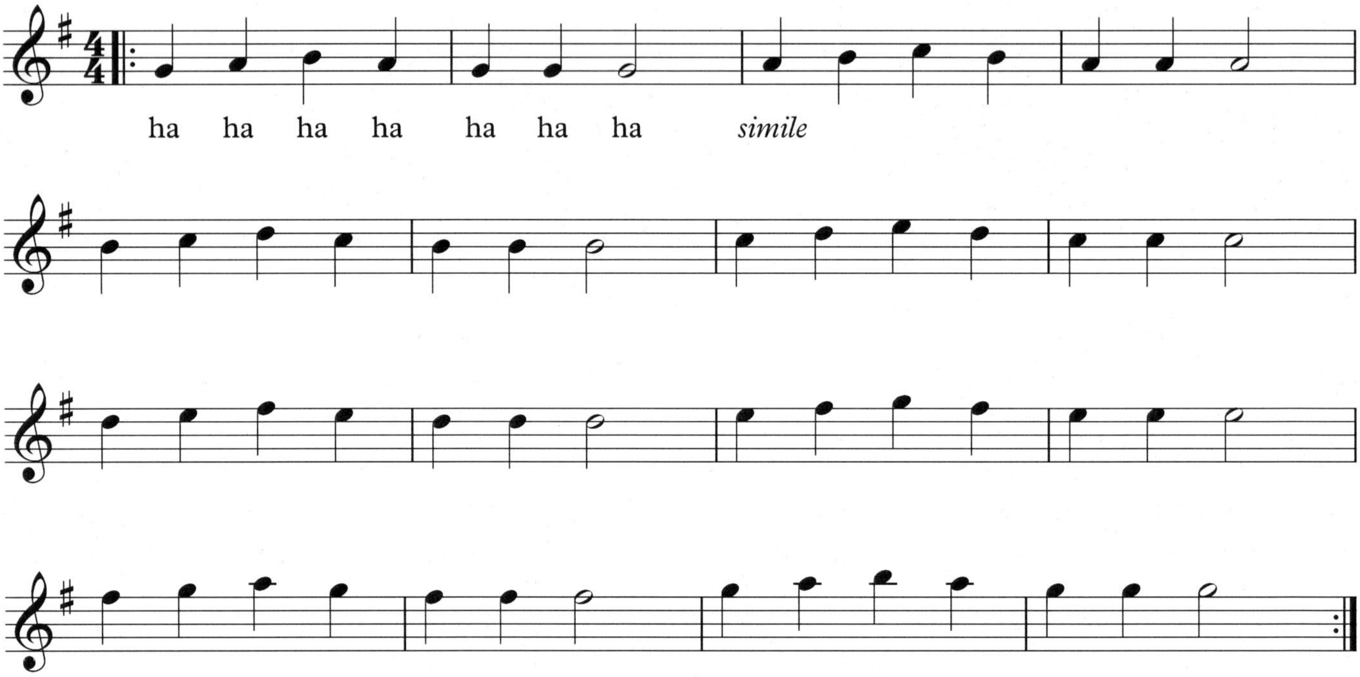

Once you are comfortable with your **ha** attacks, and therefore with the power of your abdomen, you may begin shaping this power. Without forfeiting any of the abdominal force you've just cultivated, begin replacing your **ha** attack with an **uh**. Be sure that this **uh** syllable is shaped deep in your throat and powered by a strong abdominal pulse.

TRACK 2

4. Can you hear yourself saying **uh**? You should.

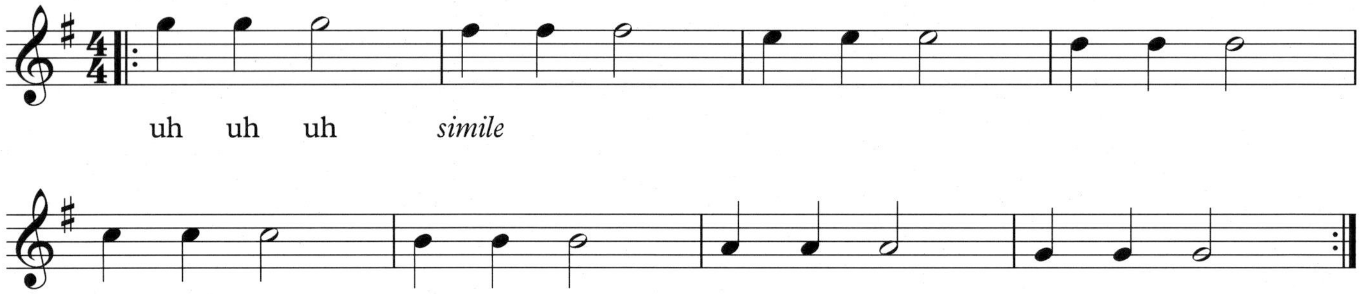

> **Boehm Tip** | Remember to search for that sweet spot right before you've rolled the flute in too far. This will be particularly important with your low range.

5. You may have noticed that this gets significantly more difficult as you descend. Be sure to keep a firm, immobile embouchure so as not to lose your low D.

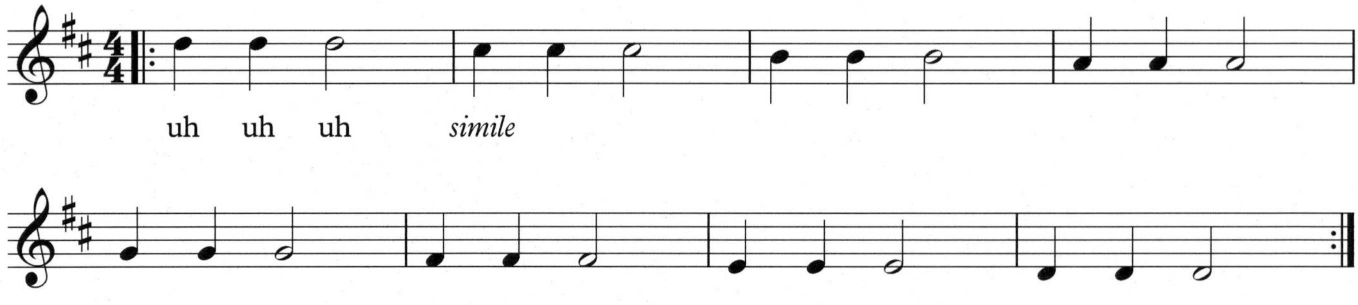

> **General Tip** | A small break in the airstream may be necessary before beginning a glottal. The strength of your **uh** attack might also need to change slightly to accommodate the octave in which you're playing. Lower octaves may require a slightly softer **uh** articulation in order to keep from cracking. To compensate for this, more abdomen may be needed on these notes.

6. The following exercise has slurs notated. You may begin the first note of each measure with a lightly tongued attack or with just your breath. To articulate the glottals on beat four, you may need to break your airstream after beat three.

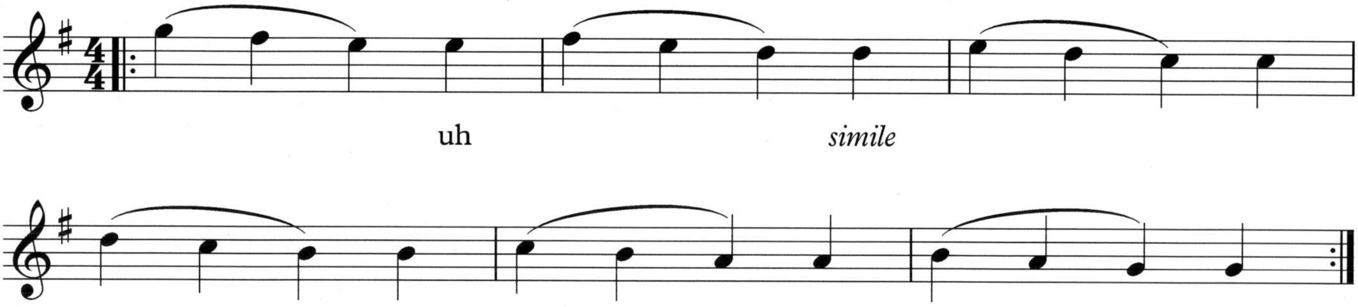

7. In the following exercise, the symbol for a glottal is introduced. Measure one and two should sound identical. Remember, except for glottals, everything can be slurred together even if not notated as such. You may begin slurs with a lightly tongued articulation, or simply with your breath.

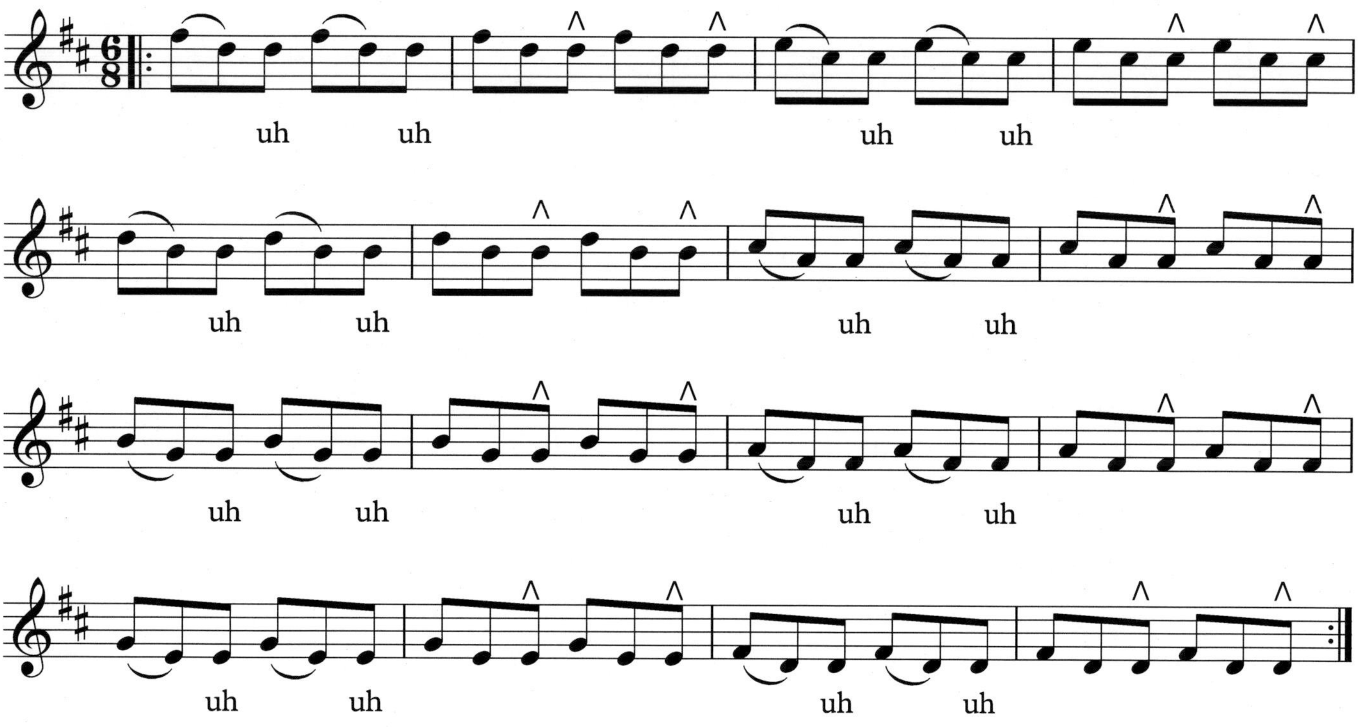

8. You'll know you have a good handle on glottals when you can play several in a row in rapid succession. Try the following exercise. Keep those scoffs coming while your abdomen stays strong and elastic. From now on, slur everything that is not marked with a glottal.

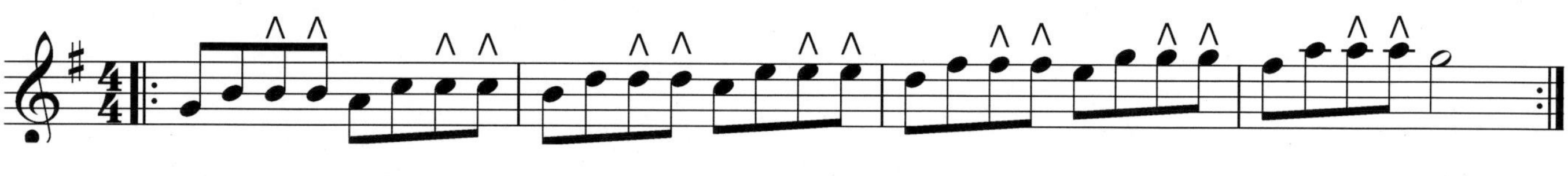

The most difficult glottal, and in my opinion the most important, takes place on hard D. Bringing a certain amount of overtones into your glottaled hard D is perfectly acceptable as long as you don't overshoot to the upper octave. With a firm embouchure, a good cough, and a strong push of air from your abdomen (as well as lots of practice), your glottaled hard Ds will begin to come through beautifully.

> **Transition Tip** | Glottaled hard Ds are where you may see the most modification to your embouchure. If you weren't engaging the center of your top lip before, you will certainly need to do so now. If this feels tricky, return to your hard D practice in *Tone, Color, and Intonation* in Volume I.

9.

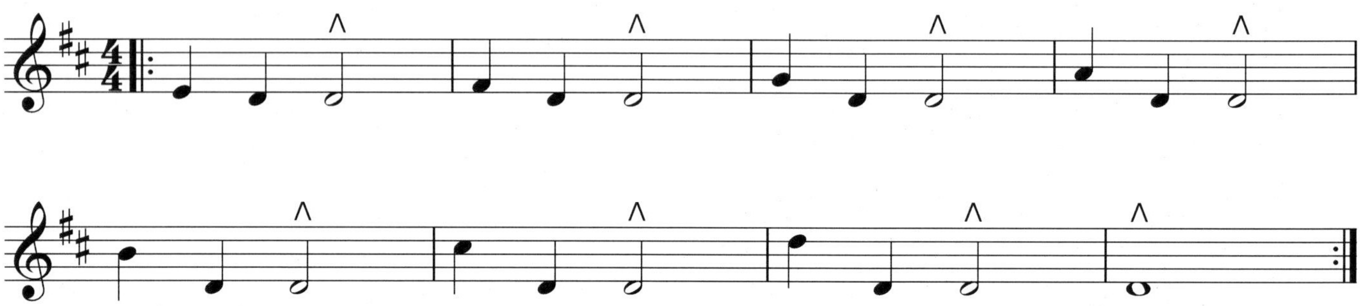

TRACK 3

10.

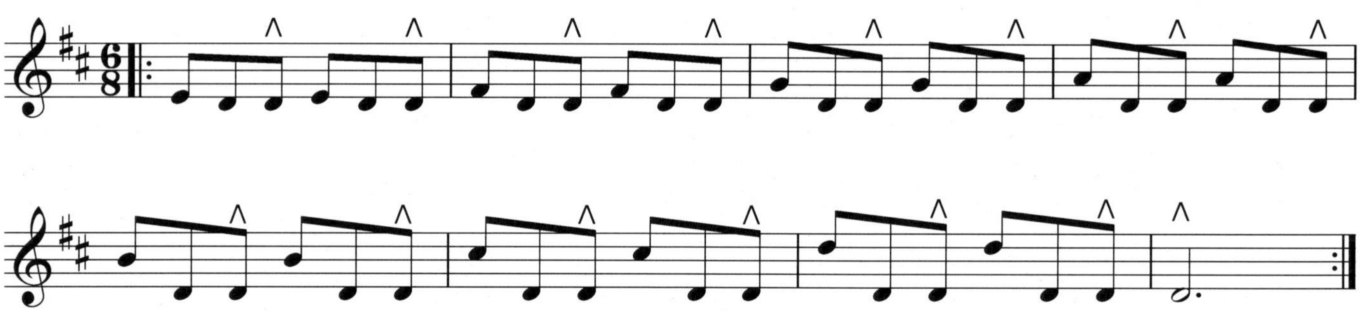

Glottals: Contextual Exercises

Now that you're becoming more comfortable with the mechanics of glottals, you can begin placing them within short melodies. Since there are no specific considerations to adding glottals to different tune types (beyond not adding them to weak beats), you will begin to see both compound and reel time signatures together here. If you are comfortable keeping your backbeat in while playing these exercises, you may certainly do so. If you'd rather focus just on glottals for now, that's fine too. There will be an opportunity to practice these techniques together later in the chapter.

> **Boehm Tip** | Remember to "bear down" on glottals by pressing your upper lip downwards and keeping the center of your embouchure very firm. Do not allow the corners of your mouth to pull back too much: this will spread your sound and lead to cracks into the upper octave.

> **Simple System Tip** | Overtones, overtones, overtones. These are the dark, edgy qualities in your tone and they will begin to come out if you play a great glottal with a firm embouchure. It's rare that one goes overboard with overtones. Embrace them.

TRACK 4

1.

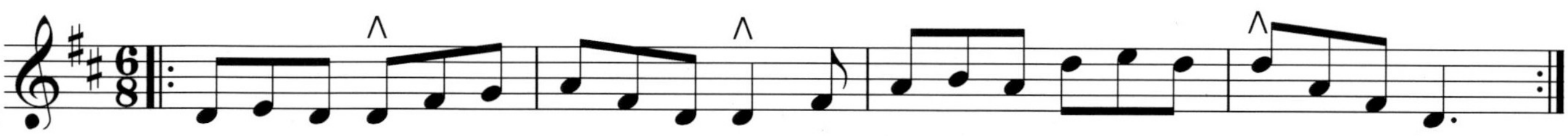

2. Glottals on downbeats may sound slightly stronger than glottaled backbeats.

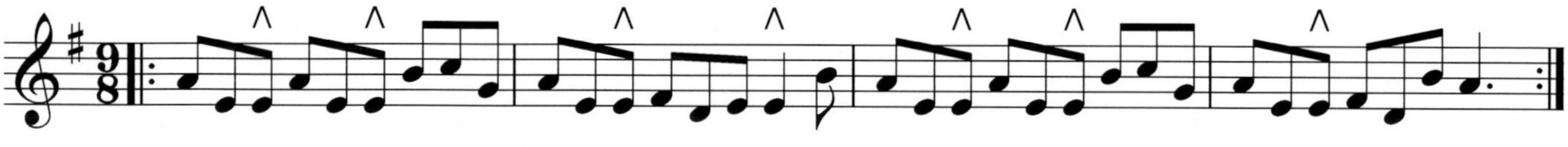

> **General Tip** | Glottals, particularly glottals that occur on big downbeats, will generally sound stronger than their surrounding notes.

3.

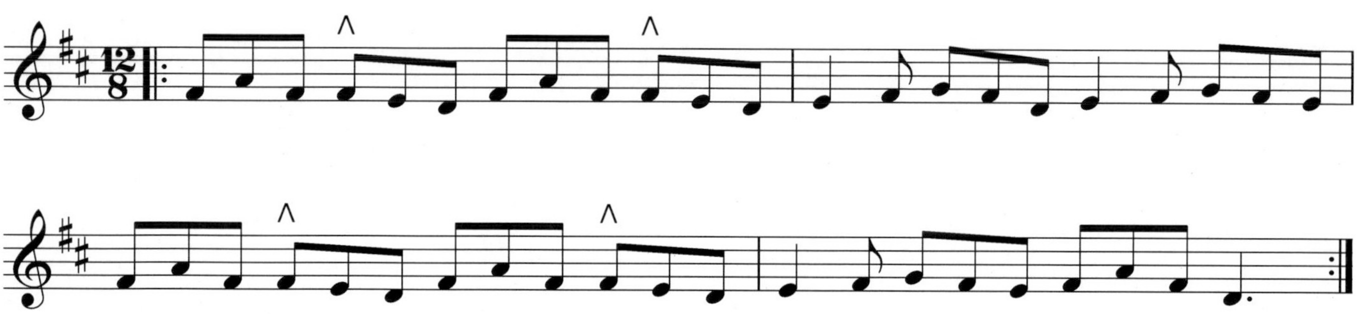

4. Add breaths if you need to. See if you can find appropriate weak beats on which to breathe.

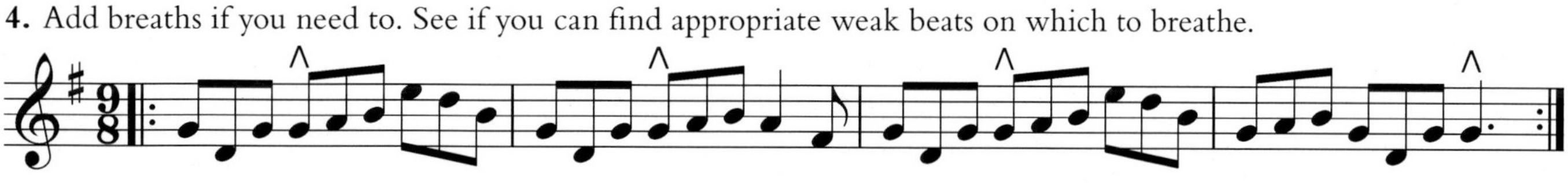

5.

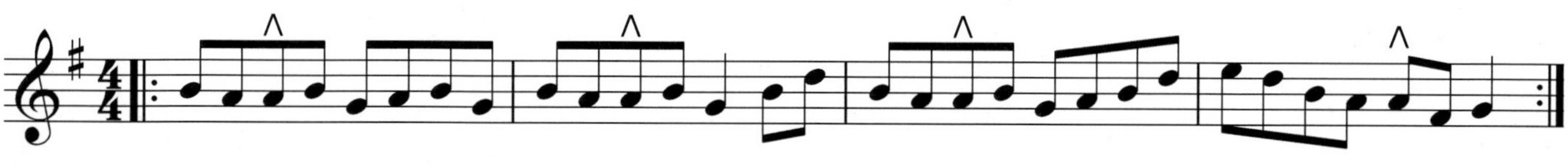

6.

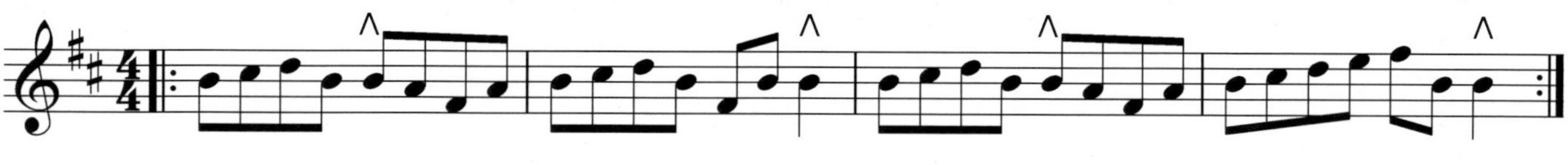

TRACK 5

7. Remember, a little break in the airstream before a glottal can be very helpful.

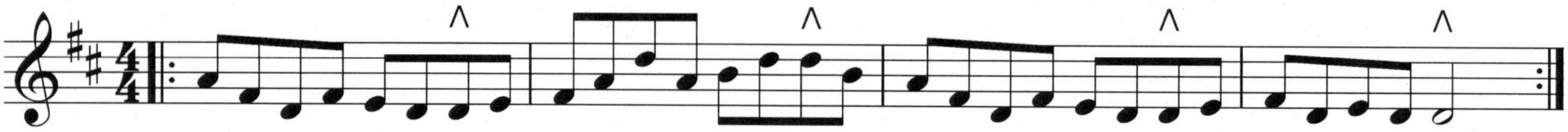

8.

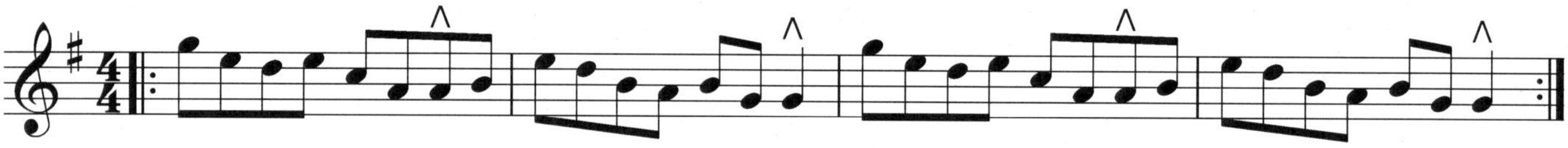

9.

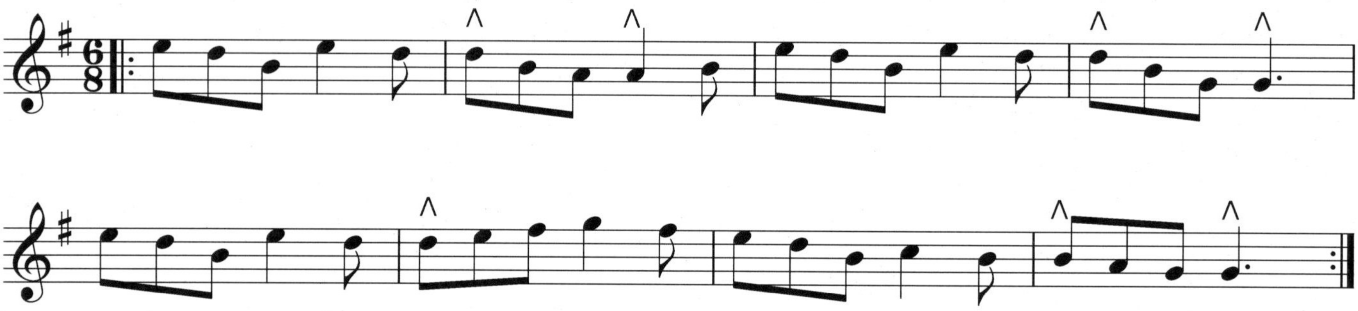

> **Boehm Tip** | If your brain (or throat) isn't too full of glottals, exercise ten is a good example of the pros of having two different F♯ fingerings available. Playing F♯ with your middle finger will lead to a problematic cross fingering between D and F♯, so I recommend using F♯ with your ring finger. Become accustomed to flipping back and forth between your two F♯ fingerings depending on what is most ergonomic for a particular passage. Further discussion of middle and ring finger F♯s can be found in *Fingerings and Technique* in Volume I.

TRACK 6

10. This last exercise uses glottals not only to separate two notes of the same pitch (in this case F♯), but also to give extra bark and bite to your hard Ds.

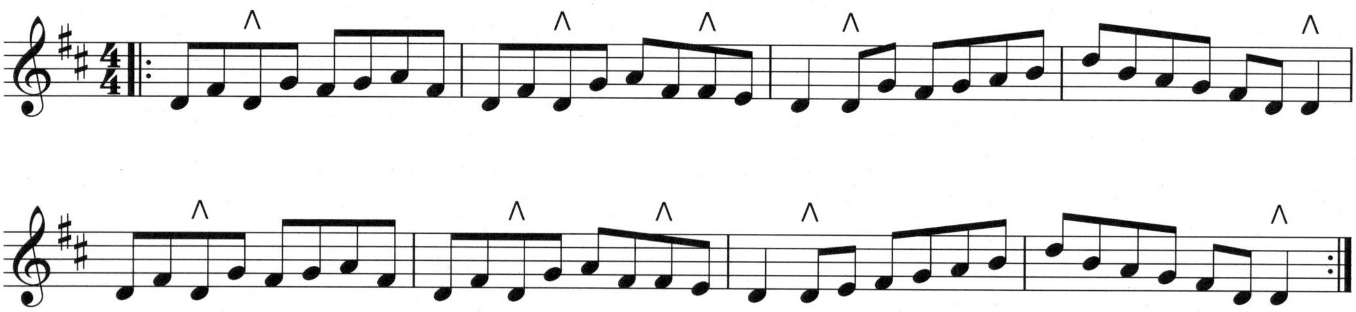

Glottals: Combined Exercises

While playing through the last ten exercises, you may have noticed that glottals require an enormous amount of air. In these next combined exercises, backbeat and rhythmically sound breaths are also provided. See if you can begin to incorporate all three techniques into your playing and pay attention to whether the breaths and backbeat *aid* the strength of your glottals. (They should.)

SYMBOLS KEY:

Volume I: Backbeat and Breathing

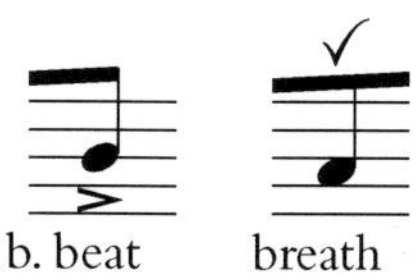

Volume II: Single Ornaments

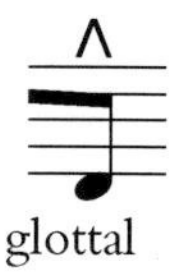

General Tip | It can be tricky when first interspersing glottals alongside backbeat. How are they different? Remember that backbeat (**ha**) is a gentle shape created by the abdomen within a breath that is already occurring. A glottal (**uh**) is a strong articulation created by the throat within either a new breath or a continuation of an existing breath. Think of your syllables again. The first four notes of measure four in exercise one would sound like: **ooo-ooo-ha-uh**. Hear the difference? Also keep in mind that glottaled downbeats may sound slightly stronger than glottaled backbeats.

TRACK 7

1.

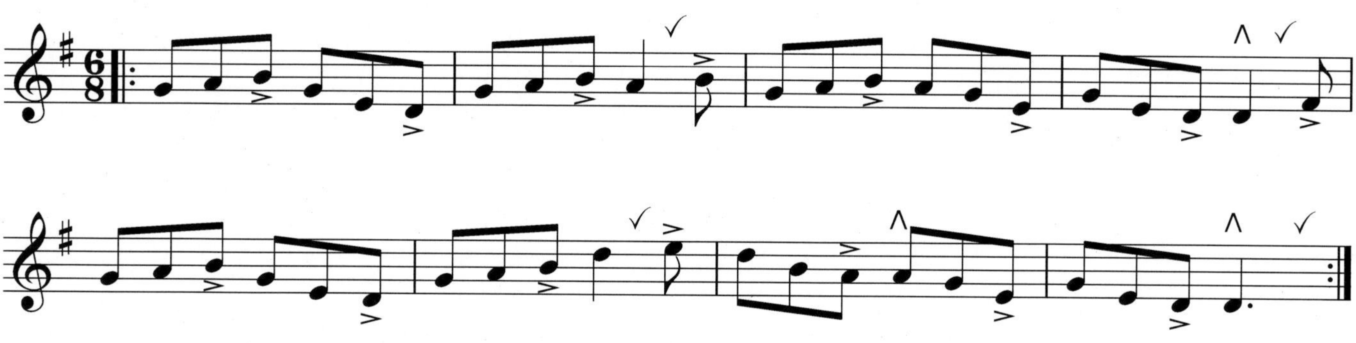

Boehm Tip | Any exercises that do not involve F♯ and D side by side are fair game for playing F♯ with your middle finger:

XXX | OXOo
ox

2.

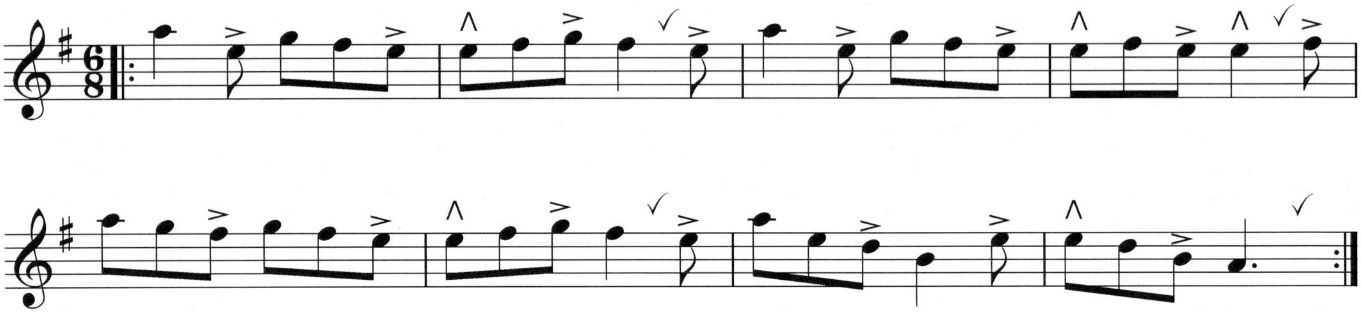

3. With everything going on now, be sure to keep an ear out for your backbeat as well.

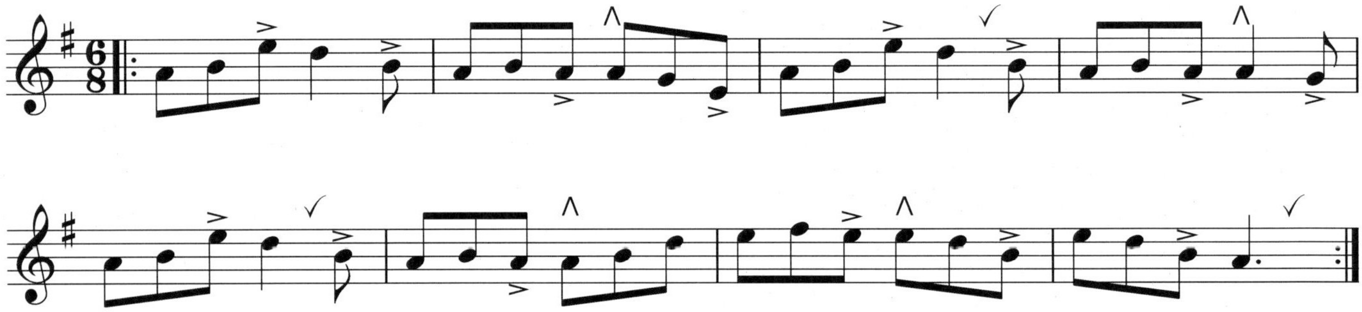

Boehm Tip | If you feel like you're breathing too often, that's great! You have good lungs and fine breath control. Boehm flute seems to require less air than simple system flute and Boehm flutists may be unused to breathing so often. You can certainly skip breaths if you truly don't need them, but remember that breaths are important to shaping phrases. Don't go too long without breathing or a tune will start to sound like a run-on sentence. When you breathe, the tune breathes too. (If you feel like you don't have enough air, no worries. Read the Simple System Tip that comes next.)

Simple System Tip | Out of breath? Yes, that will happen. Throw in backbeat, some glottals, and a simple system flute, and you'll be using quite a lot of air. Just be sure to keep breathing in rhythmically weak places (review our *Breathing* chapters in Volume I if need be), and it will simply sound like the tune is breathing with you. (Already feel like you have enough air? Sweet. Check out the previous Boehm Tip.)

4.

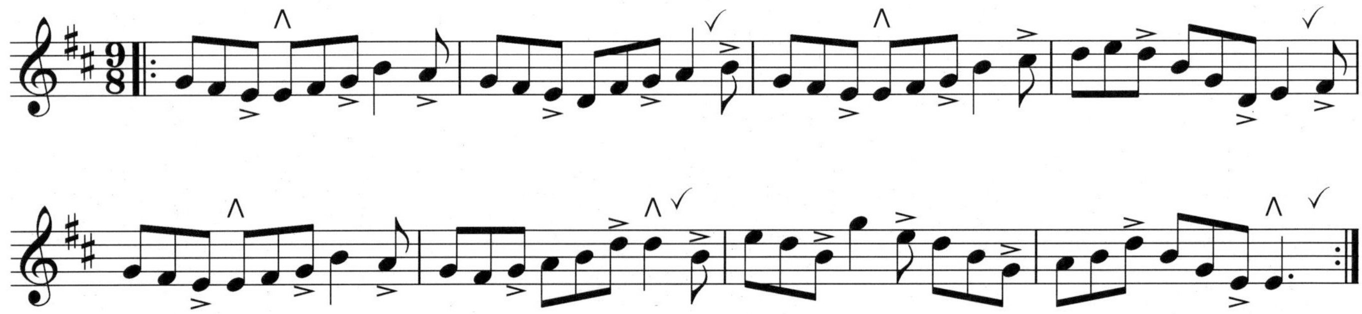

5.

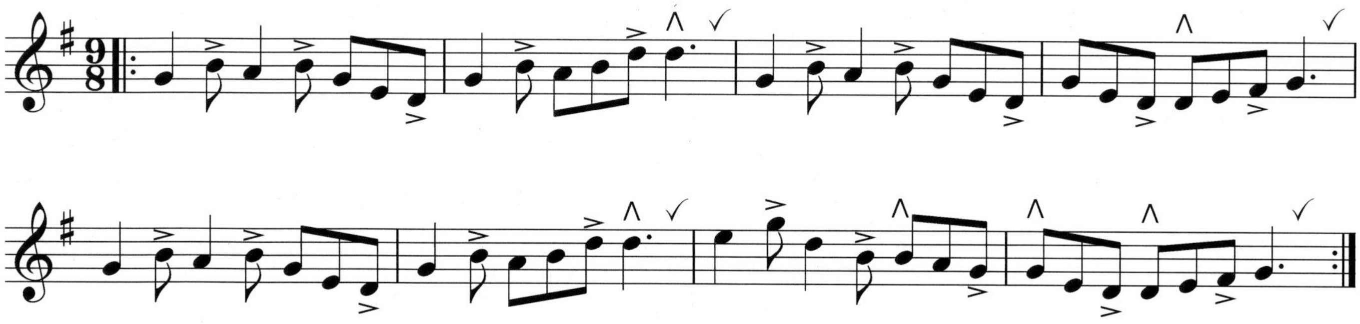

6.

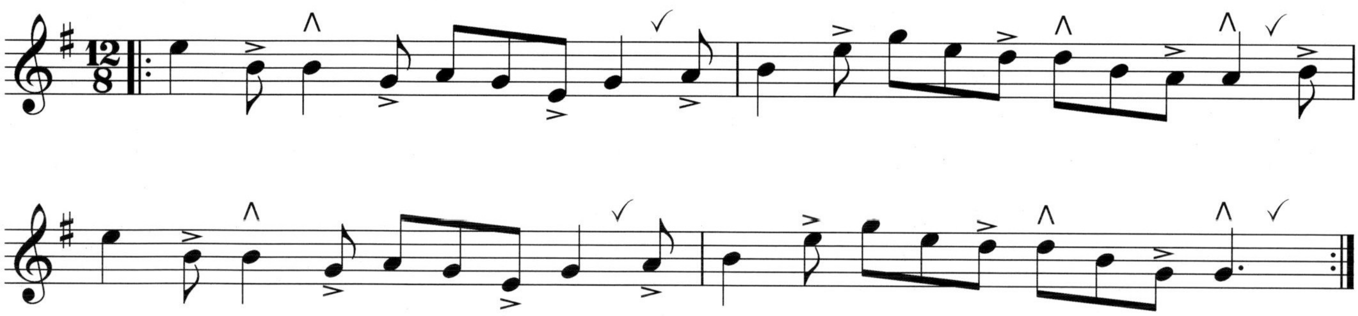

General Tip | If you're lucky, sometimes you'll line up backbeats *and* glottals at the same time. Combine your **ha** backbeat pulse with a whopping **UH** glottal attack: **UHHA**!

7. These next exercises offer simultaneous glottals and backbeats.

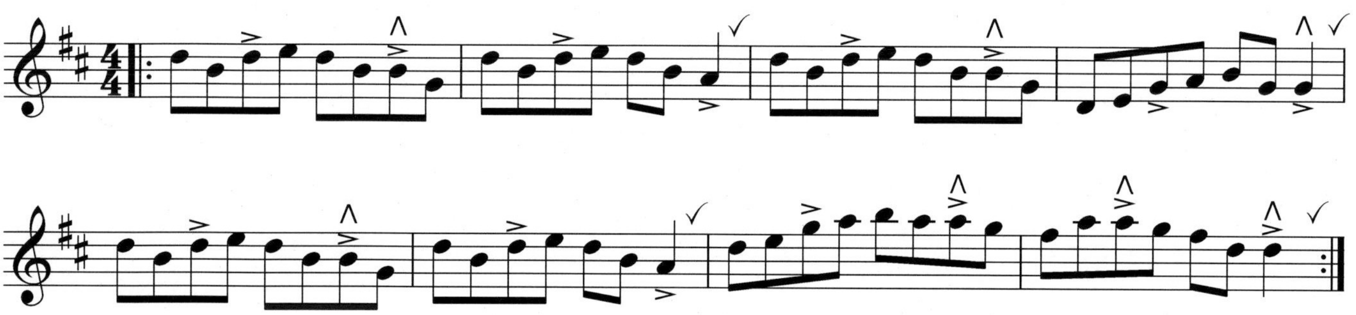

TRACK 8

8. Be careful of the last measure of this exercise. It is very easy to incorrectly accent the high A instead of the G since it is the melodic height of this phrase.

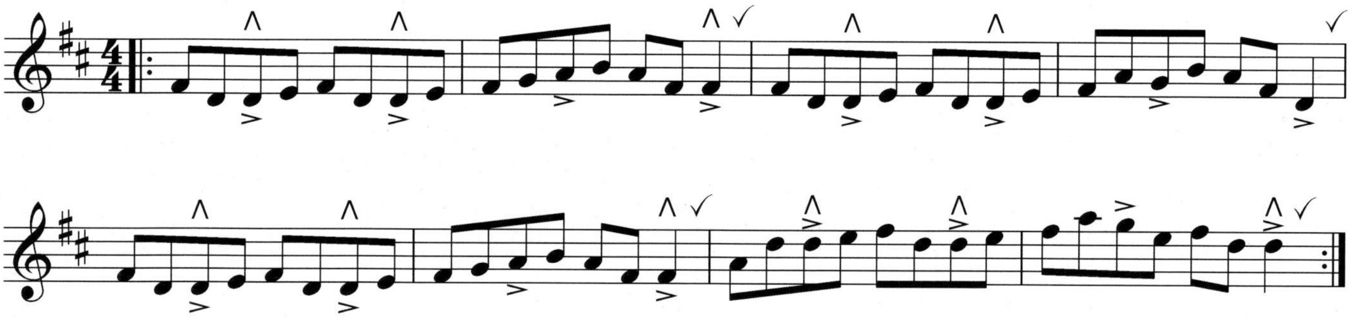

9.

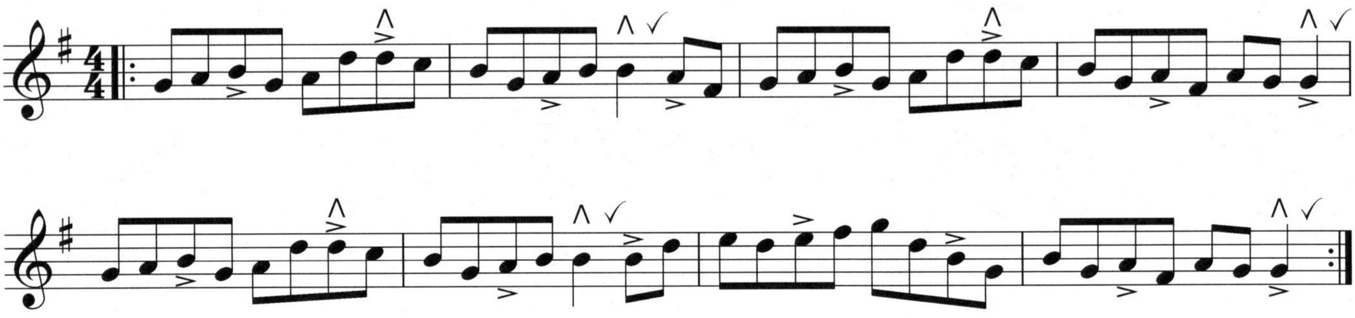

10.

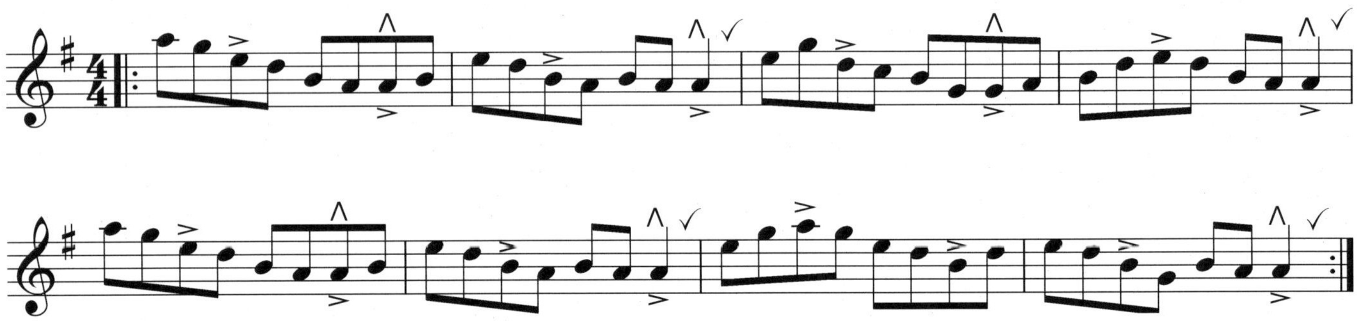

Glottals: Tunes

These tunes should look familiar from Volume I. We will continue to follow all six tunes throughout the remainder of the series. There are a number of repeated notes in these tunes that are not always marked with the glottal symbol. You can backbeat and glottal where marked and lightly tongue the rest for now. If you are ambitious and would like to practice more glottals, however, feel free to add this technique where you think appropriate (on those repeated notes, for instance). We'll be learning some great techniques for those notes in the coming chapters though, so if you'd only like to glottal where marked, rest assured that we'll soon be filling in the blanks. There will also be further discussion of these sorts of decisions (to glottal or not to glottal) in *Painting Our Own Tunes: Versions and Variations* in Volume IV.

SYMBOLS KEY:

Volume I: Backbeat and Breathing	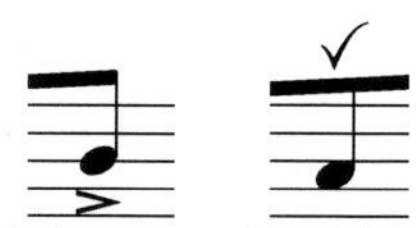 b. beat breath
Volume II: Single Ornaments	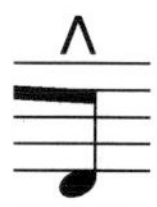 glottal

Glottals: Boiled Goat's Milk

Glottals could be added to many places in this jig. Feel free to do so, but we'll be adding some different techniques to this tune as we go along. At the very least, you may practice adding the glottal marked in the last line.

TRACK 9

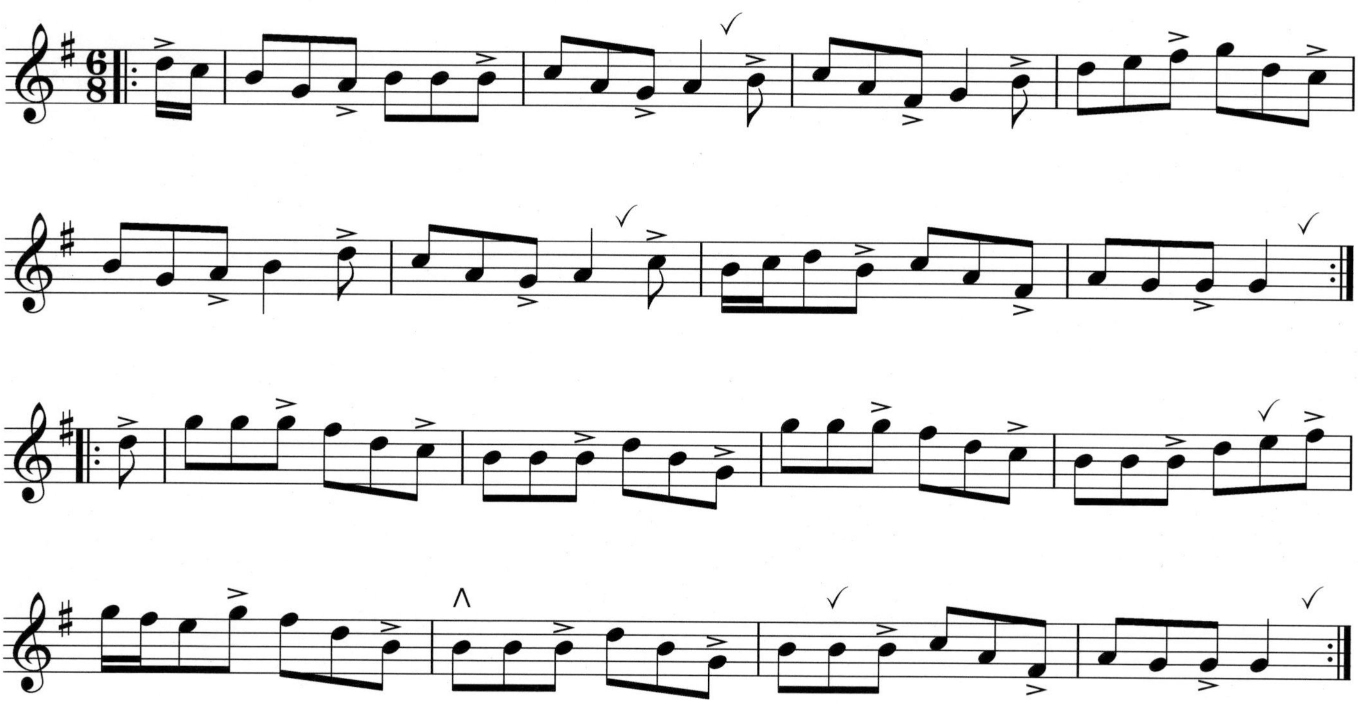

Glottals: Dever the Dancer

Many repeated Es fall on the backbeat in this slip jig. Adding glottals to these backbeats separates these notes and provides additional drive and lift to the tune.

TRACK 10

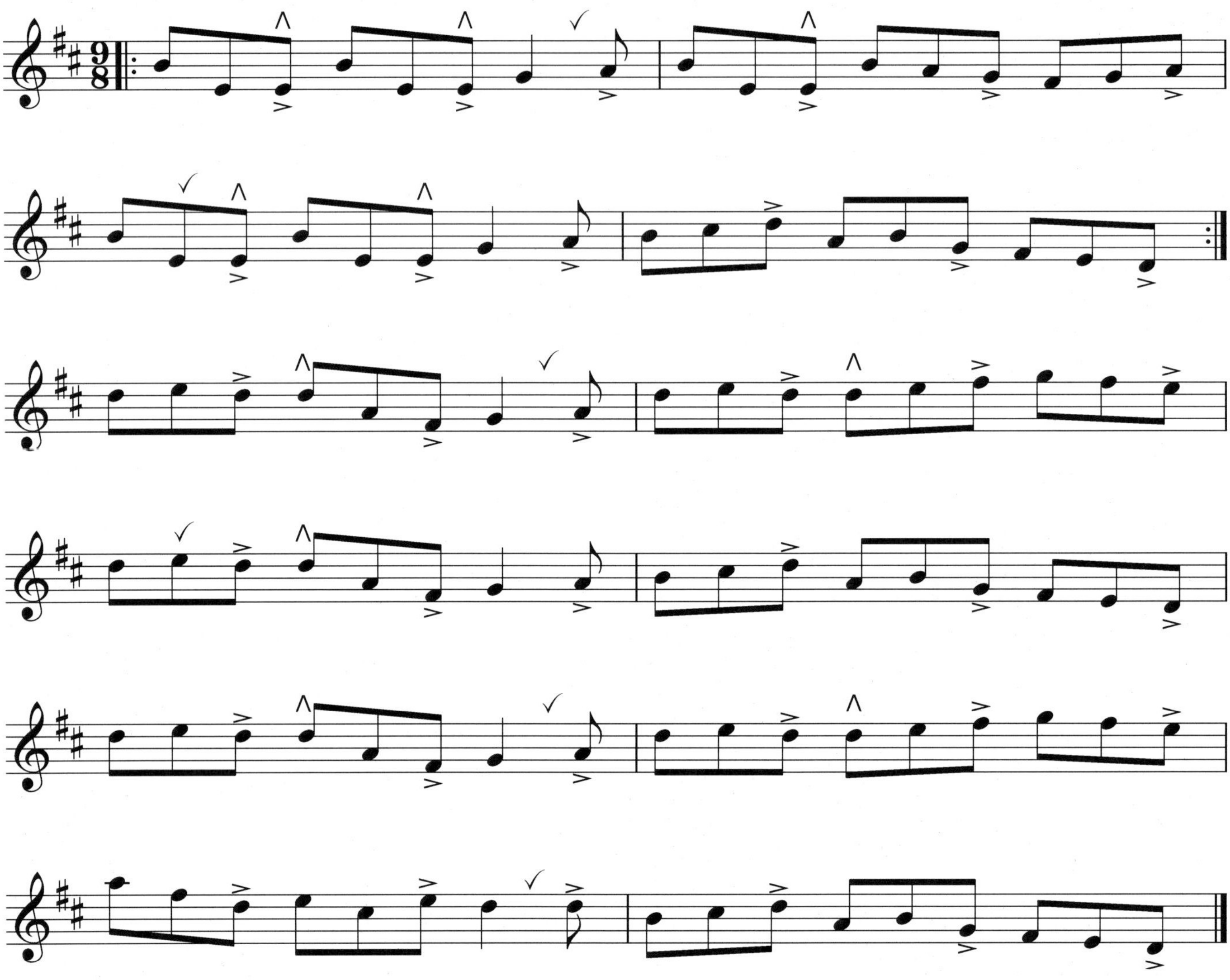

Glottals: The Dingle Regatta

This slide uses glottals to separate repeated Ds in the B part. Remember that tunes are separated into multiple parts, with each part named for a letter of the alphabet. In this tune, the A part is the first four bars, the B part is the middle four, and the C part is the last four. If you'd like a more in-depth review of parts and tune types, see *Tunes* in Volume I.

TRACK 11

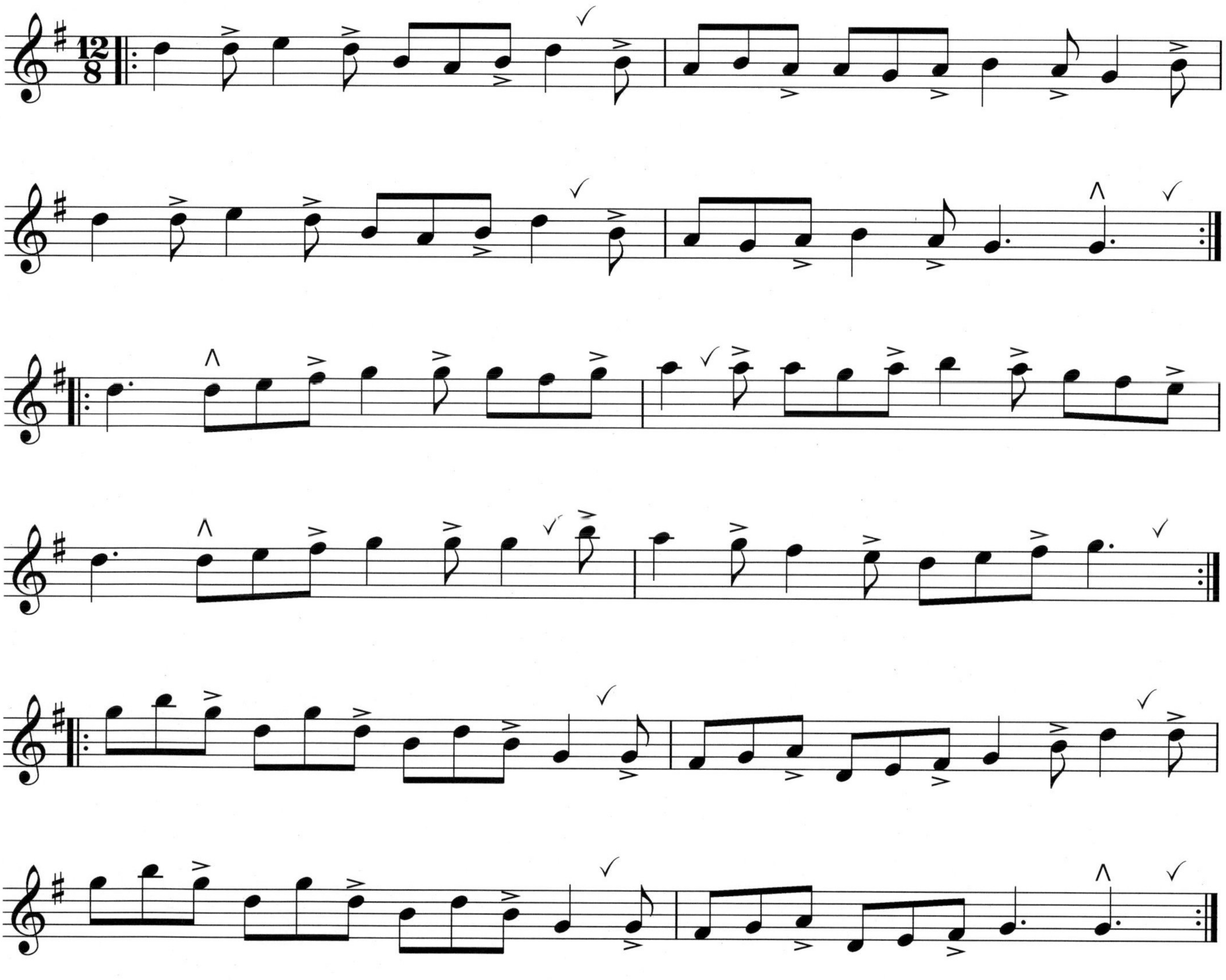

Glottals: My Love is in America

These next three tunes are reels. *My Love is in America* has a number of repeated Ds that sound particularly fine when glottaled.

TRACK 12

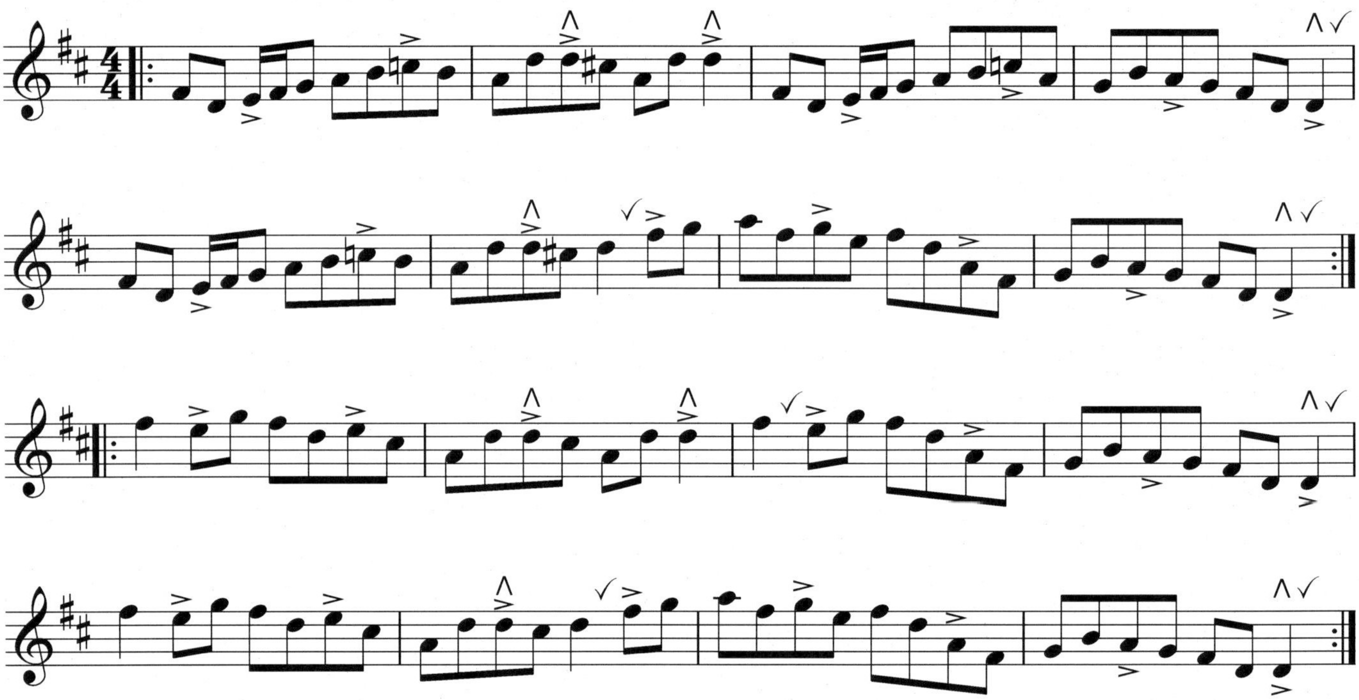

Glottals: The Pretty Blue Seagull

A glottal can be used to great effect to separate some of the repeated hard Ds in measure two of *The Pretty Blue Seagull.*

TRACK 13

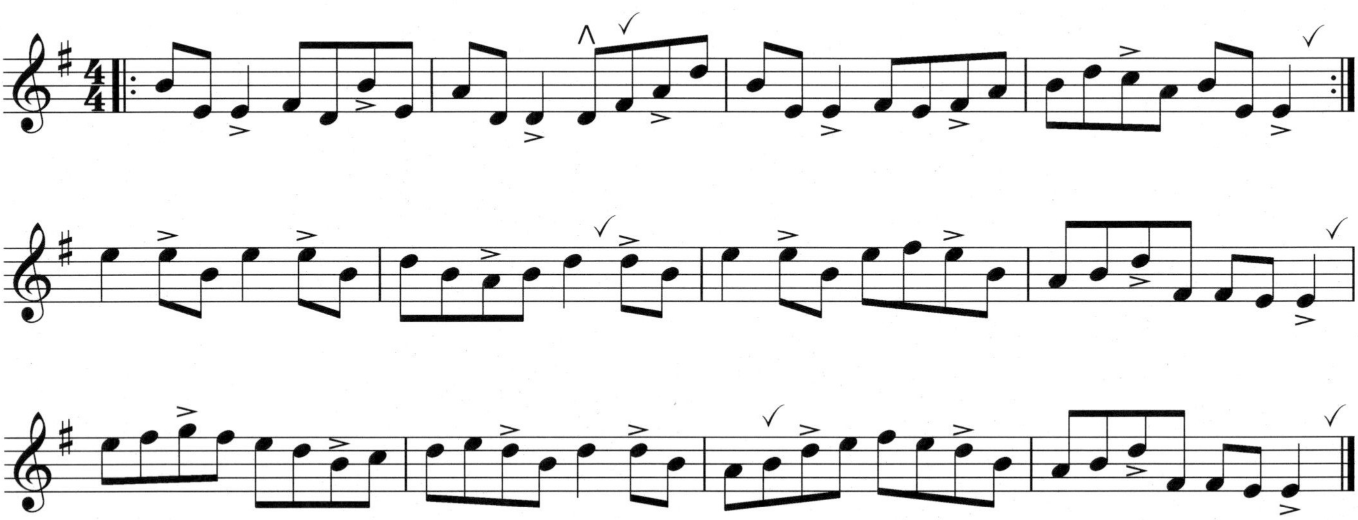

Glottals: The Congress Reel

The Congress Reel is a great example of using glottals to make a part of the melody pop out. These will also be combined with an additional ornament down the road.

TRACK 14

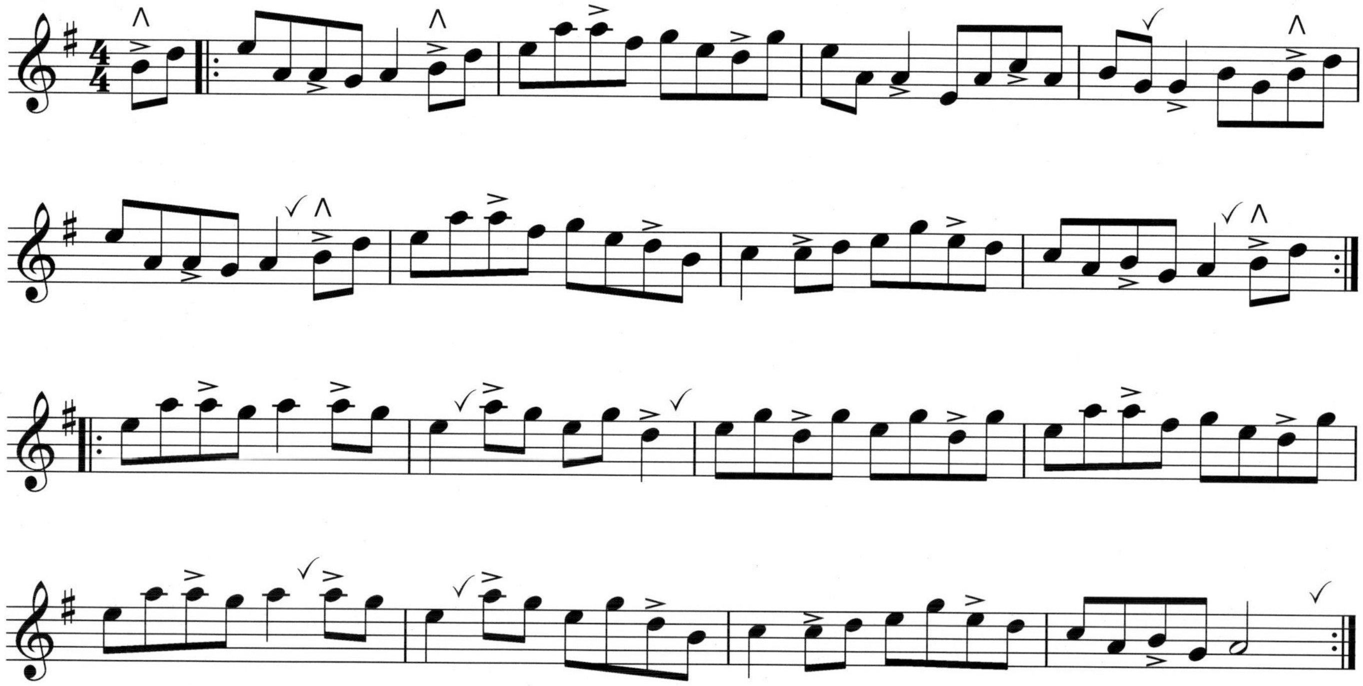

Chapter 2: Finger Vibrato

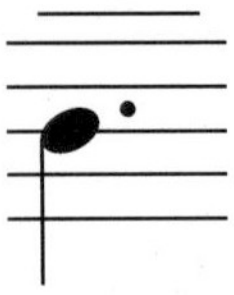

Finger vibrato was the ornament that motivated me to find and buy my first simple system flute. It is certainly possible to emulate the sound on a Boehm flute, but to me it just didn't *feel* quite the same. Finger vibrato is created on the simple system flute by fluttering a finger against an open hole (some players even call the technique "fluttering"), and it is used to soften and embellish long notes. This is very similar to the finger vibrato, or *flattement,* used on Baroque flutes. Finger vibrato can be found most commonly in slower tunes, such as airs, but it can also be used to great effect in the faster tunes we are examining in this book. When listening to great fiddle players, you'll sometimes hear them add a long note or double stop in the middle of a fast jig or reel. Using a long note and finger vibrato is a great way to mimic this sound.

Finger vibrato on the simple system flute is faster and narrower than most throat vibratos, and generally starts as soon as the note begins. While throat vibrato moves above and below the primary pitch, finger vibrato only moves below. I often think of it as adding a "shimmer" to a note, and nothing more. Finger vibrato requires an open hole on which to flutter a finger, so it is possible on every note except D (some flutists instead use a very tight, fast throat vibrato on D in order to mimic the sound of finger vibrato). For many of the notes on simple system flute, you can skip a hole after your last closed finger and flutter on the next. Doing so will allow you to (usually) cover the entire hole as you flutter and therefore provide a very pleasing "shimmer."

Executing finger vibrato on the Boehm flute can feel a little awkward at first, and it does take practice to feel comfortable with the technique. On the Boehm flute, I find it best to flutter multiple fingers in unison against the keys without adding enough weight to close them (depressing keys widens the vibrato too much and makes an unappealing clacking sound). You may find that you're creating the vibrato as much from the resulting "shake" of the flute as you are from fluttering your fingers. As long as the sound is fast and narrow, this is fine. If you are tempted to emulate the sound of finger vibrato with a fast throat vibrato instead, I would advise against it. It does not create the same style of sound, particularly on a Boehm flute.

Finger Vibrato Fingering Chart

Finger vibrato is made much easier when you internalize which fingers are used to ornament which pitches. Go through this chart carefully, paying particular attention to the note about ornamenting E/E'.

Boehm Tip | Do not close the designated keys. Instead, flutter your fingers gently against the keys without closing them. If more than one finger is being used, they should move in unison. Remember that this type of vibrato should sound fast and narrow. It is also possible for Boehm flutists to add finger vibrato to more notes than listed in the fingering chart. As previously discussed, however, if playing in the Irish Traditional Tonality Set (see *Scales and Modes* in Volume I), using those additional notes will be largely unnecessary.

Simple System Tip | Since there are not enough remaining open holes to skip a hole and then add vibrato to the next, E vibrato involves fluttering on only half of the remaining open hole. Otherwise, flutists will play a very diatonic sounding trill, not at all what the music calls for. I've found it is easiest to half-hole the E by dropping my wrist down and fluttering on the hole at a 45° angle, rather than coming at it straight on and trying to accurately cover 50% of the hole.

Finger Vibrato Fingering Chart:

To read this fingering chart, place all X fingers down, then flutter your finger(s) on **O**. Boehm flutists, you will be fluttering against the marked keys, not closing them. Simple system flutists, there is a specific technique for fluttering on E/E' that is explained on the previous page.

E/E'

Boehm

X X X | X X **O** o
o x

Simple System

X X X | X X **O**

F♯/F♯'

Boehm

X X X | **O O** X x
o x

or

X X X | **O** X O o
o x

Simple System

X X X | X O **O**

G/G'

Boehm

X X X | **O O O** o
o x

Simple System

X X X | O **O** O

A/A'

Boehm

X X O | **O O O** o
o x

Simple System

X X O | **O** O O

B/B'

Boehm

X O O | **O O O** o
o x

Simple System

X O **O** | O O O

C

Boehm

X O O | **O O O** o
o O

Simple System

O X X | **O** O O

C♯

Boehm

O O O | **O O O** o
o O

Simple System

O **O** O | O O O

Finger Vibrato: Preliminary Exercises

It is awkward indeed to arrive on a note forgetting which finger to use, particularly in faster tunes when there is little time for error. It is therefore important to develop muscle memory for your finger vibrato.

> **Boehm Tip** | Keep your fingers in the position that you're using. If you are using flattened fingers, for instance, keep them flat when executing vibrato. In fact, using flattened fingers to flutter *against* the hinging mechanism of the keys can be extremely helpful, as it prevents the fingers from closing the keys. Your vibrato should be similar in speed to a trill, if not faster, and should start from the beginning of the note. This type of vibrato is rarely added in later with a gradual increase of speed, like you may hear in classical throat vibrato.

> **Simple System Tip** | Playing a C♯ with finger vibrato can feel like a bit of a balancing act. Maintain a great left hook and good contact with the thumb (and if necessary, the pinkie) of your right hand. If the flute still feels unbalanced, now is a good time to review *Posture* in Volume I.

TRACK 15

1. As you can see, the rhythm of these exercises becomes progressively quicker. Becoming comfortable with adding finger vibrato to long and short notes alike will be very helpful.

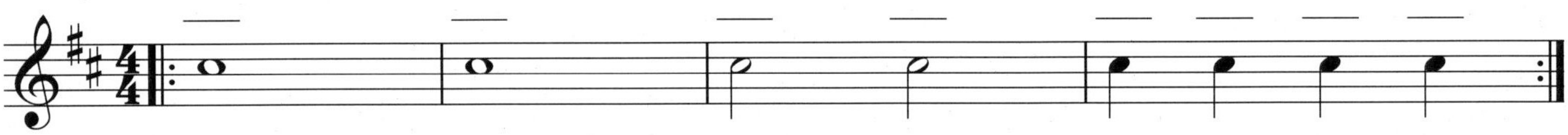

2.

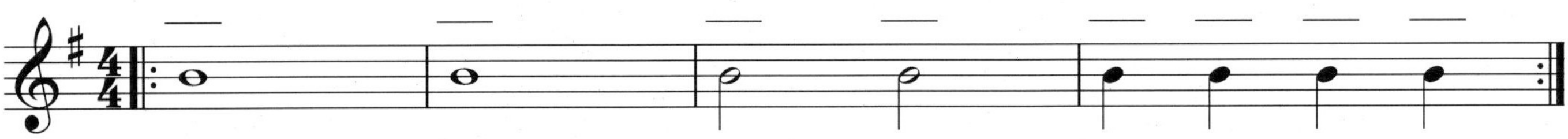

3.

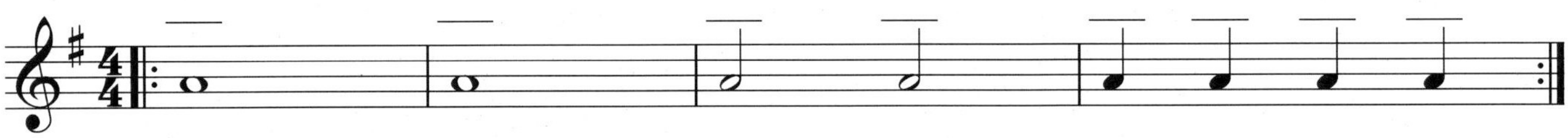

> **General Tip** | It is important to control the end of each note by making sure you finish the vibrato with your fluttering finger raised to its original position. This will be especially important when adding this ornament to fast tunes, as it provides a clean exit strategy and will allow you to continue swiftly and accurately.

4.

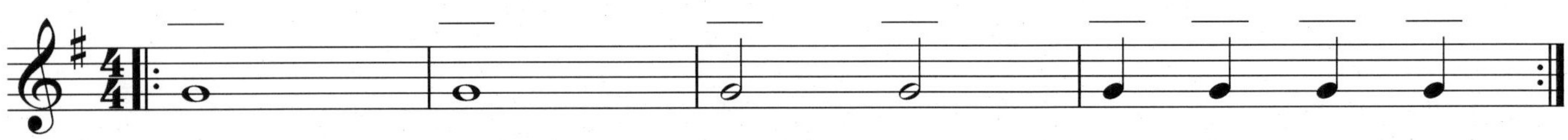

Boehm Tip | Make sure both F♯ vibrato fingerings feel fluent to your fingers:

XXX | OOXx
ox

or

XXX | OXOo
ox

5.

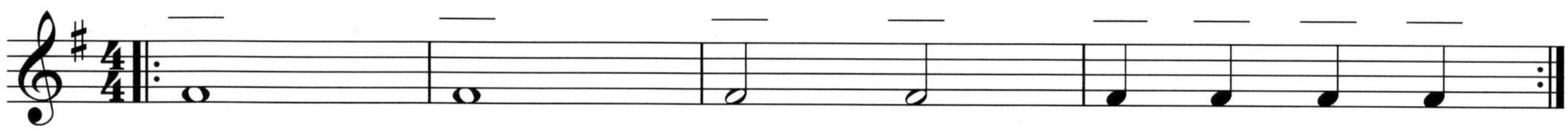

Simple System Tip | This is a good opportunity to practice your half-holed E vibrato. Experiment both with fluttering at a 45° angle and with covering 50% of the hole straight on. Choose what works best for you and your flute.

6.

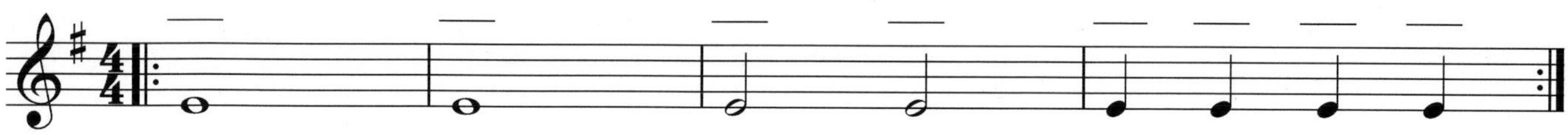

7. If this feels unstable on the Boehm flute, supporting with the right hand pinkie can help.

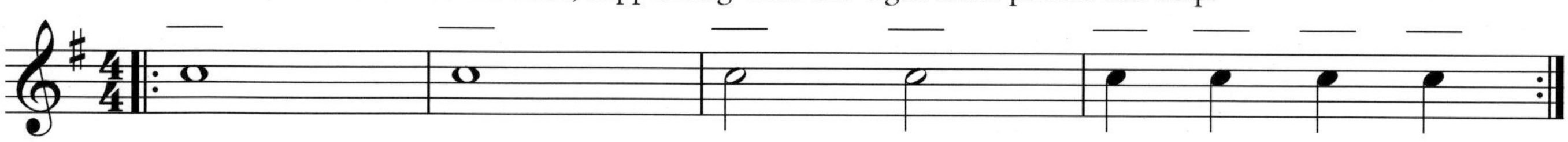

8. E and C natural are the two outliers in the vibrato fingering pattern on simple system flute. Make sure you feel confident with executing both of them.

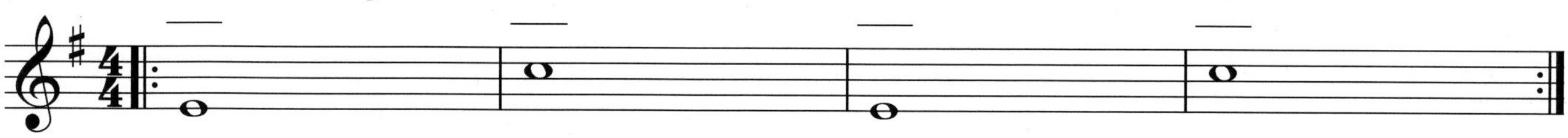

9. E and F♯ are two outliers in the vibrato fingering pattern for Boehm flutists. Be sure to feel comfortable with both, as well as with both F♯ vibrato fingerings.

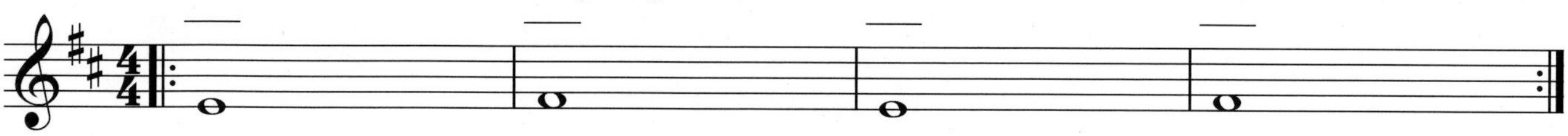

TRACK 16

10. This is a great opportunity to develop your muscle memory. Can you remember which fingers go where?

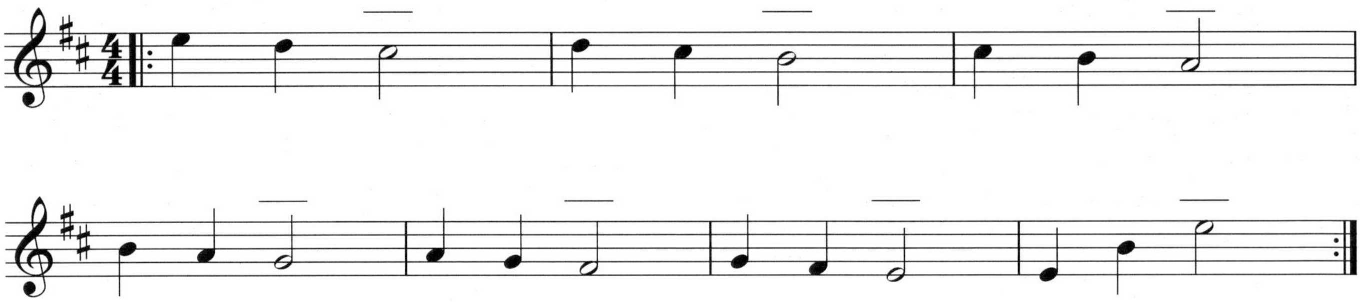

Finger Vibrato: Contextual Exercises

Now that you're more confident with your finger vibrato, you may begin using it in more complicated contexts. As you increase your speed, you'll notice that you often only have time for a few quick flutters of vibrato.

TRACK 17

1.

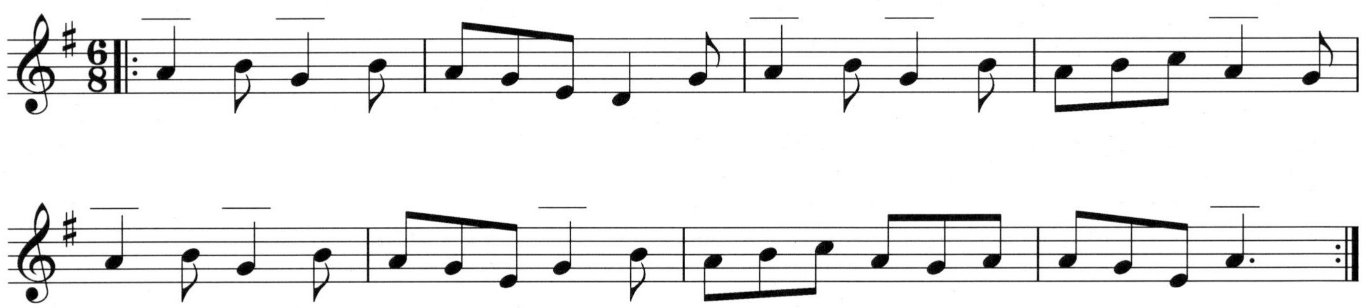

2.

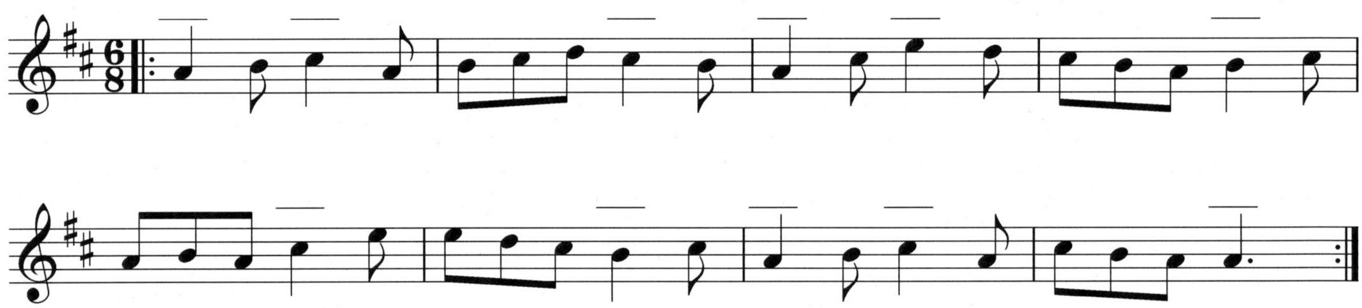

> **Boehm Tip** | If adding finger vibrato at speed without closing keys feels too difficult, think instead of aiming for the bar behind the keys. Allowing your fingers to graze this bar slightly as you're fluttering provides immediate feedback and ensures the keys won't fully close.

3. Boehm flutists, you may find that your ring finger F♯’ works better here. It will avoid a cross fingering with the D’ that follows.

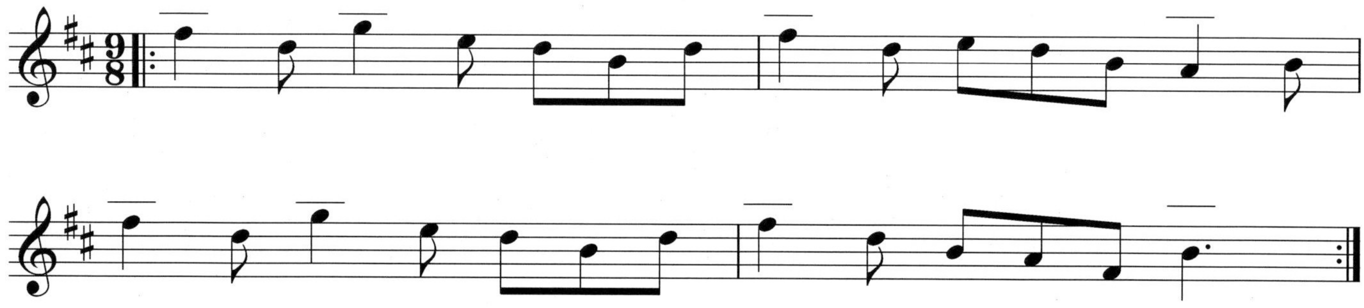

TRACK 18

4. Simple system flutists, be sure to half-hole your E.

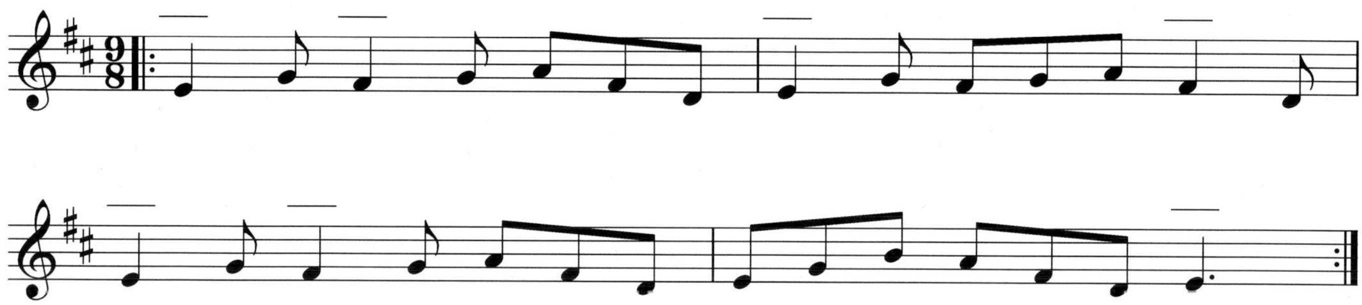

5. The same concept of half-holing applies to the higher E’ on simple system flutes.

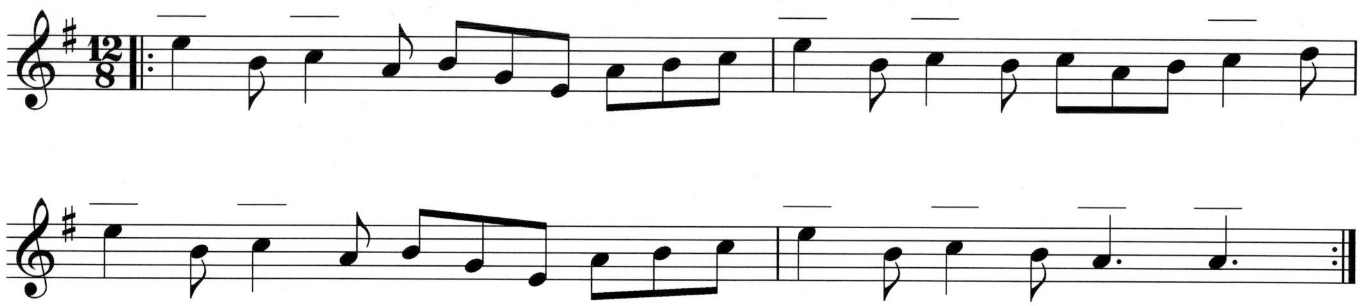

6. Use a firm left hand hook to support your flute while executing vibrato on C♯s.

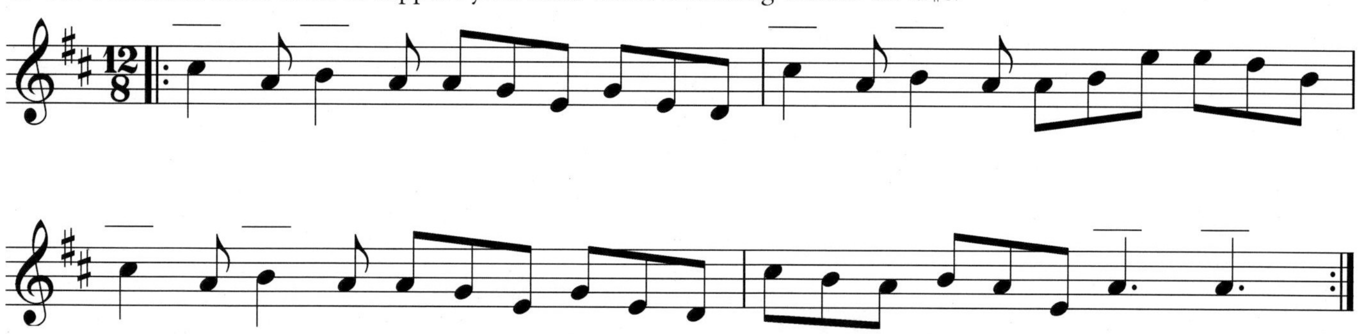

7.

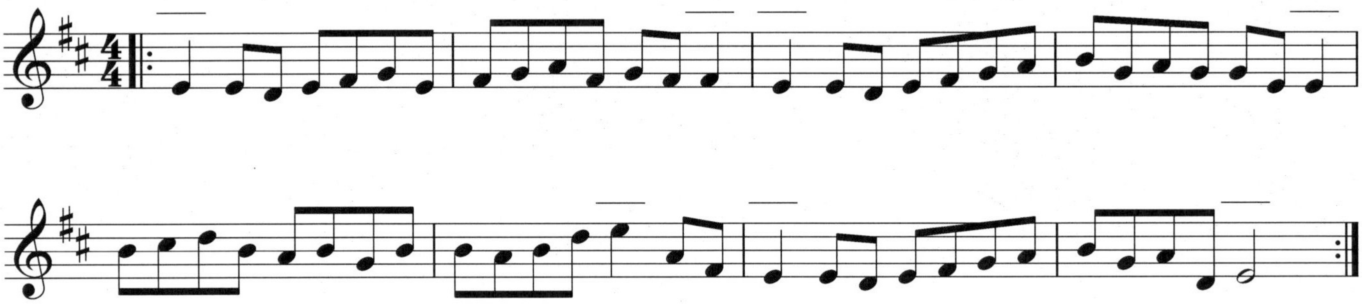

8.

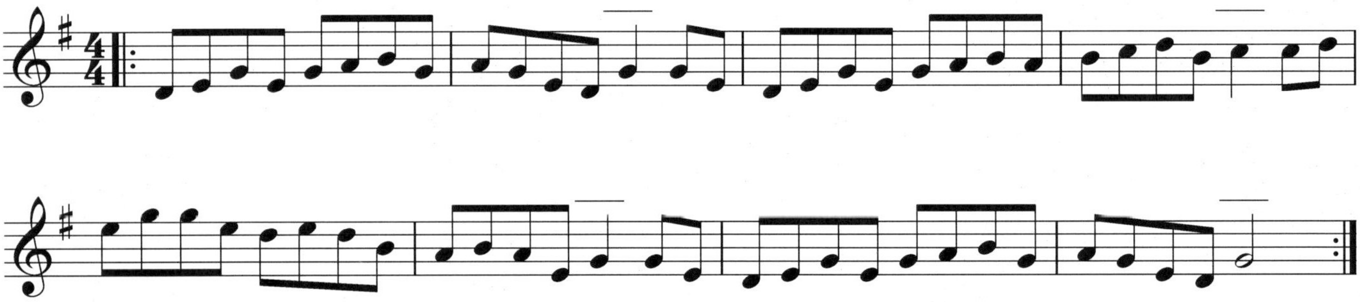

9.

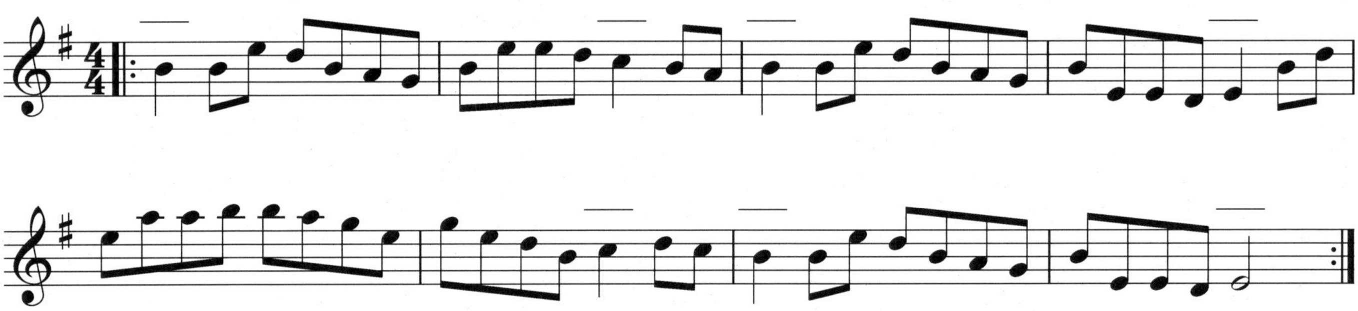

10.

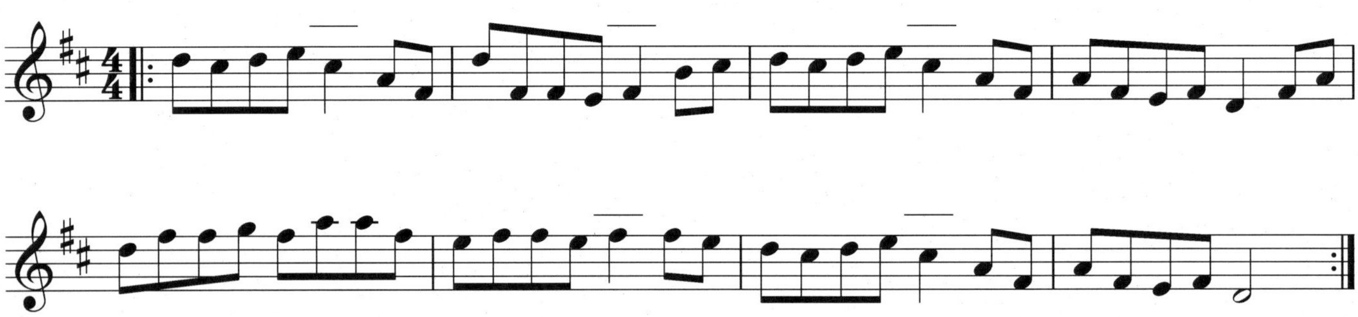

Finger Vibrato: Combined Exercises

We will now add finger vibrato to our previous techniques. Begin slowly and consult the Symbols Key when you need to.

SYMBOLS KEY:	
Volume I: Backbeat and Breathing	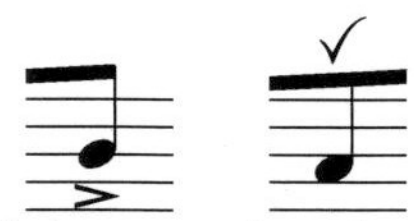 b. beat breath
Volume II: Single Ornaments	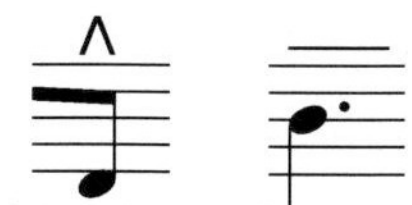 glottal finger vibrato

TRACK 19

1. Notice the combined glottal and backbeat in measure one. ***Uhha!*** If you haven't been doing so already, you'll also need to cut your vibrato notes short in order to breathe.

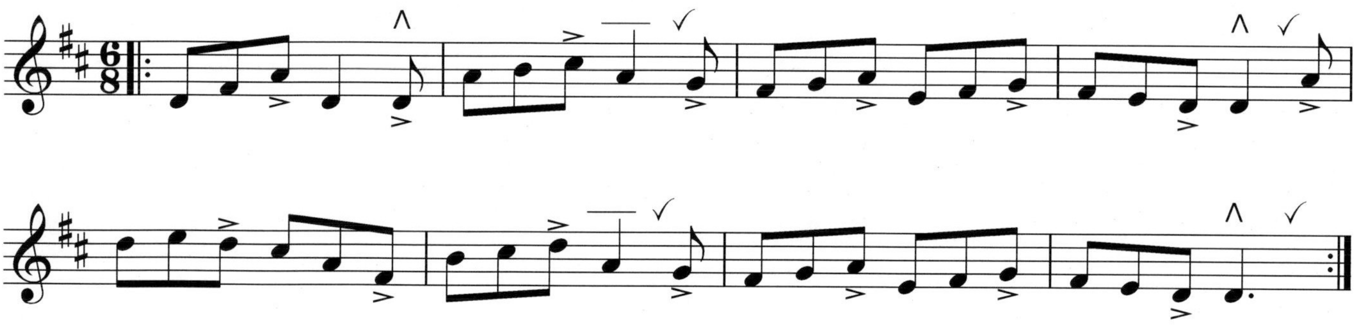

2.

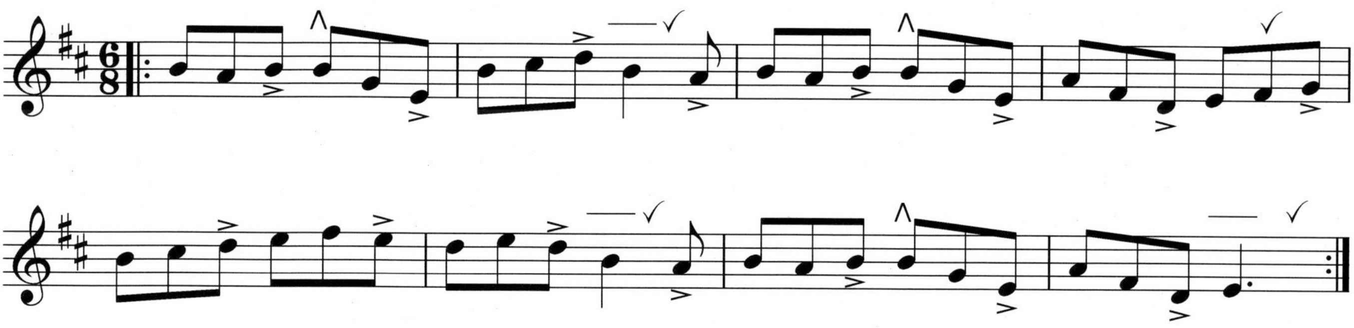

3. Boehm flutists, except for any F♯ to D motion, your middle finger F♯ will work very well here.

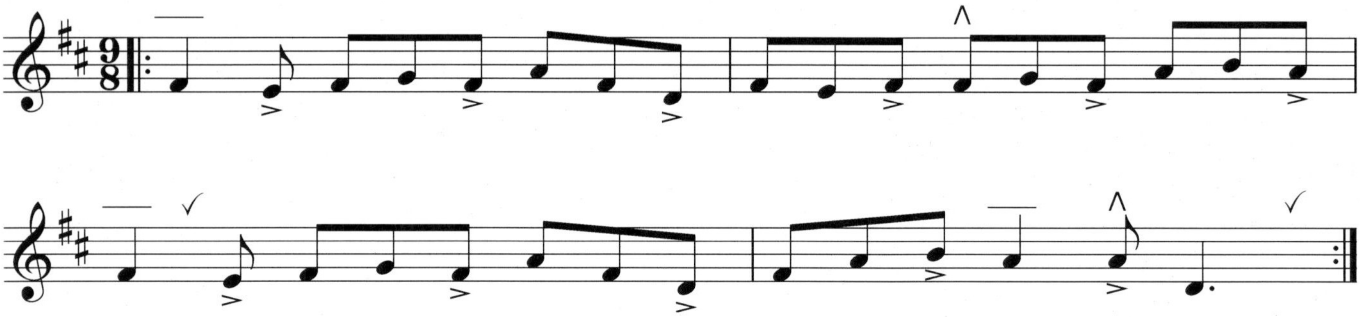

4. Notice the combination of symbols on the C in measure two. A glottal starts the note, and finger vibrato is added to make it shimmer.

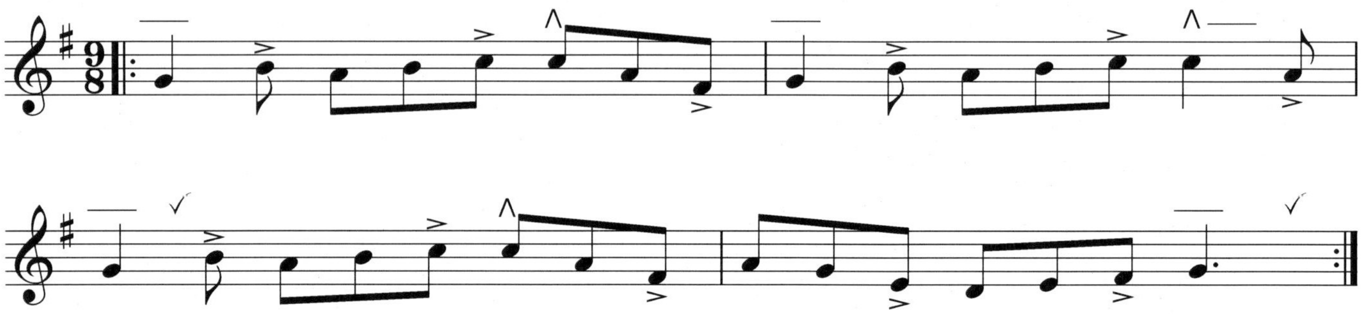

5. While there is more finger vibrato added to these exercises than you might ordinarily use in tunes, it is good practice.

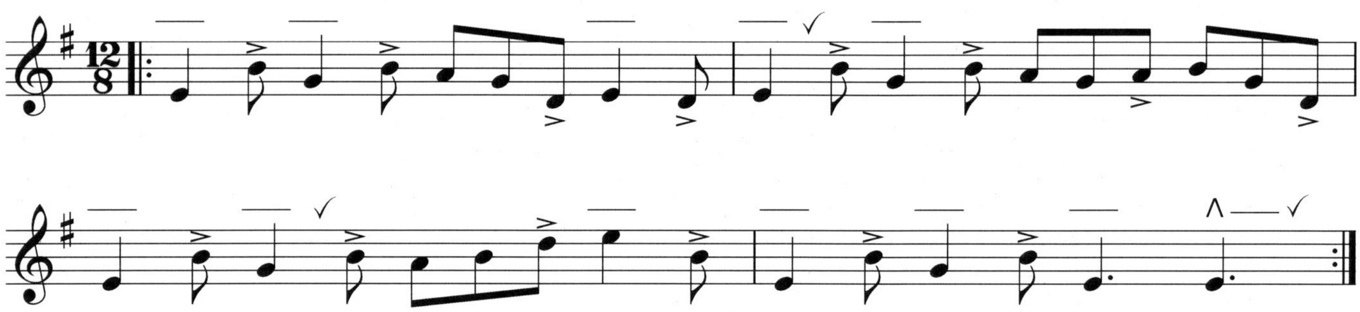

6. Although it might make sense to breathe after the D quarter notes in measures one and three, the breaths are instead placed differently so as to allow for backbeat and glottaled Ds. This is an example of planning breaths to accommodate the ornaments you choose.

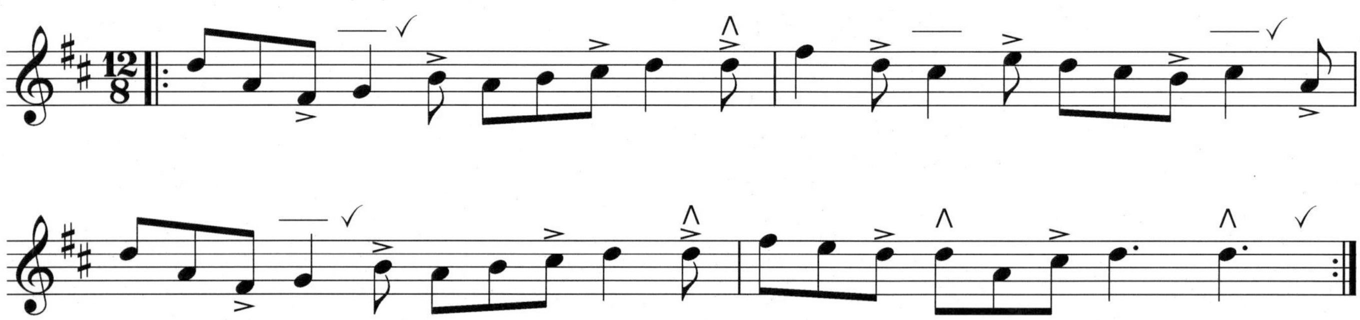

7. Although it is less common to see dotted quarter notes in reels, they do allow more time to execute finger vibrato and a breath in a busier time signature. They are also a good approximation of how fiddle players may add longer notes to tunes.

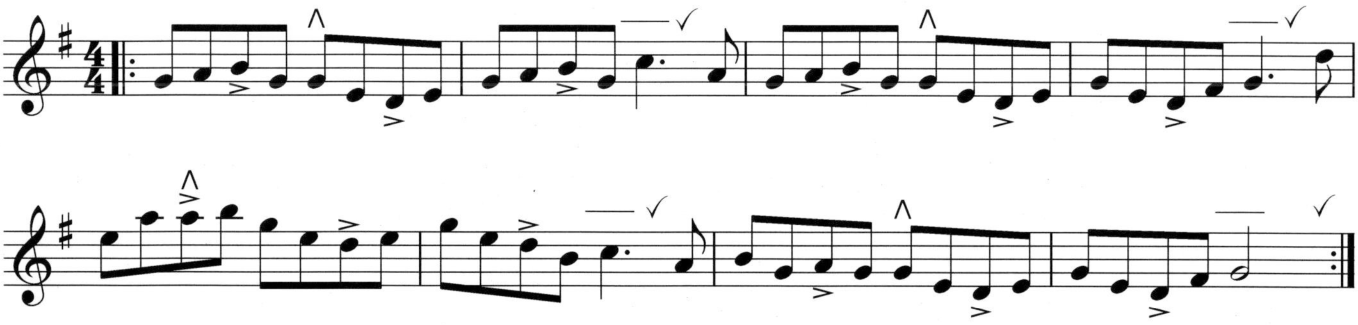

8. Boehm players might consider using their ring finger F♯' to at least navigate the transition between measures two to three and six to seven.

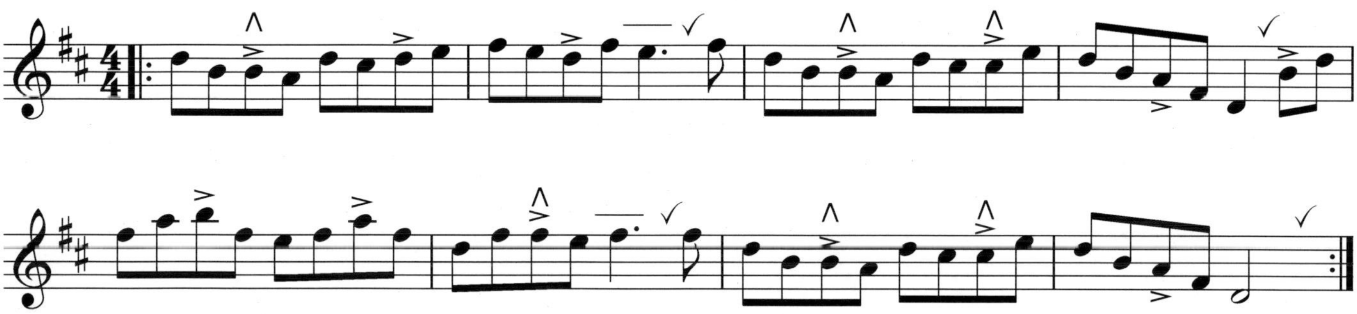

TRACK 20

9. These will be a little more challenging now that the dotted quarters are gone. You'll only have time for a quick flutter of vibrato before taking a breath.

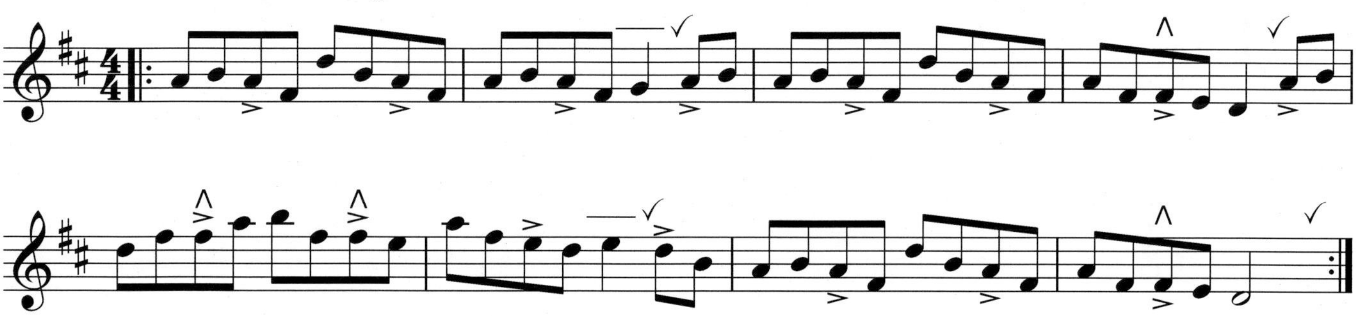

10.

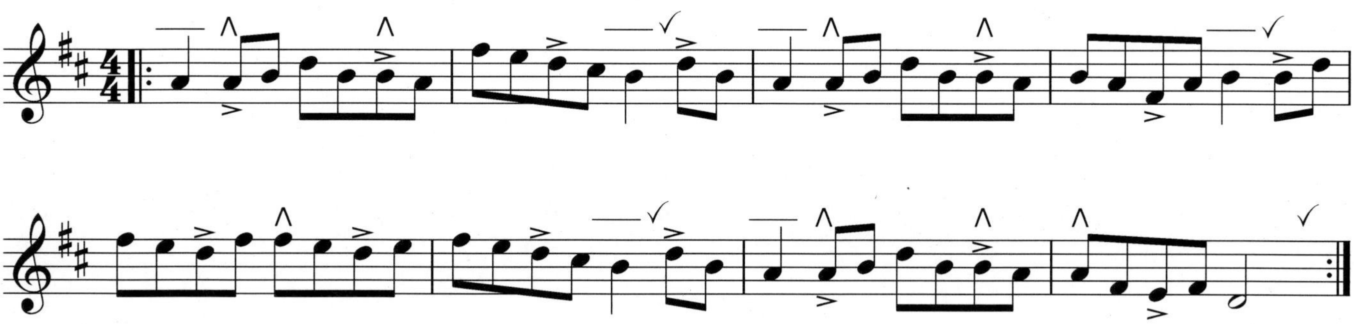

Finger Vibrato: Tunes

Although these tune types tend to be played quite quickly, adding quick turns of finger vibrato can provide wonderful lift to the melody. You may find that using finger vibrato just before a breath can also help shape the tune in such a way that the breath is less noticeable.

SYMBOLS KEY:

Volume I: Backbeat and Breathing	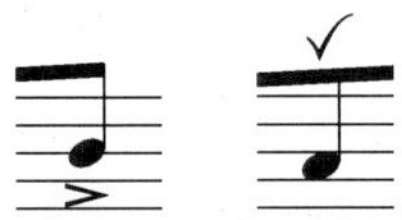 b. beat breath
Volume II: Single Ornaments	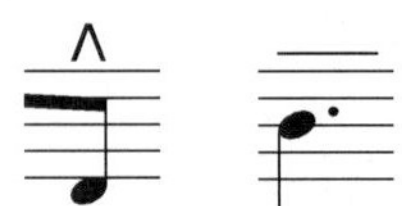 glottal finger vibrato

Finger Vibrato: Boiled Goat's Milk

This jig benefits from a quick shimmer of vibrato on some occasional long notes. You won't have much time for them, especially since they're followed by breaths, so you'll have to move quickly. You may add more vibrato as you see fit, but other ornaments will soon be added to the remaining long notes in this tune.

TRACK 21

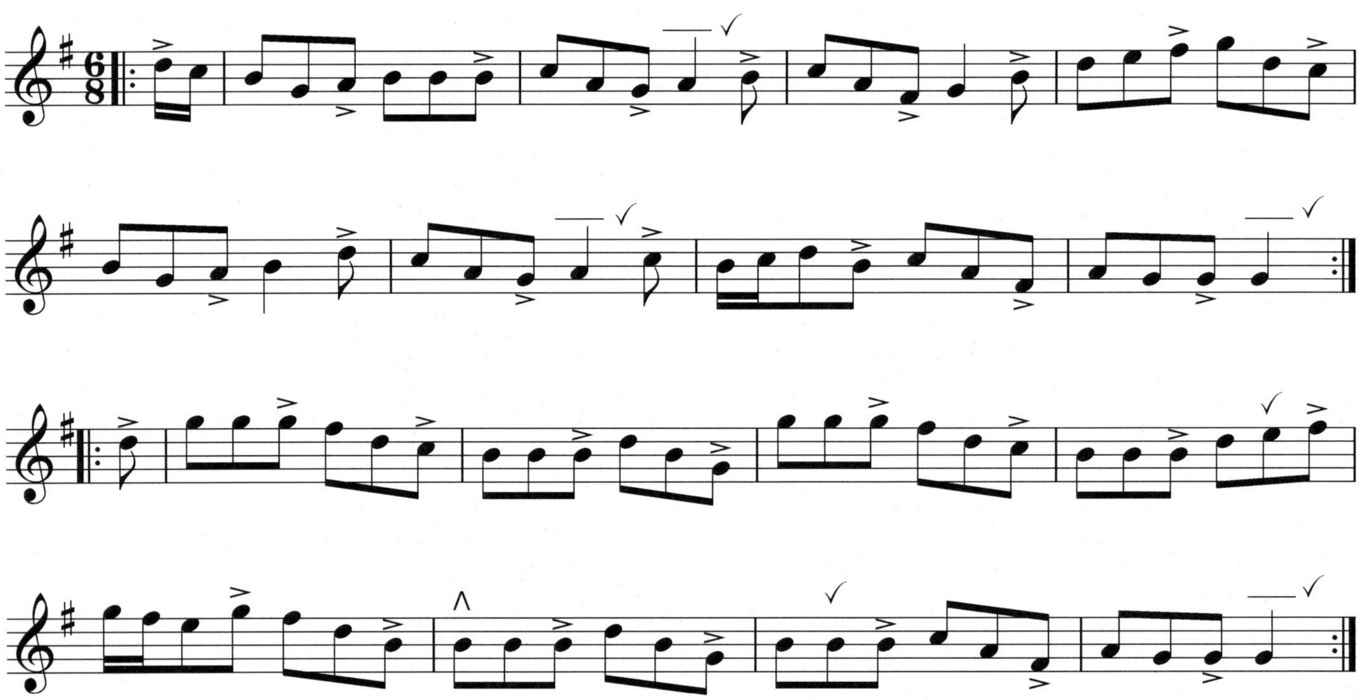

Finger Vibrato: Dever the Dancer

You may certainly add finger vibrato to any of the Gs beyond the few already marked in. However, we'll soon be learning other ornaments to add to those Gs as well. Note that finger vibrato is not possible on the long D' in the penultimate measure.

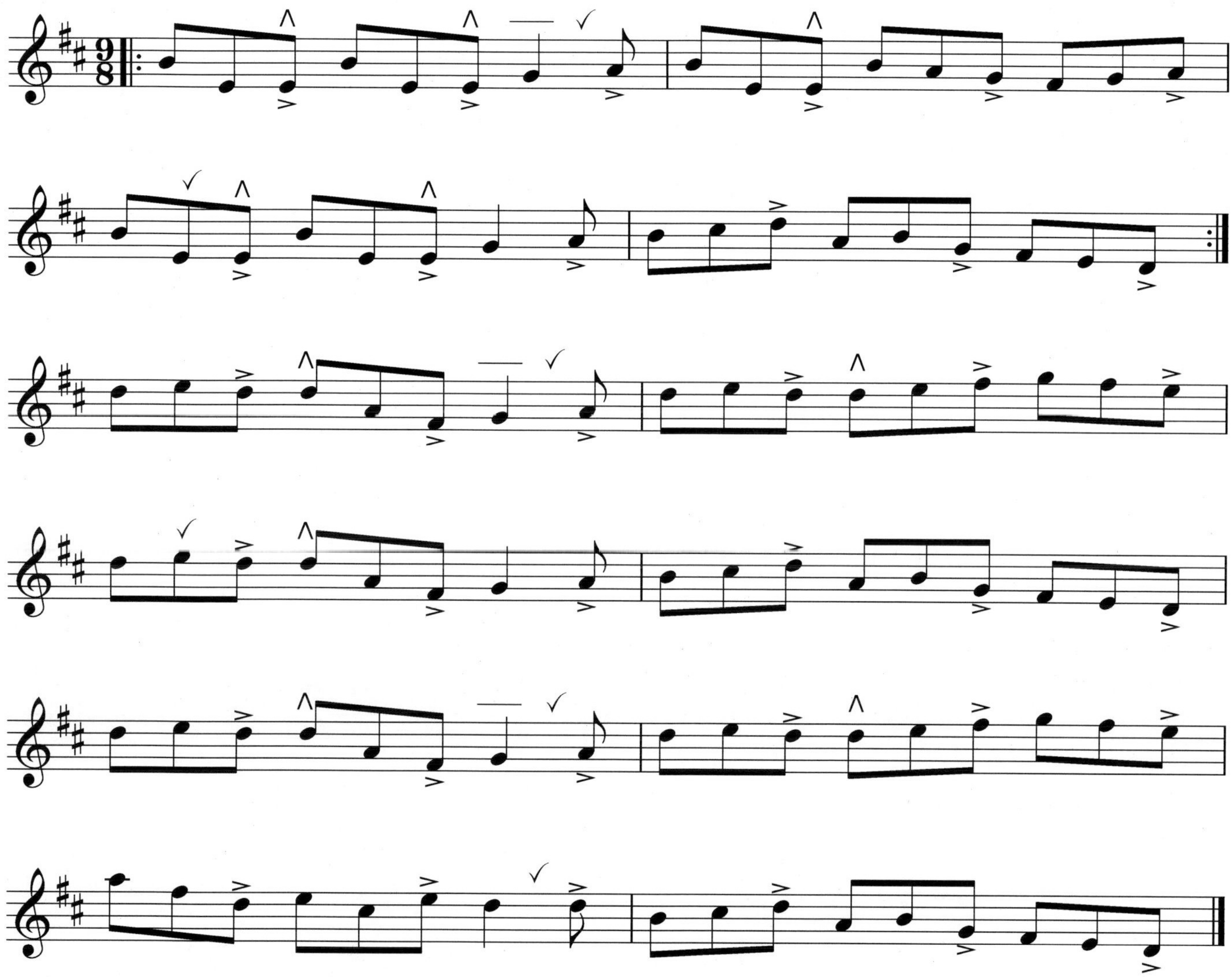

Finger Vibrato: The Dingle Regatta

Here is an example of how sparingly finger vibrato can be used. Notice that the finger vibrato at the end of the A and C parts is combined with a glottal.

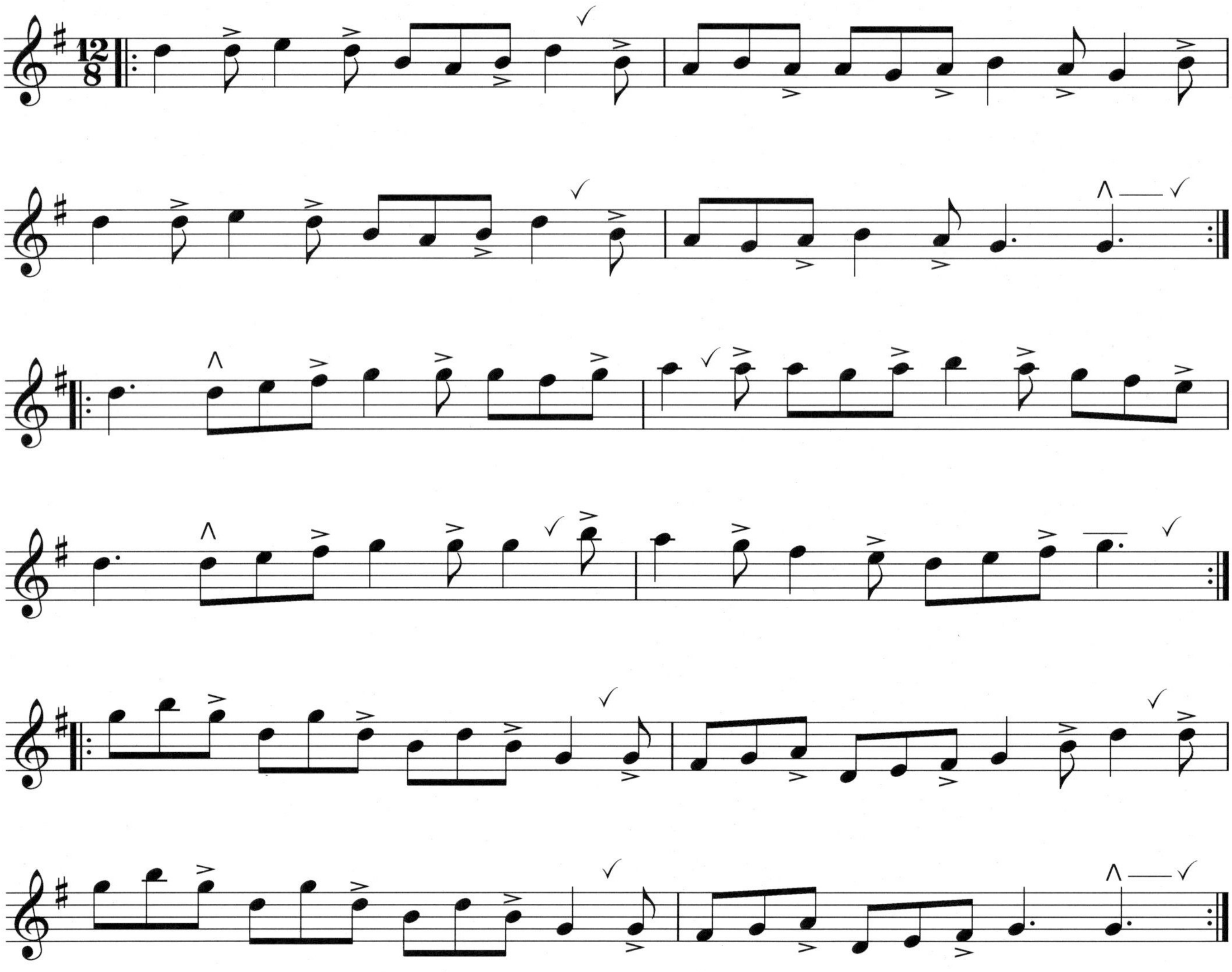

Finger Vibrato: My Love is in America

Finger vibrato in the B part provides a welcome respite in an otherwise busy tune, as well as a lovely contrast to the sixteenth note passages that begin the A part. It's also a nice imitation of those long fiddle notes we discussed at the very beginning of the chapter.

TRACK 22

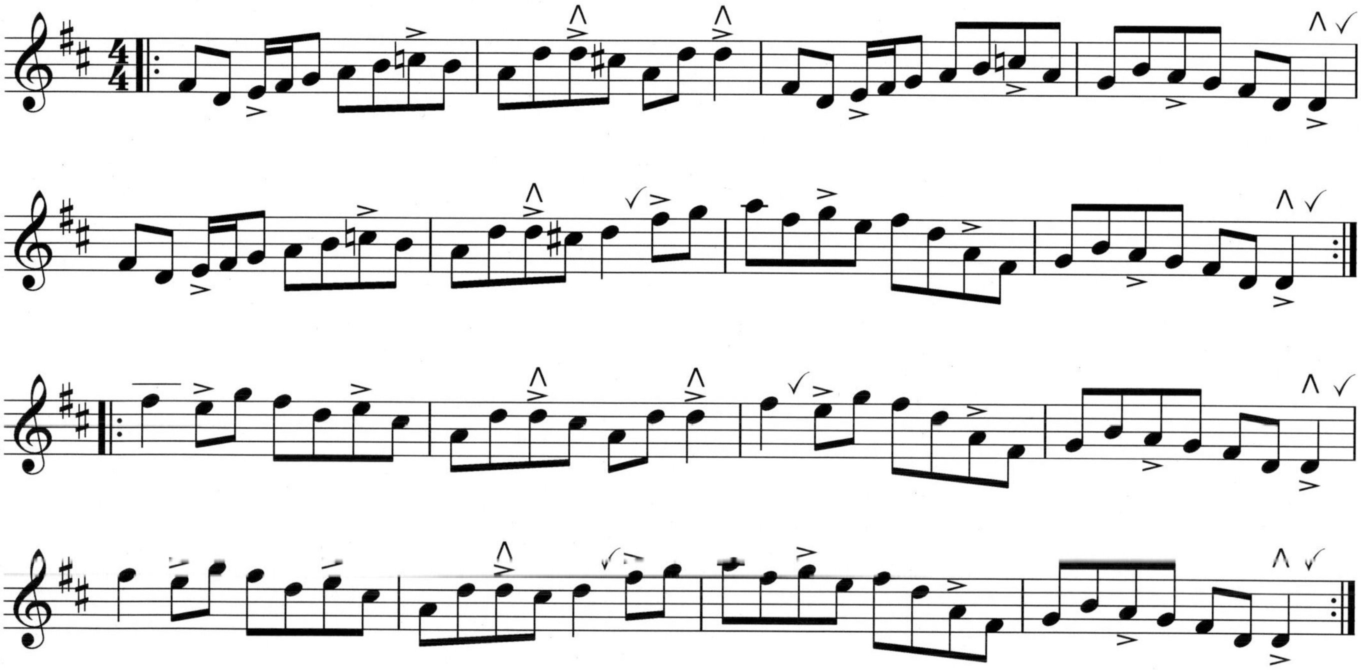

Finger Vibrato: The Pretty Blue Seagull

This tune is a great opportunity to practice your half-holed E vibrato. Add as much as you'd like to unmarked Es. We'll add more ornaments to them in coming chapters.

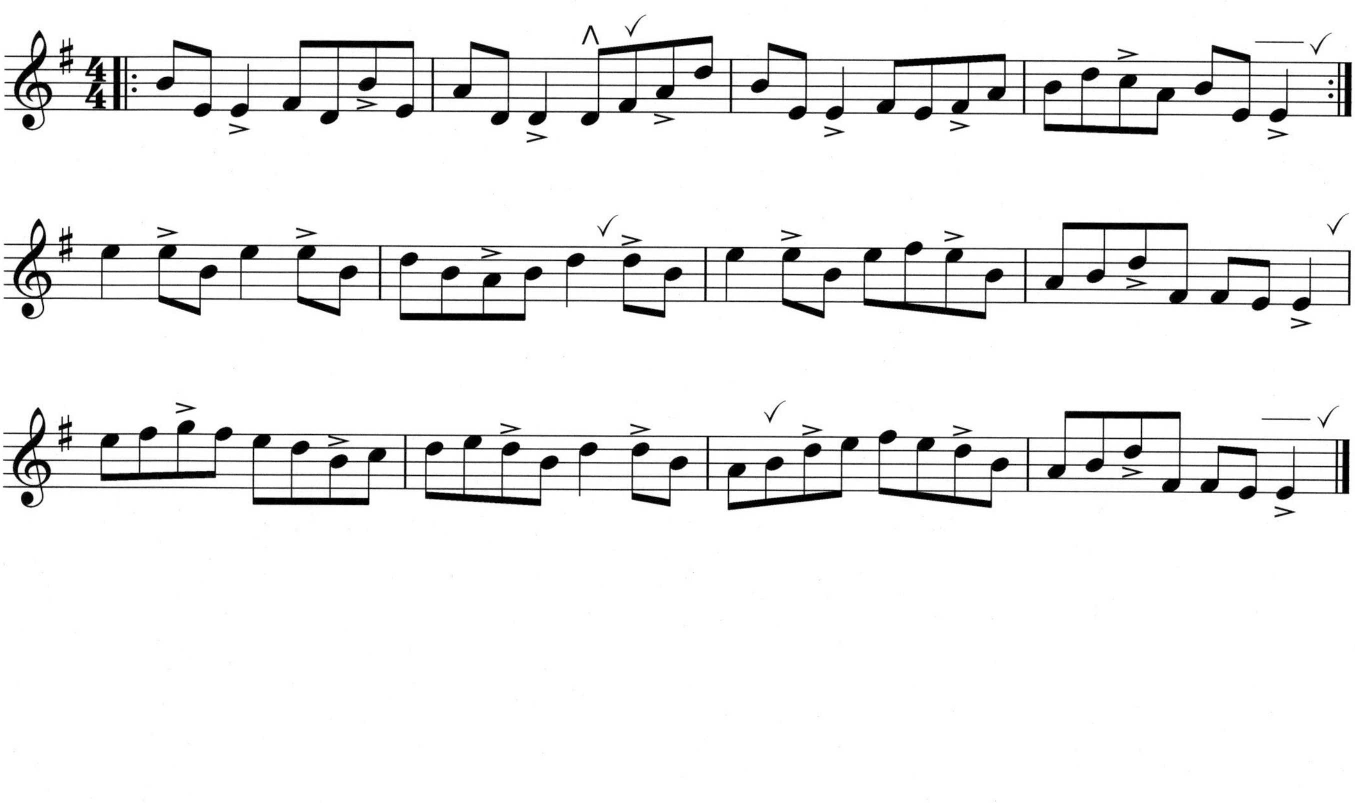

Finger Vibrato: The Congress Reel

Certainly feel free to add finger vibrato to any long As, Es, and Cs that are not marked. We'll be learning additional ornaments for those notes in the coming chapters.

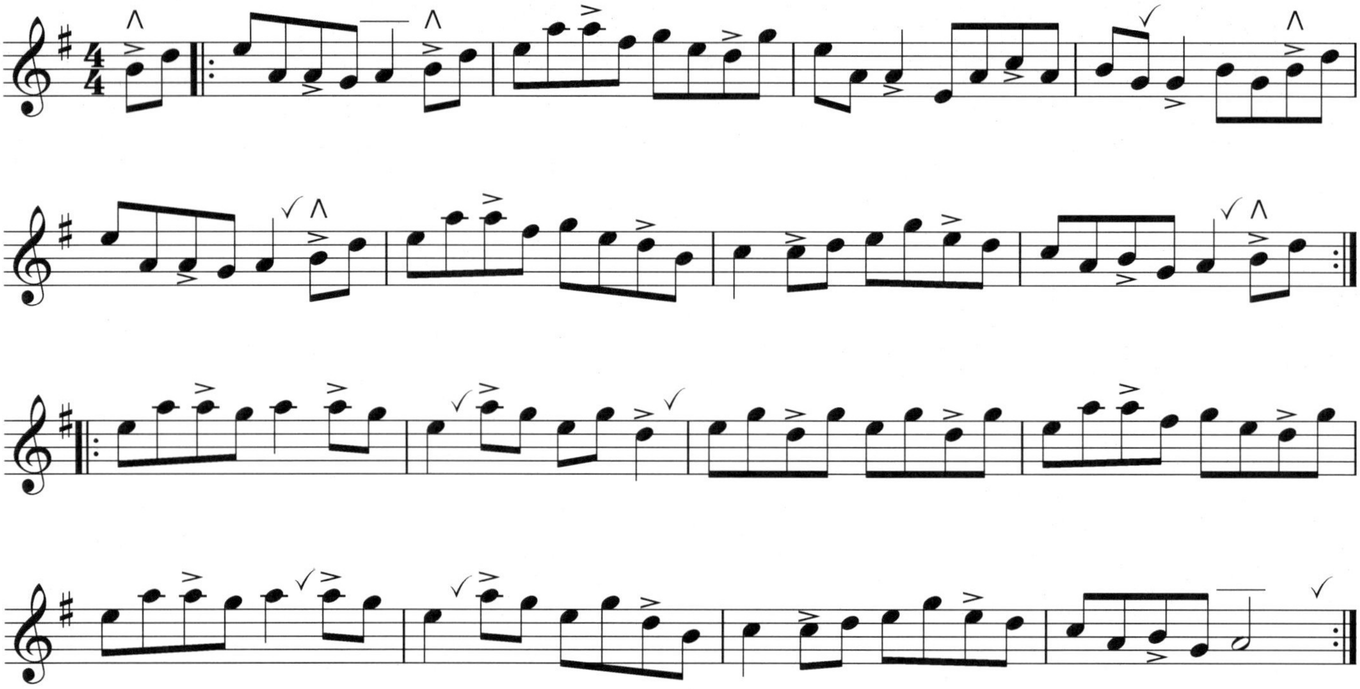

Chapter 3: Slides

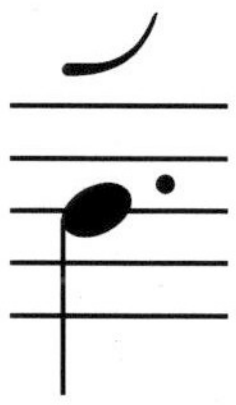

Slides (not to be confused with the tune type) are exactly what they sound like: sliding a finger off the flute in order to arrive at a primary note. A slide is similar in execution to a *glissando* (sliding between two notes), but in faster tunes is rhythmically comparable to a *scoop* (beginning below pitch slightly before the beat and quickly sliding up to the intended note). Like the scoop, it is more common (and for flute players, more ergonomic) to move up to a note rather than down. Slides are often used in slow tunes, such as airs, but they also have great application in faster tunes like jigs, slip jigs, slides (the tune type, not the ornament), and reels. While slides can be used to ornament most notes, especially rhythmically longer notes, they can also be used more specifically to embellish the high register, soften octave or wide interval jumps, and resolve up from lower neighbor notes.

Slides can also be paired with other ornamentation, such as finger vibrato (see *Finger Vibrato* on page 18) or more advanced rolls (see *Advanced Rolls* in Volume III). Because of the motion involved, it is not possible to create quite the same sound between C to D' or C♯ and D', so slides are mostly used on E, F♯, G, A, B, and C♯. B to C slides are possible, but the fingering is slightly more complicated on both flutes. Although slides are easier to maneuver on simple system flute or open hole Boehm flutes, they are also possible on closed hole Boehm flutes.

It is possible to execute slides moving in either direction, and I tend to categorize slides as *push slides* (pushing my fingers away from my hand and off the holes or keys) and *pull slides* (pulling my fingers back towards my hands). I recommend that all flutists experiment with both directions. The notes around a slide will often determine the best direction for the ornament.

In order to play a slide, start on the note below the primary note and slide into the primary note. For instance, if you want to execute a B slide, play an A and gradually slide your left hand middle finger off the flute until you've arrived on a B. Some flutists do slide between wider intervals by starting with more fingers down and sliding and lifting these additional fingers off simultaneously. While you are certainly welcome to experiment with this, it is easier to learn how to slide with one finger first (particularly for Boehm flutists who are navigating around their keys).

Boehm Tip | Slide your finger off the hole (if playing an open hole flute) as you gradually raise the key. This will take practice and coordination. Be careful not to move your finger too abruptly or your slide will become a series of bumpy steps. The smoothest ornaments may come from push slides on some fingers and pull slides on others. Sometimes, moving *away* from the hinging mechanism of the keys creates the smoothest slide, which means that the left hand will execute pull slides (curling inwards) while the right hand performs push slides (straightening outwards).

Transition Tip | If you are playing a closed hole flute now, a sliding motion will seem unnecessary since there is no hole from which to slide. However, I do recommend using the motion as it will not only assist in raising keys with the necessary gradation, but it will also allow you to transition these slides directly to simple system or open hole flute in the future. If you are transitioning between Boehm and simple system flutes now, you may find that while the sliding motion may stay mostly the same, the direction you prefer (push vs. pull) may be different.

Simple System Tip | Experiment with both push and pull slides. Many players will develop a preference for one direction or the other, with this preference sometimes changing from finger to finger. There are benefits to developing fluency in either direction, as the notes around a slide often dictate whether a push or pull is more ergonomic.

Slides Fingering Chart

Slide can be a little tricky to execute, and feel pretty different between the flutes. I've therefore included a number of tips to take into consideration when you start playing through the fingering chart.

Slides Fingering Chart:

To read this fingering chart, place all X fingers down, then slide your finger off **X**.

	Boehm	Simple System
E/E'	X X X | X X **X** o o x	X X X | X X **X**
F♯/F♯'	X X X | **X** X O o o x	X X X | X **X** O
G/G'	X X X | O O **X** x o x *or* X X X | O **X** O o o x	X X X | **X** O O
A/A'	X X **X** | O O O o o x	X X **X** | O O O
B/B'	X **X** O | O O O o o x	X **X** O | O O O
C/C'	Boehm* X O O | O O O o o **x**	Simple System** **X** O O | O O O
C♯/C♯'	X O O | O O O o → **X** O O | O O O o o **x**	**X** O O | O O O

On the Boehm flute, C natural slides work best by sliding the thumb sideways.

***C natural slides on simple system flutes require removing the index finger from only half of the B hole, either by sliding halfway or rotating the finger off the hole.*

Slides: Preliminary Exercises

Slides can happen before or after the beat, with different lengths depending on the speed of the tune and what the musician would like to imply. In a slow tune, for instance, musicians may create tension by using a slower slide that begins on the beat. In faster tunes, however, musicians may use quicker slides that begin just before the downbeat. Developing a familiarity with varying speeds and rhythmic placements is very beneficial. To this end, the exact rhythm of these exercises is not notated, and it is left up to you to experiment with how and where you would like to execute these ornaments.

In the first two measures of these exercises for example, you may experiment with beginning the slide on the downbeat and not resolving until the second beat of the half note. In the last two measures, you could practice a quicker version of the same ornament by beginning the slide just before the beat and resolving the slide on the downbeat. Each measure is repeated twice so that you can practice push or pull slides if you'd like (I recommend that you do).

> **General Tip** | Be sure to start from the note below the one written in these exercises. While you will need to curl or straighten slide fingers, you shouldn't have to change the position of your other fingers in order to do so.

> **Simple System Tip** | Due to the wider circumference of simple system flutes, players with smaller hands may find it difficult to execute C♯ pull slides. You can experiment with pulling your finger to the side, or simply use push slides on your C♯s instead.

TRACK 23

1. There's no need to tongue your slides. Simply rearticulate them by beginning the ornament again.

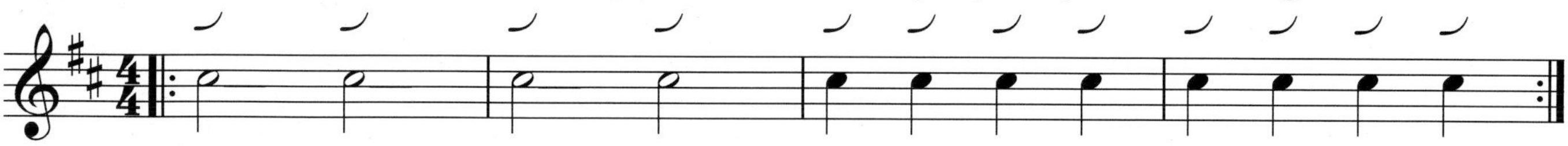

2.

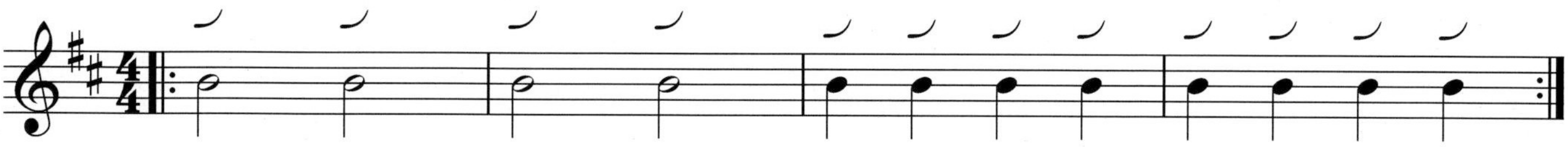

> **Simple System Tip** | If you have smaller hands, you may find that your ring fingers are already completely straightened. Since push slides involve straightening fingers, this means a standard A or E push slide may be difficult. It is possible to experiment with pushing your fingers to the side and creating a push slide in this way instead. If this sound or action is not agreeable, however, it is certainly fine to use only pull slides on As and Es.

3. For flutists with small hands, a pull slide may be the best option for A slides.

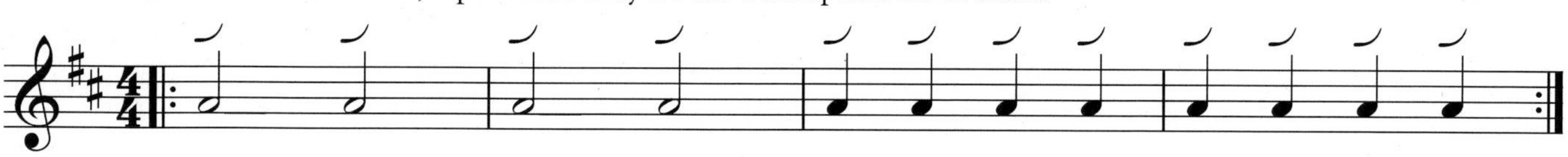

Boehm Tip | If you are hearing distinct steps instead of a smooth glissando, concentrate on curling or uncurling your fingers rather than lifting them. This can be very helpful in smoothly raising the keys.

4.

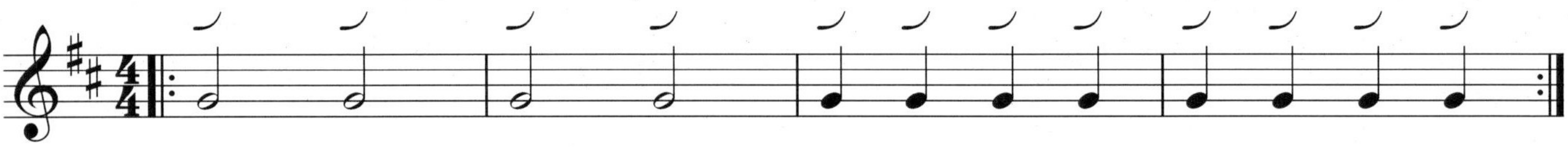

5.

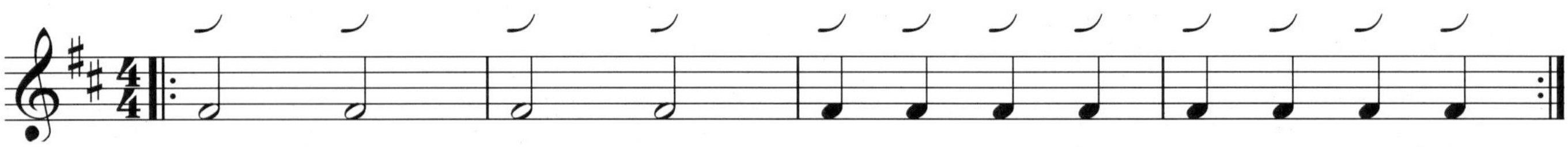

6. As previously mentioned with A, an E pull slide may work best for smaller hands.

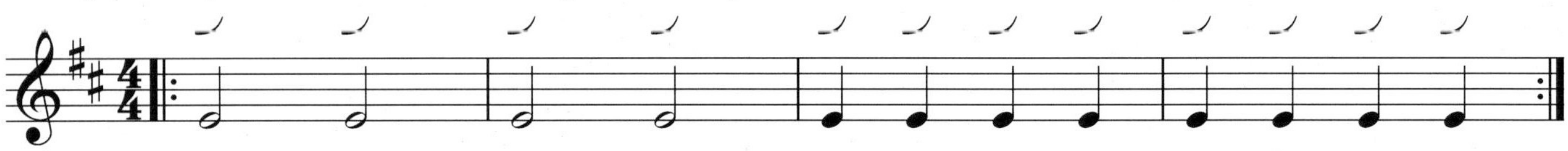

Simple System Tip | Due to the circumference of the flute, it may not be possible to execute traditional push or pull slides on C natural. These slides may therefore involve pulling your finger to the side, or even rotating your entire hand slightly. Make sure you are only opening the hole half way.

7.

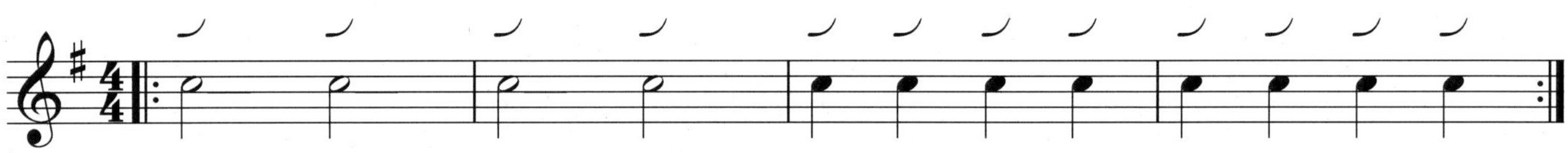

8. Your goal is to automatically know which finger must be used to create each slide.

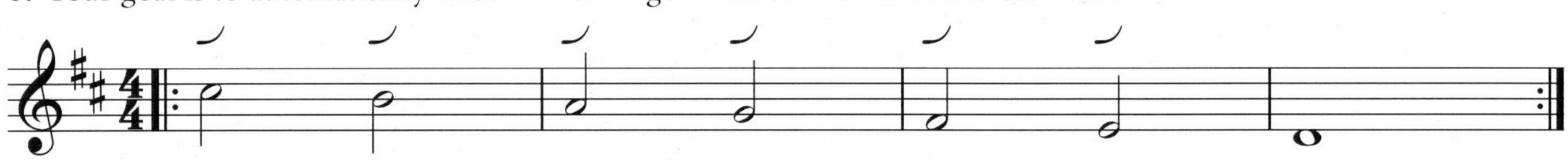

Boehm Tip | As you saw on the fingering chart, a C♯ slide requires moving two fingers at once, and may therefore be slightly less smooth than other slides.

TRACK 24

9. Practice sliding up from a lower neighbor note.

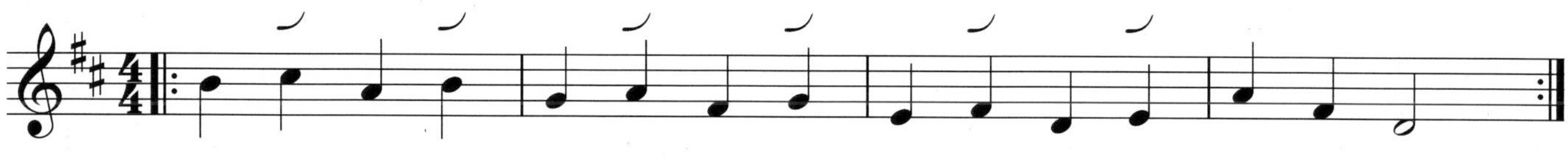

TRACK 25

10. Now try using slides to ornament these higher notes.

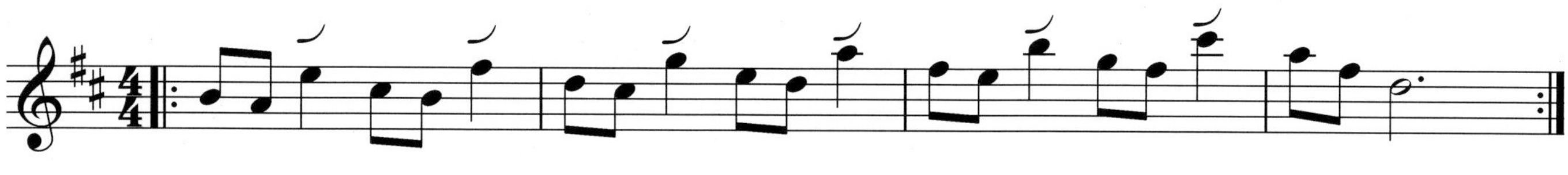

TRACK 26

11. Octave jumps are a great example of using slides to simultaneously define and soften wide intervals.

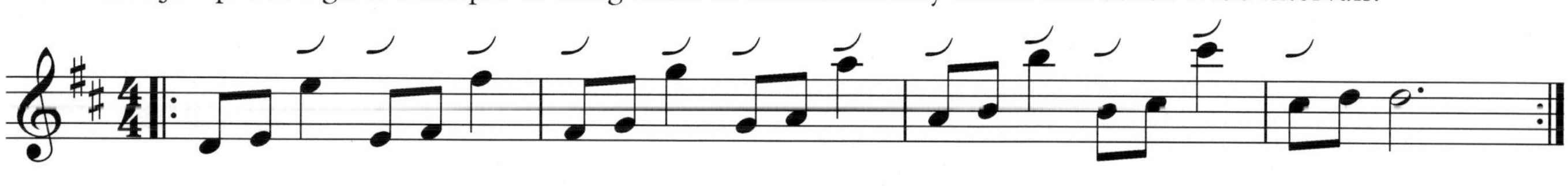

Slides: Contextual Exercises

These next exercises will provide a chance to incorporate your slides into simple melodies. You'll also practice using slides to slide up from a lower neighbor note, soften octave jumps, and embellish high notes.

1.

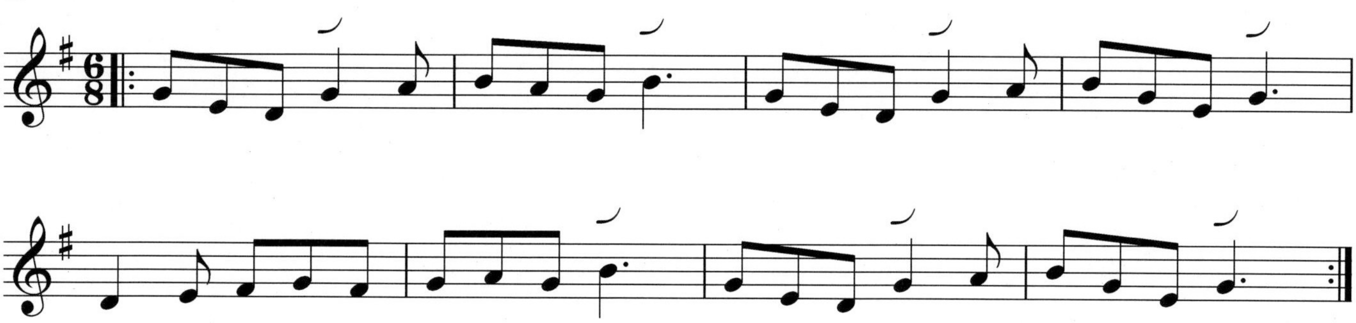

Boehm Tip | Be sure your F♯ slides end on your alternate fingering:

X X X | O X O o
o x

2.

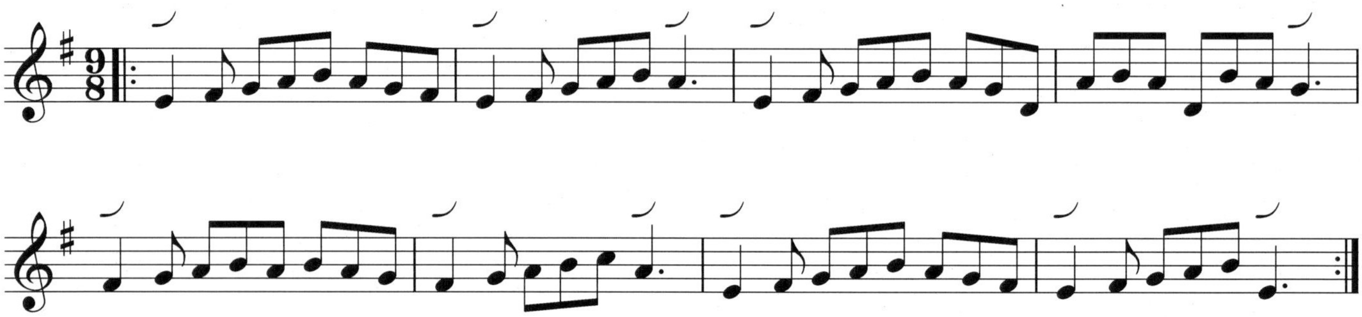

3.

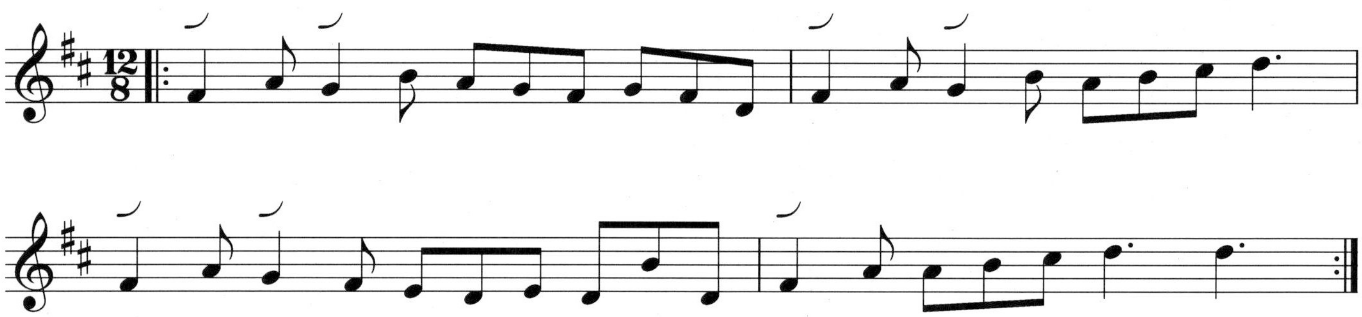

4. Faster slides placed right before the beat work best in reels.

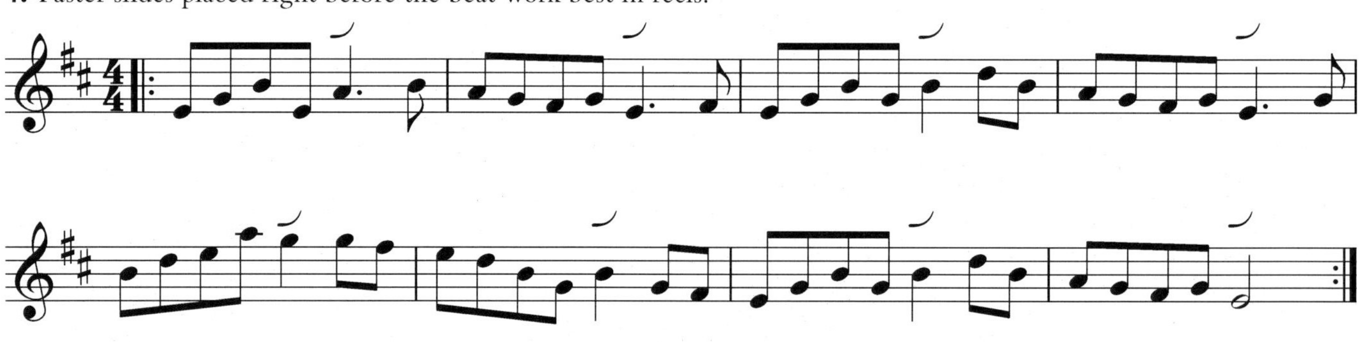

5. There are plenty of opportunities to practice lower neighbor note resolutions in the next two exercises.

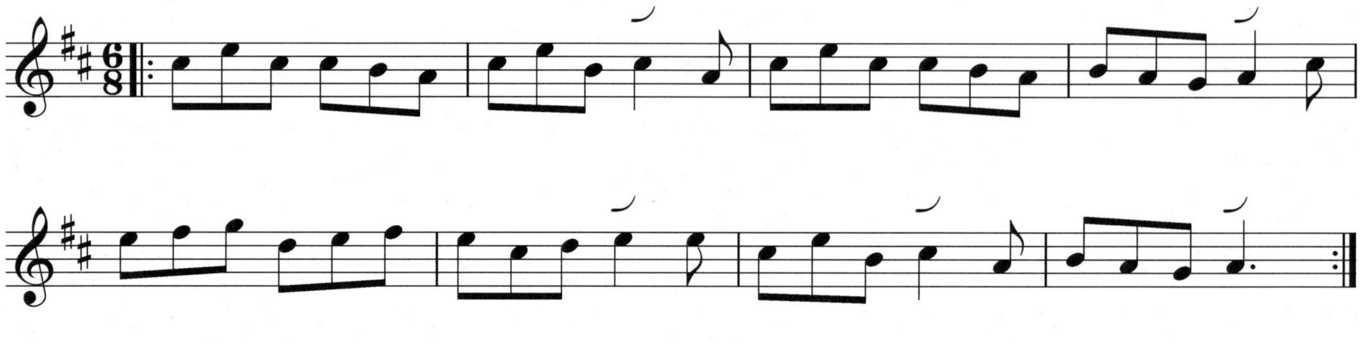

6.

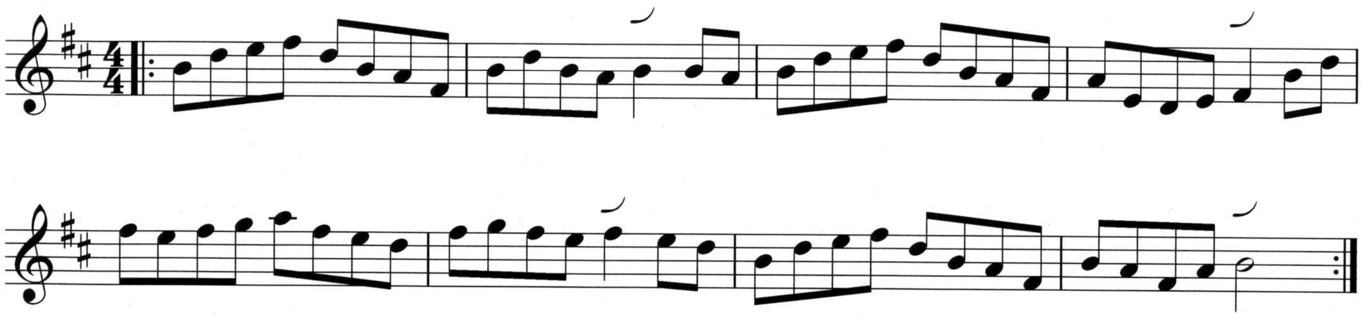

7. Exercises seven and eight are a chance to practice using slides to embellish long high notes.

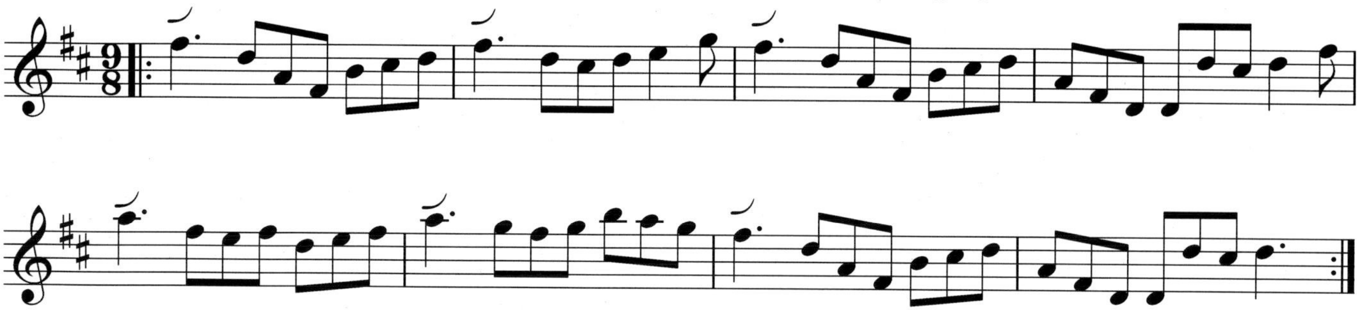

TRACK 27

8.

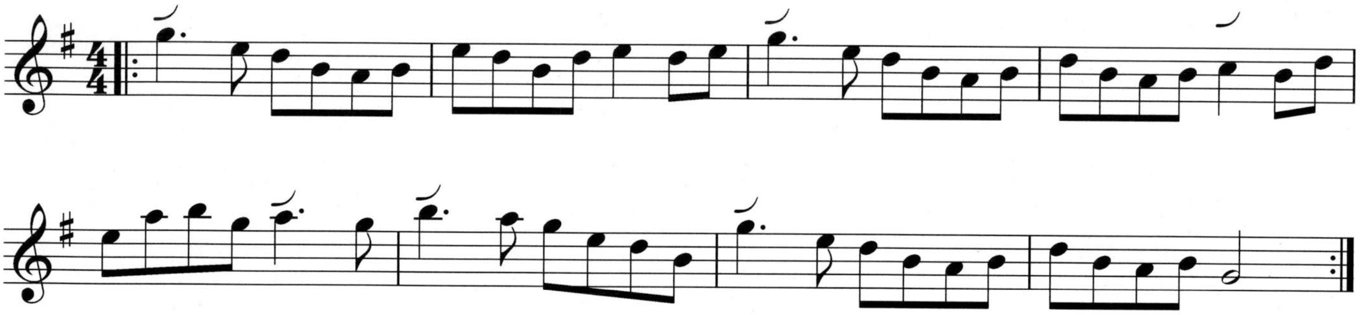

TRACK 28

9. Exercise nine and ten provide plenty of octave leaps in which to add slides.

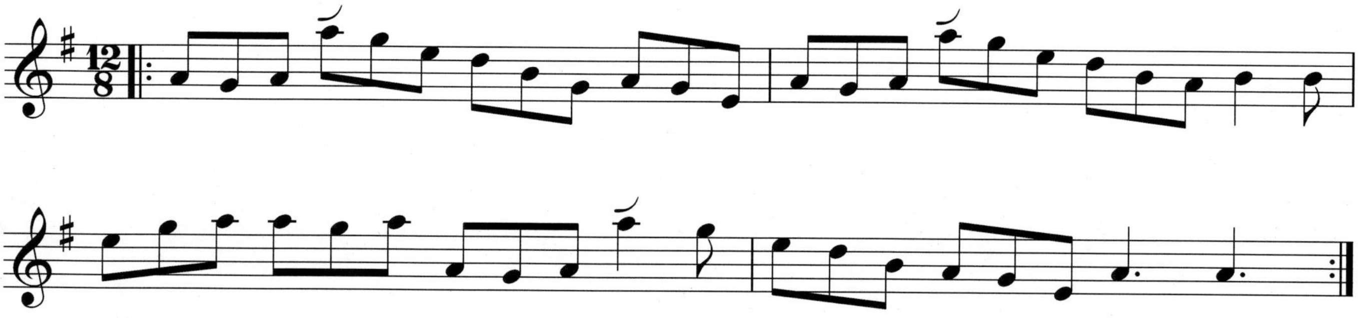

10.

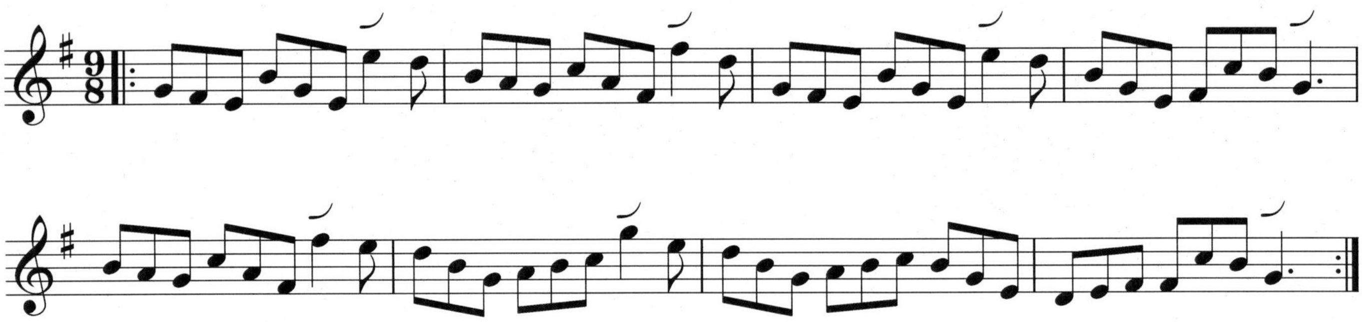

Slides: Combined Exercises

As we progress through the book and add a new ornament in each chapter, our combined exercises will become increasingly complicated. Please feel free to add ornaments gradually, starting with just a few in each exercise if necessary. Ornamentation is intended to embellish and *aid* a tune. A little bit can go a long way, and ornamentation should never make a tune sound overloaded or frenetic. Also keep in mind that these exercises are intended to help your fingers become agile and fluent and may therefore contain more repetition of the same ornaments than would ordinarily be used in a tune.

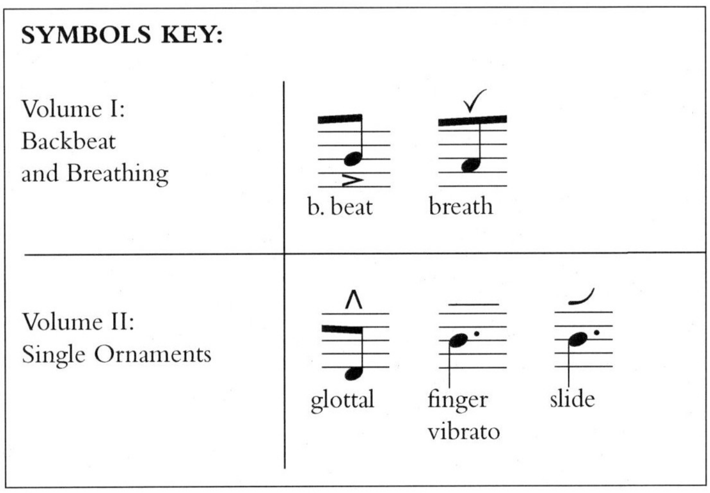

Boehm Tip | This is the first time you'll see slides combined with finger vibrato, a very common combination, and one that can be challenging on the Boehm flute due to the keys. Practice slowly and patiently. Keep your slides short, remember your good finger vibrato technique from the previous chapter, and break the exercises down into small chunks as needed.

Simple System Tip | Be sure to only slide halfway off the hole when executing C natural slides.

1. A quarter note that uses a slide and finger vibrato combination will necessarily require that each technique be executed quickly and cleanly.

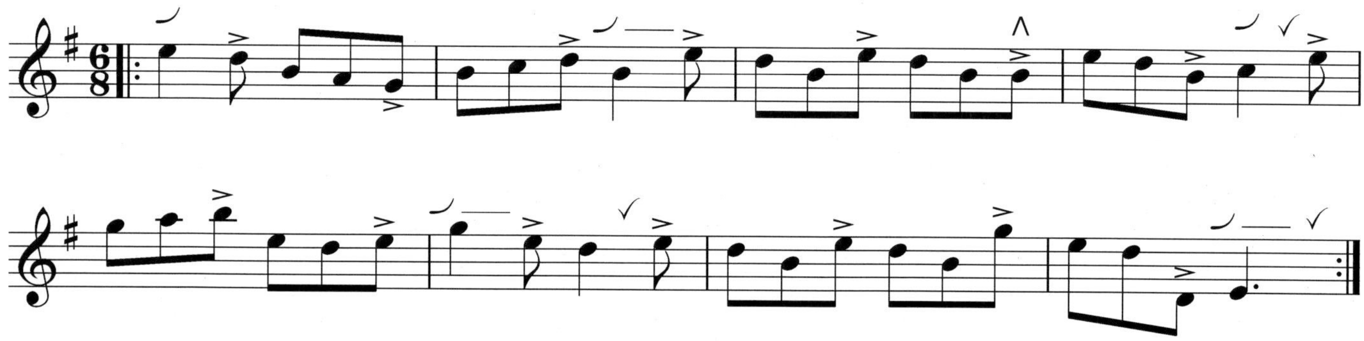

TRACK 29

2. Notice the breath in the second to last measure. Adding ornaments to rhythmically longer notes will begin to cover possible breathing spots and will require dropping eighth notes for breaths instead.

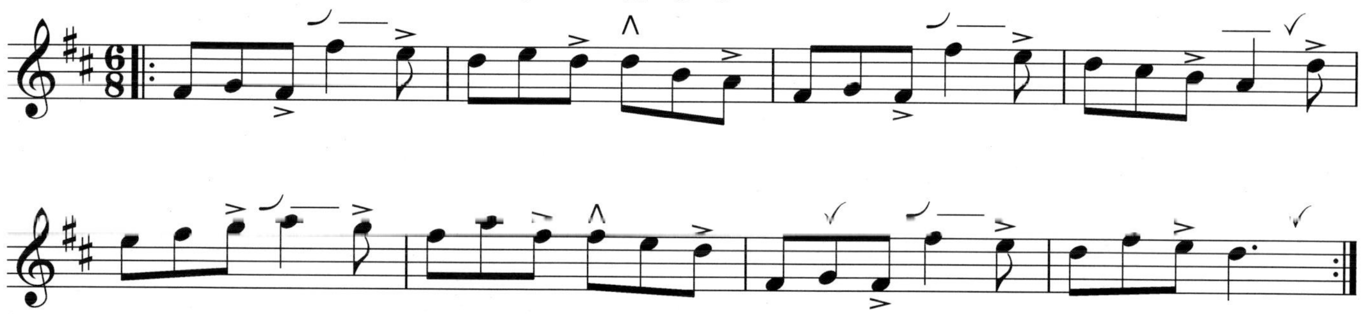

3. If you intend to breathe after a quarter note, it will be difficult to also fit in both a slide and finger vibrato. For this reason, any quarter notes followed by breaths use only a slide *or* finger vibrato.

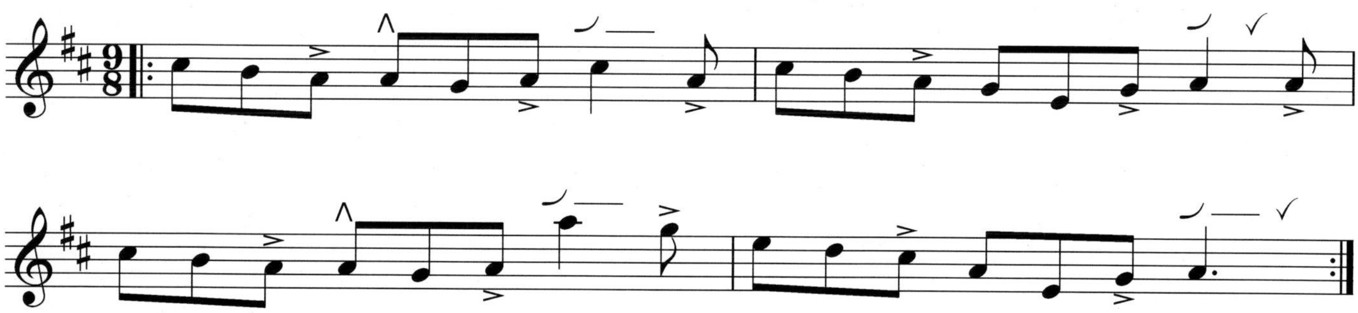

4.

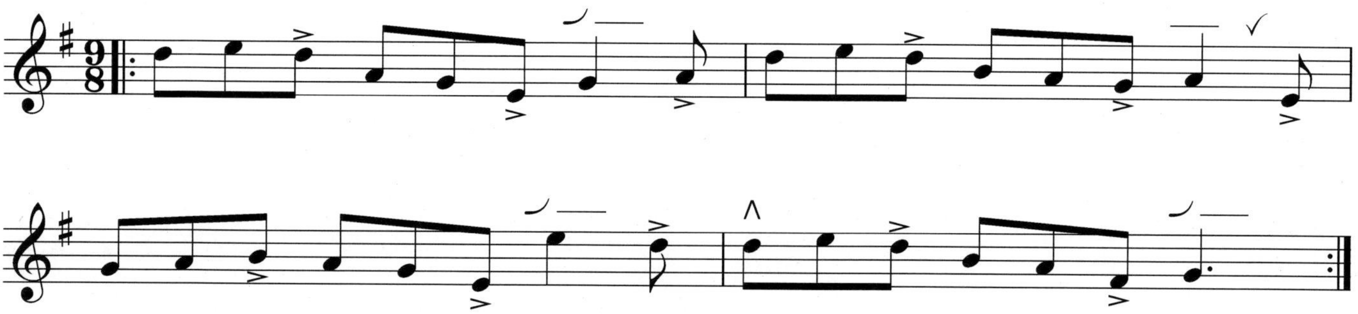

5. Now practice slides without a finger vibrato pairing.

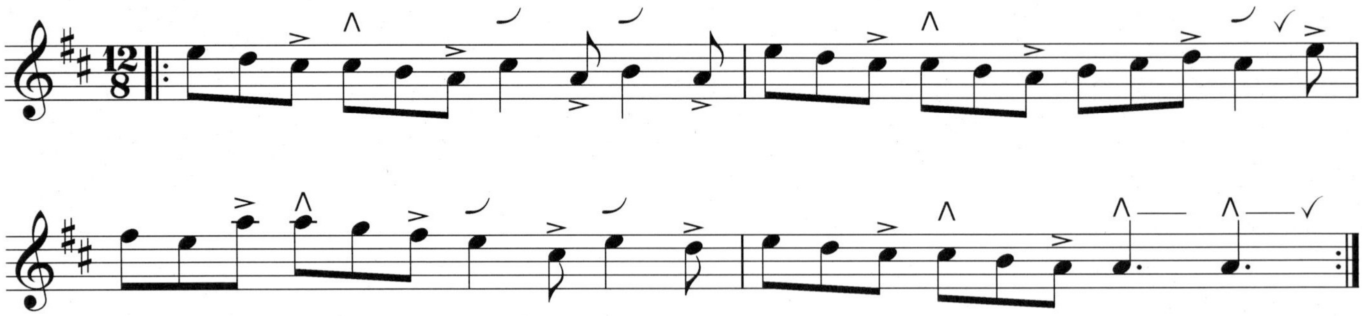

6. In contrast, pairing slides with finger vibrato creates a different sound. It is also much more challenging. While it would be unusual to use this figure so often in a single tune, it is good practice for now.

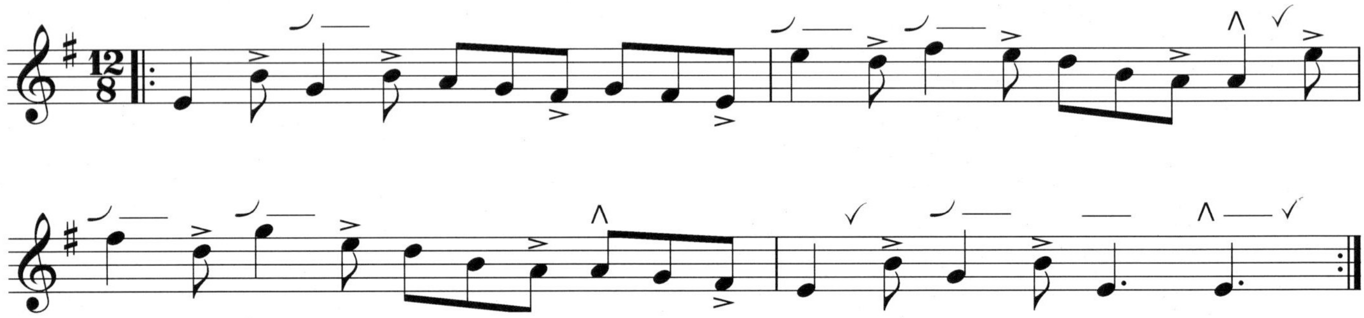

> **General Tip** | Sliding up to a high B requires good breath support and a strong embouchure. This is also a nice opportunity to revisit your glottals in the top octave. Glottals can be quite emphatic or fairly smooth. What's your preference?

7. As they are often played faster, reels may offer less space for ornament combinations on a single quarter note.

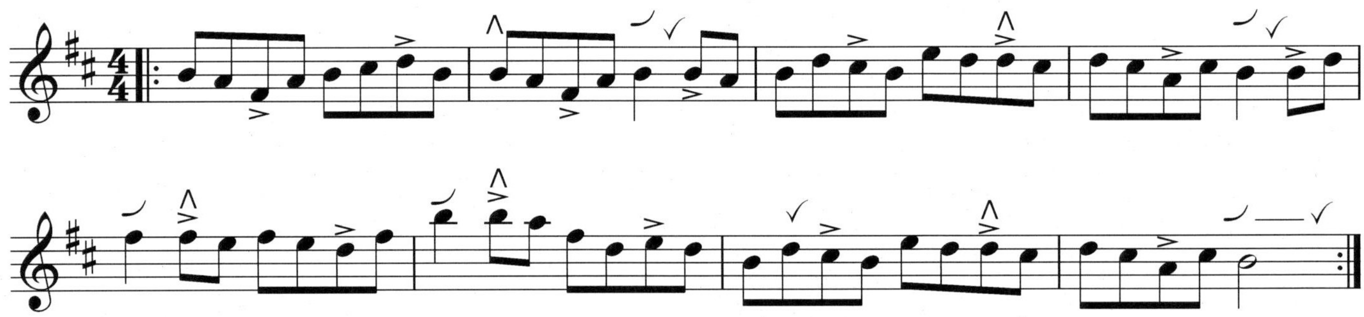

TRACK 30

8. Dotted quarters in reels are a great opportunity for ornament combinations, as seen in measure five. They also provide a wonderful contrast to the constant eighths of the tune.

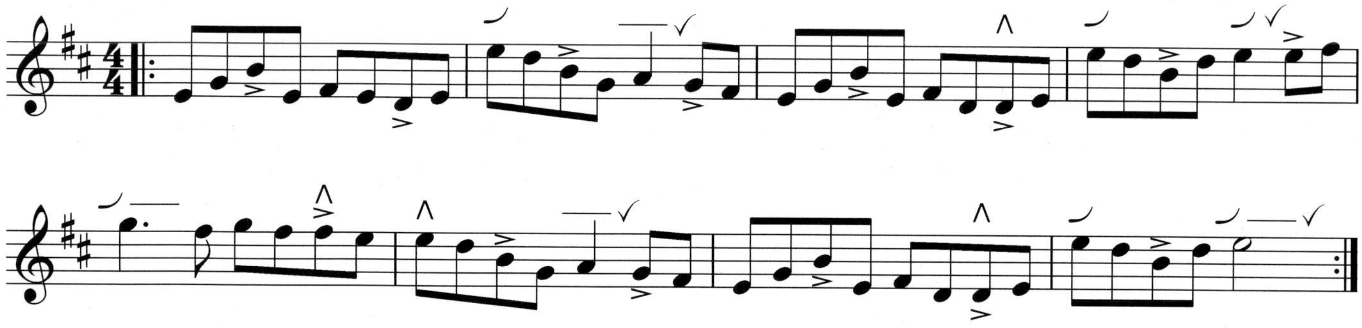

9.

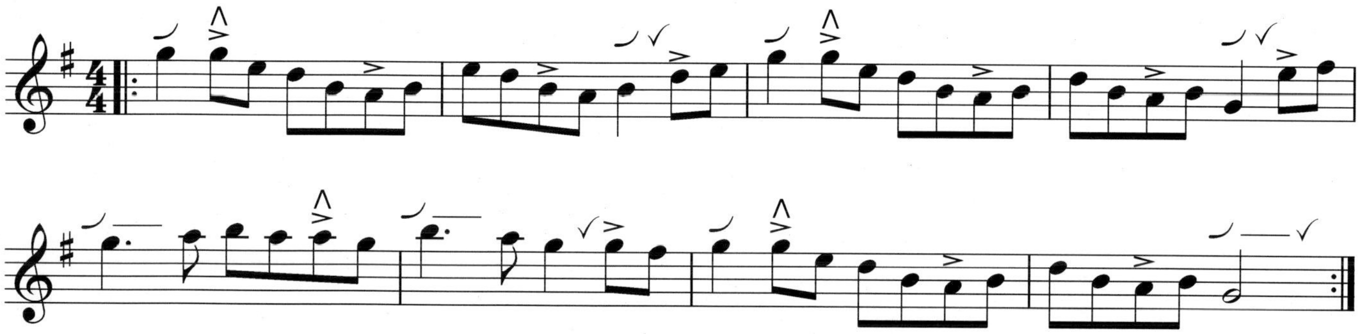

10.

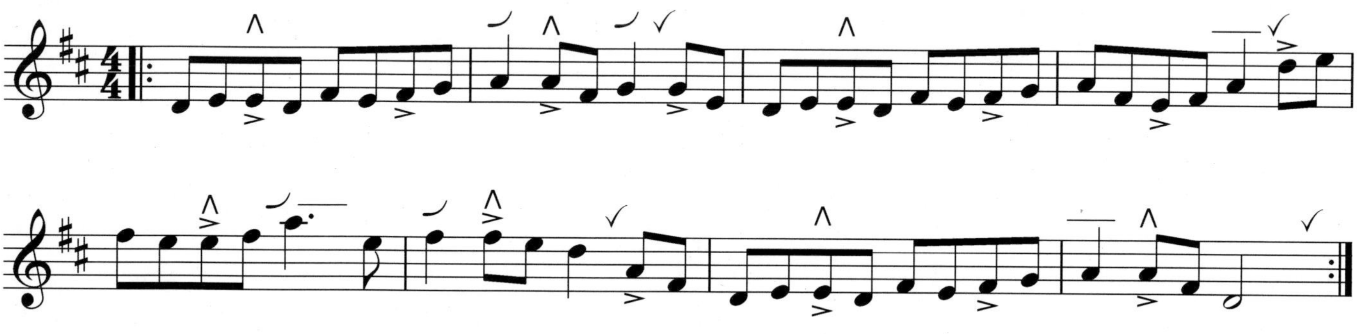

Slides: Tunes

Let's now take a look at how slides can be added to our selection of tunes. Refer to the Symbols Key if you need to, and work through the tunes slowly until you feel confident incorporating everything.

SYMBOLS KEY:

Volume I: Backbeat and Breathing	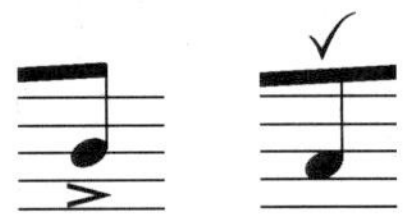 b. beat · breath
Volume II: Single Ornaments	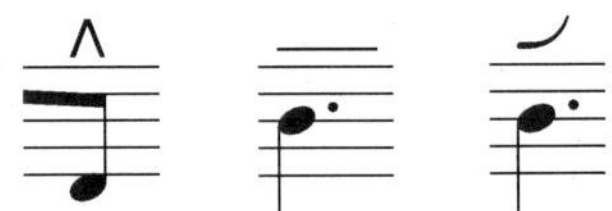 glottal · finger vibrato · slide

Slides: Boiled Goat's Milk

Slides in faster dance music will necessarily have to be quick, but if you've perfected the action by now, they can fit in quite effectively. This is true for the slides in the B part of this tune, which we will pair with an advanced roll in Volume III (see *Advanced Rolls*).

TRACK 31

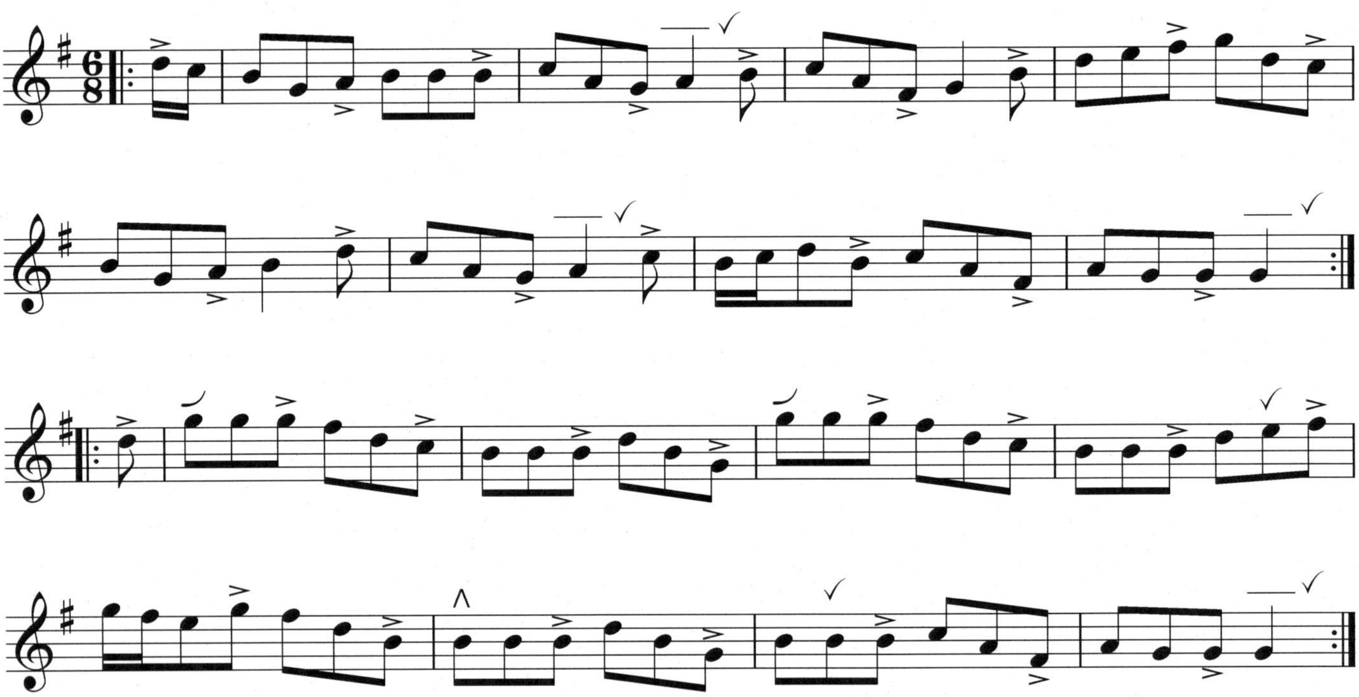

Slides: Dever the Dancer

A quick slide into the first note of a tune can be a great attention getter, and there are also opportunities for lower neighbor note slides in the B part. Remember that *Dever the Dancer* should resolve to an E the last time through the tune. If you are so inclined, you could slide into this final E as well.

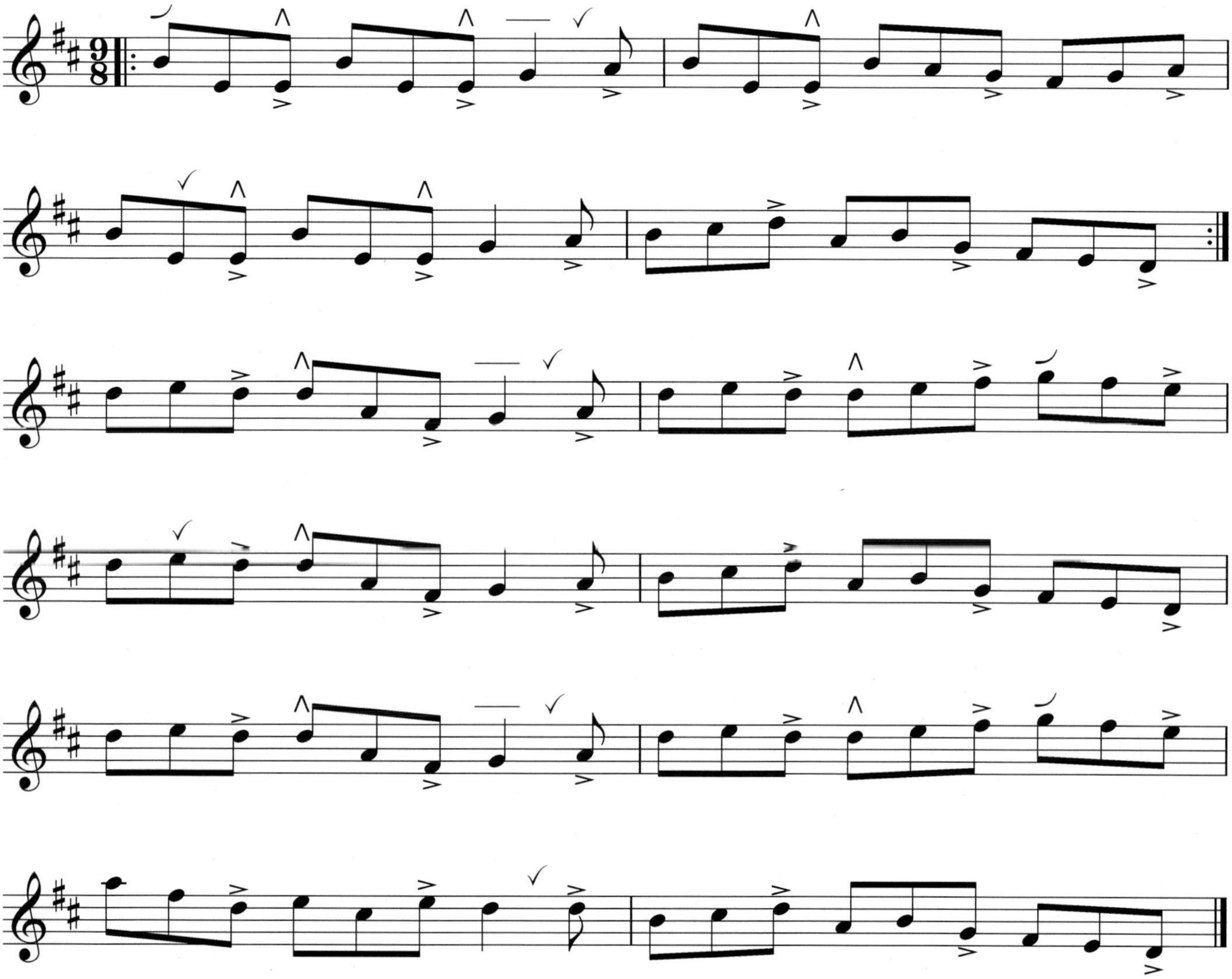

Slides: The Dingle Regatta

There are several opportunities for slides (the ornament) in this slide (the tune type). You may notice that measures one and three, while identical, do not both use slides on the E quarter note. You may certainly practice a slide on that second E for now, but we will add a different ornament to that note in Volume III.

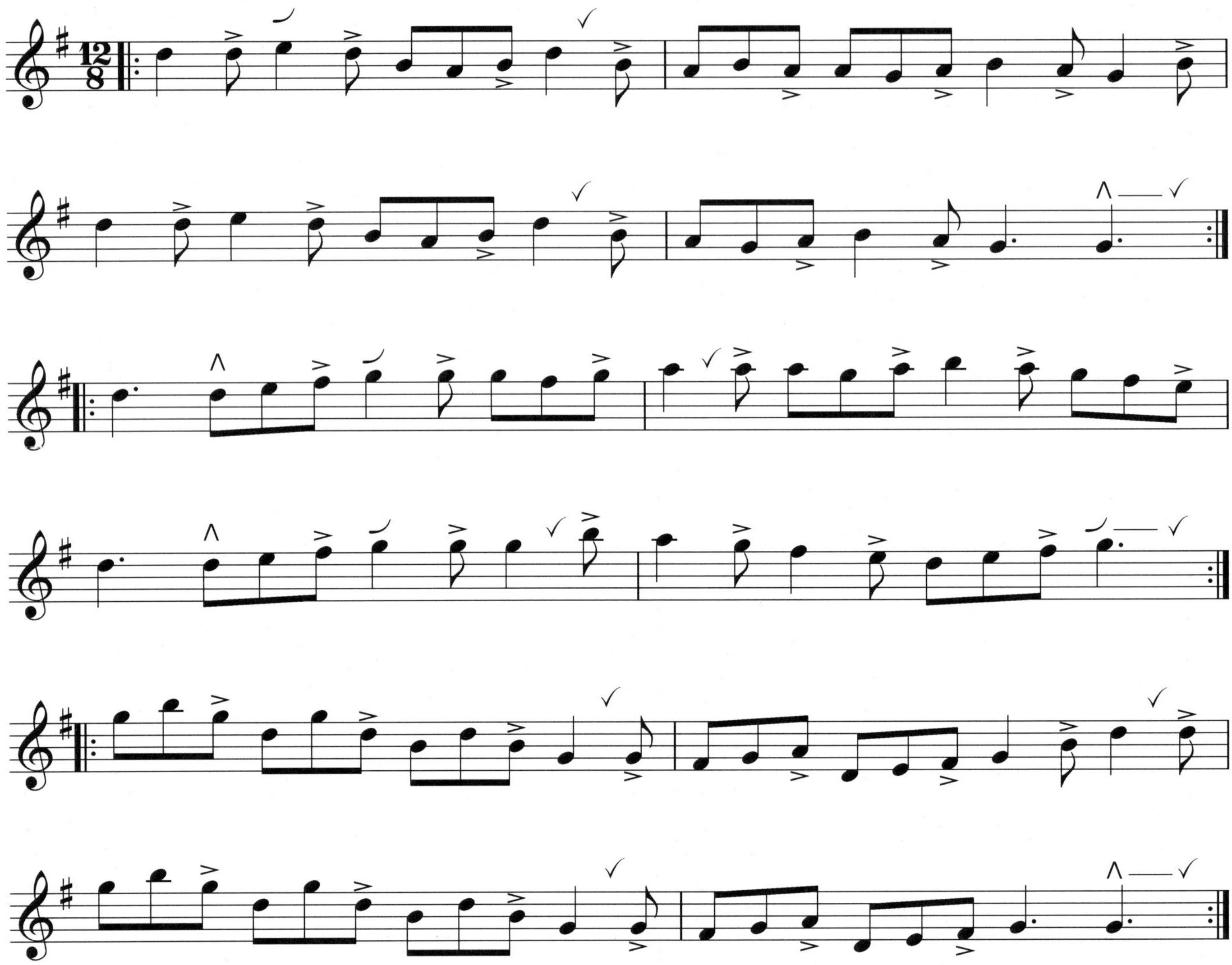

Slides: My Love is in America

Slides can also contribute to a breath of calm. We've already discussed adding finger vibrato to the B part of *My Love is in America* as a contrast to the busier A part. Sliding into this long note of finger vibrato helps pull the ears into this moment of respite.

TRACK 32

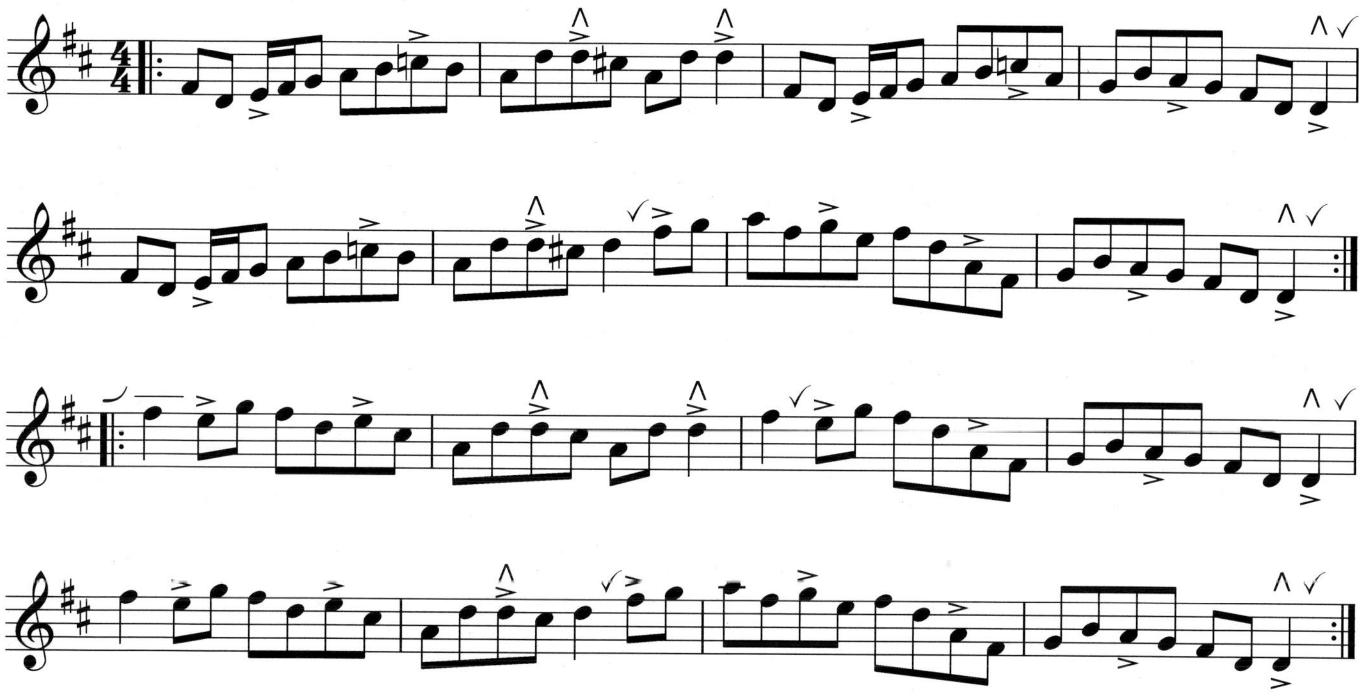

Slides: The Pretty Blue Seagull

The slides in the B part draw the ear to the tonal center of *The Pretty Blue Seagull*, as well as provide a springboard for advanced roll possibilities which we will explore in Volume III.

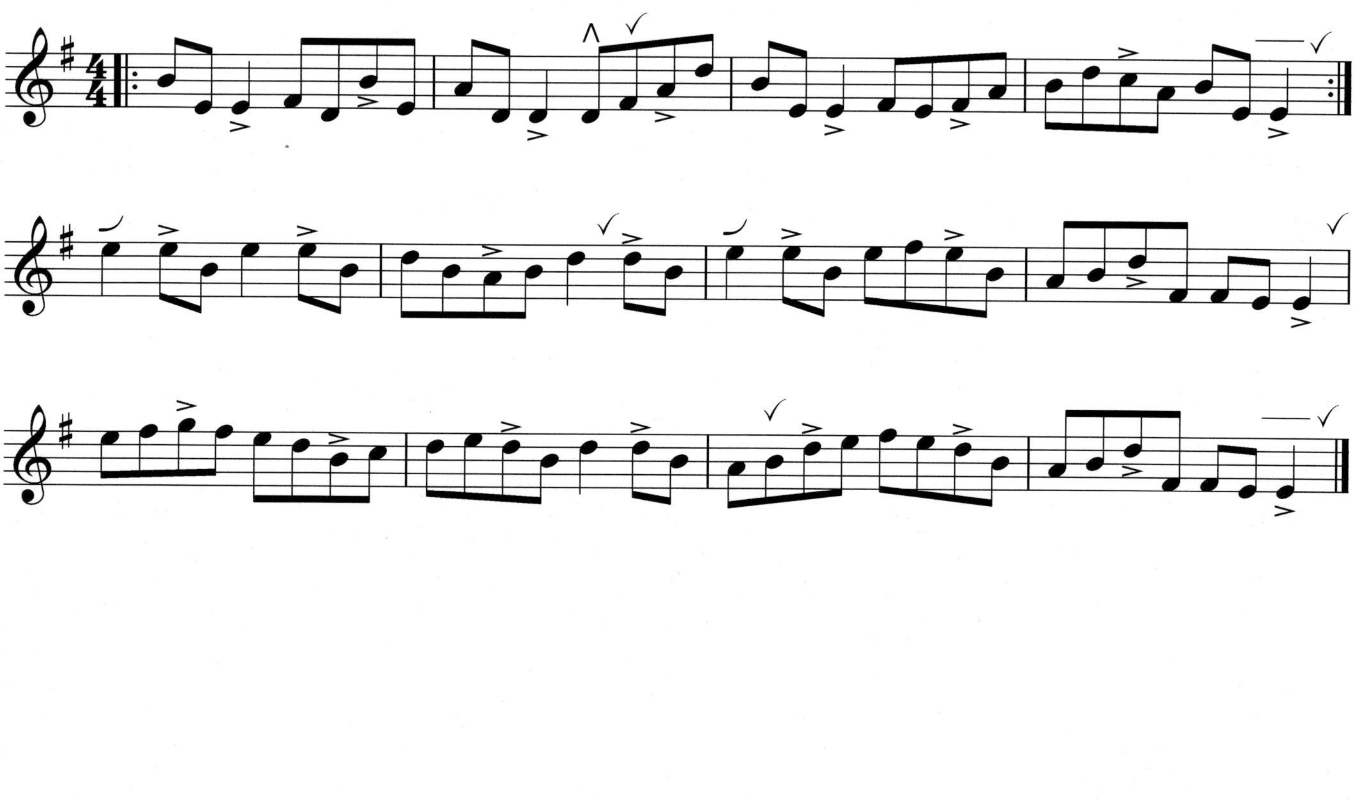

Slides: The Congress Reel

Sliding into As is a great way of providing tension and pull around this tune's tonal center. It will also provide an opportunity for advanced rolls in Volume III.

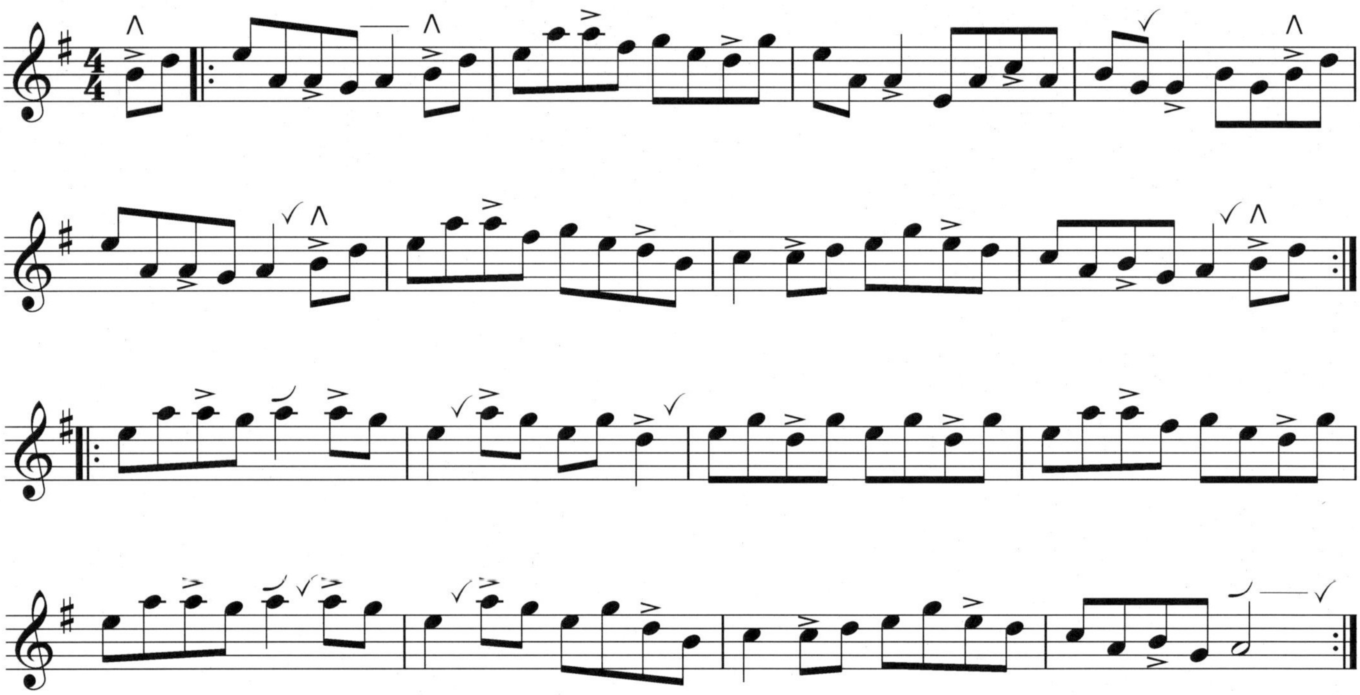

Chapter 4: Cuts

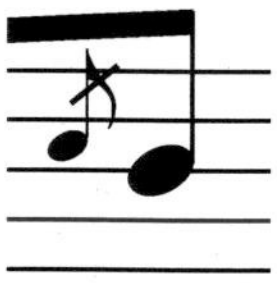

Cuts are upper grace notes that are often used to separate two notes of the same pitch, or to give articulation and emphasis to rhythmically and melodically important notes. Cuts can also add a lot of pop and sparkle to a tune. These ornaments require a quickly lifted finger, so they tend to work very well when ascending (if you're already lifting fingers to move upwards, cuts fit into this motion quite nicely). Since cuts require at least one closed hole or key, they work on any note except C♯ (although unlike simple system flutists, Boehm flutists do actually have a nifty C♯ option).

Cuts should be sharp and crisp in articulation, and rhythmically they should be executed as close as possible to the note they are intended to modify. In other words, cuts are a finger articulation that starts a note, and they are not necessarily a melodic embellishment. Since cuts are intended to be a fast articulation, it is unnecessary to worry excessively about the pitch of the cut (so long as it is higher in register than the note it is modifying). This means you do not need to change the pitch of a cut to fit the key of a tune. When played well, the snap of a well-articulated cut will make any pitch considerations unnecessary. Developing good, snappy cuts now will also be very important for more advanced ornamentation later, such as rolls, short rolls, and crans (we'll cover these ornaments in Volume III).

Cuts Fingering Chart

Although the pitch in cuts is difficult to discern, you may choose certain fingerings based upon whether you prefer a narrow (small interval) or wide (large interval) sound, and there are also many available fingerings between these two extremes. The options on this fingering chart start with the narrowest sounding cuts and move progressively towards the widest. As you sort through these fingerings, you may notice a very persistent logic: the closer your cut finger is to the last open hole, the narrower the cut will sound; the farther away your cut finger is from the last open hole, the wider the cut will sound. This also means that notes with fewer fingers down have fewer cut options. Most fingerings will work for both your low and high octaves, although they may sound slightly different or have a unique response in each octave. For your D' fingerings, remember you have the option of raising your left index finger.

I've made a note of my preferences in case they can be of any guidance, but I recommend choosing the option that feels ergonomic and pleasing to your own hands and ears. Be willing to experiment and take time making your choice. You may want to refer to this fingering chart while playing the exercises later in this chapter in order to best determine where your preferences lie.

Cuts Fingering Chart:

To play a cut, place all X fingers down, and then quickly pop **X** up and then back down. This chart begins with the narrowest options, and then moves progressively to the widest. My preferences are starred.* (Occasionally I have more than one.)

D/D' Cuts**	Boehm	Simple System
Option 1 (narrow)	X X X | X X **X** o o x	X X X | X X **X**
Option 2*	X X X | X **X** X o o x	X X X | X **X** X
Option 3	X X X | **X** X X o o x	X X X | **X** X X

Option 4	X X **X** | X X X o o x	X X **X** | X X X
Option 5 (wide)	X **X** X | X X X o o x	X **X** X | X X X

***These cut fingerings will also work for D'. Experiment with raising the first finger of the left hand for a crisper D'.*

E/E' Cuts	Boehm	Simple System
Option 1 (narrow)*	X X X | X **X** O o o x	X X X | X **X** O
Option 2	X X X | **X** X O o o x	X X X | **X** X O
Option 3	X X **X** | X X O o o x	X X **X** | X X O
Option 4*	X **X** X | X X O o o x	X **X** X | X X X
Option 5 (wide)+	**X** X X | X X O o o x	**X** X X | X X O

+This fingering is not always as clear for Boehm flutes in the top octave.

F♯/F♯' Cuts	Boehm	Simple System
Option 1 (narrow)	X X X | O **X** O o o x	X X X | **X** O O
Option 2	X X **X** | O X O o o x	X X **X** | X O O
Option 3*	X **X** X | O X O o o x	X **X** X | X O O
Option 4 (wide)	**X** X X | O X O o o x	**X** X X | X O O

G/G' Cuts	Boehm	Simple System
Option 1 (narrow)	X X **X** | O O O o o x	X X **X** | O O O
Option 2*	X **X** X | O O O o o x	X **X** X | O O O

Option 3 (wide)	**X** X X | O O O o o x	**X** X X | O O O

A/A' Cuts	Boehm	Simple System
Option 1 (narrow)*	X **X** O | O O O o o x	X **X** O | O O O
Option 2 (wide)	**X** X O | O O O o o x	**X** X O | O O O

B/B' Cuts	Boehm	Simple System
Option 1 (narrow)*	X O O | O O O o o **x**	**X** O O | O O O
Option 2 (wide)	**X** O O | O O O o o x	

C/C' Cuts	Boehm	Simple System**
Option 1 (narrow)*	**X** O O | O O O o o o	O X X | X **O** X *or* O X X | **O** X X
Trill Key Option (wide)†	X O O | O**o**O O o o o	

***Simple system flutists can execute a C cut by placing all X fingers down and quickly lowering and raising O.*
†Boehm flutists can also cut a C by quickly tapping the first trill key.

C♯ Cuts	Boehm†	Simple System
Option 1 (narrow)	X X X | X **X** X o o o x x	None available+
Option 2 (wide)*	X X X | **X** X X o o o x x	

Trill Key Option (wide)   O O O | OoO O o
o o

†*Boehm flutists can cut C♯s by fingering a low register C♯, overblowing to the middle octave, and cutting with one of the closed fingers. It is a more cumbersome fingering, particularly at speed, but it is certainly an option.*
+*Simple system flutists with a low C♯ key can use Boehm Option 1 or 2 for C♯ cuts.*

As you decide on cut fingerings, keep in mind that it can be helpful to learn several options for each note. The ease of cutting with one finger over another may change depending on the melodic shape of the tune you are playing.

Cuts: Preliminary Exercises

In some of these exercises, tongued measures alternate with cut measures. Since a cut is replacing a tongued attack, the two measures should sound rhythmically identical, with the cut as close to the downbeat as possible. To ensure rhythmic accuracy, try these exercises with a metronome. Remember that the pitch of a cut is unimportant when compared to its ergonomic ease and rhythmic accuracy. You are not playing a diatonic grace note; you are simply popping a finger up and down to quickly create an articulation. This means that it is perfectly acceptable to play a C♯ cut in the key of G, for instance. In other words, the cut fingerings you settle on will work in any key.

Now is the perfect time to refer to the fingering chart and experiment with different cuts. Once you have settled on your favorite cuts, your long-term goal will be to work those fingerings into your muscle memory.

General Tip | Support your air stream smoothly and consistently: this will help your cuts speak clearly. Do not tongue cuts.

1. Play the second and fourth measures with one continuous breath. The cuts will provide the necessary articulation. Although the cuts are all notated as As, they could be a variety of pitches above G, depending on which fingering you choose to use.

TRACK 33

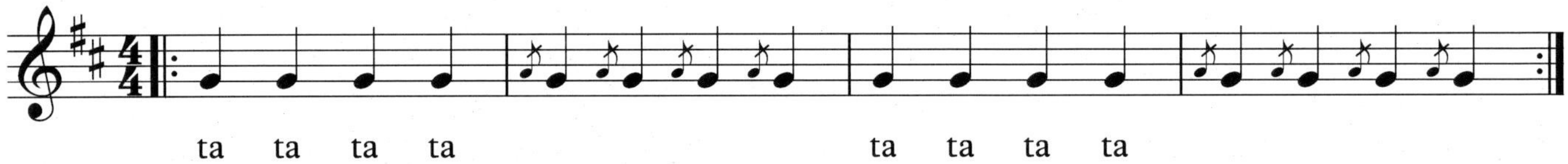

Simple System Tip | Keep your fingers light when playing cuts. If you are holding your flute firmly enough to hyperextend your knuckles (bending your knuckles backwards against the joint), this can lead to much slower cuts since forcibly hyperextended fingers have to flatten back out before they can lift. While hyperextension is a natural feature of some players' hands, *forced* hyperextension is a more cumbersome process and is not helpful when trying to play cuts with "snap." If you are forcing hyperextension into your fingers, revisit *Posture* in Volume I.

Boehm Tip | As you progress through this series, you should become accustomed to flipping back and forth between your middle and ring finger F♯s depending on which is most ergonomic for a phrase. Most cut fingerings will work on both F♯s without needing any modification.

2.

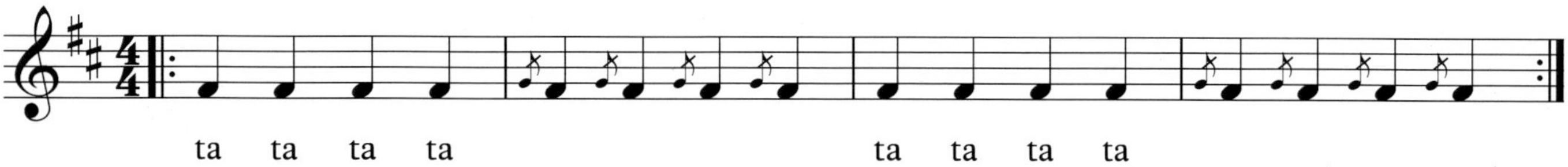

3.

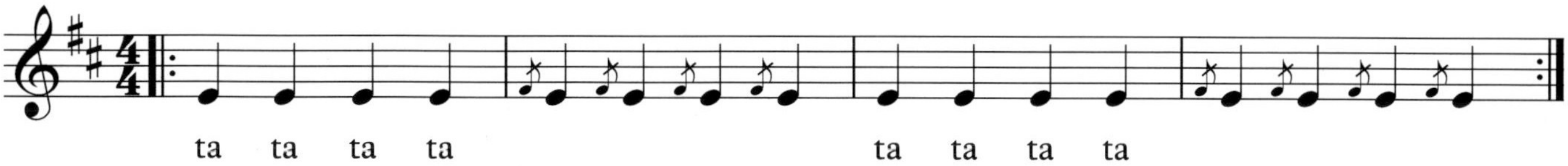

4. Keep a firm upper lip for your low D cuts.

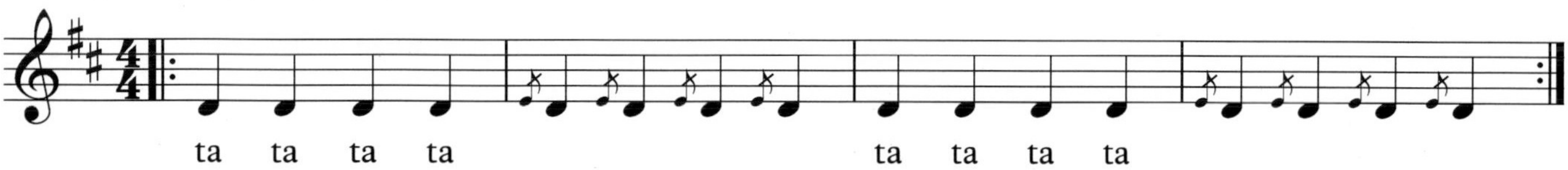

General Tip | If you are struggling to place your cut just before the downbeat, think "snap" when executing your cuts. The "s" begins the cut, and the "p" ends the cut on the downbeat. "Snap" also perfectly describes the motion of your finger: quick and snappy.

5. Left hand cuts can be a bit of a balancing act. Stay relaxed, but keep a firm left hook.

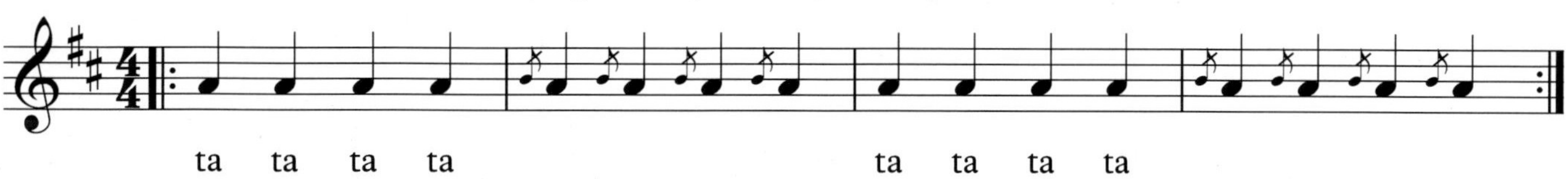

Boehm Tip | Maintaining low action will help keep cuts short and snappy. Raise your cut finger just high enough to open the key. If you lose contact with the key, you've gone too far.

6.

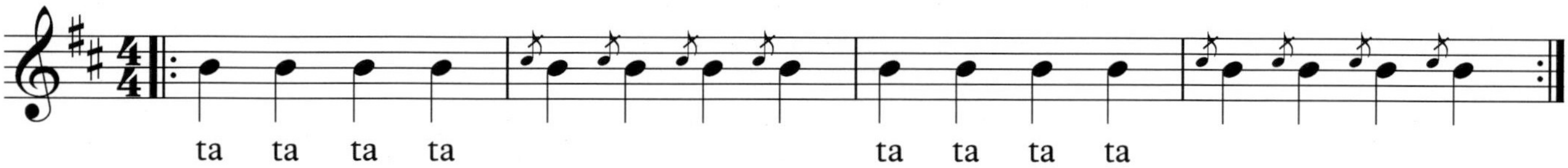

7. Since keyless simple system flutes cannot cut C♯s, this exercise is exclusively for Boehm players (or simple system players with a low C♯ key). As mentioned in the fingering chart, Boehm flutists can either cut on an overblown low C♯ or cut a middle register C♯ with a trill key.

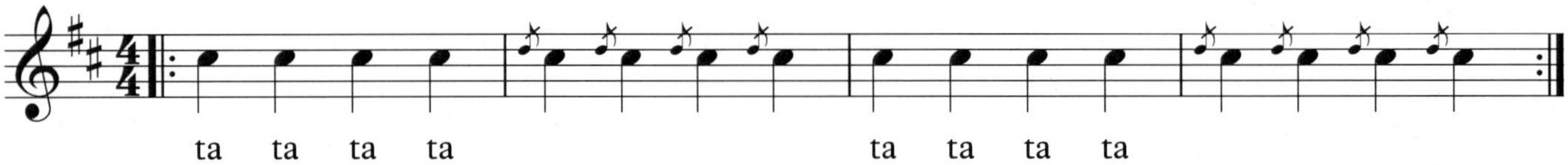

Simple System Tip | Remember that your C natural cut fingering is different than your other cuts, and requires tapping O down and then up:

O X X | X O X

or

O X X | O X X

8.

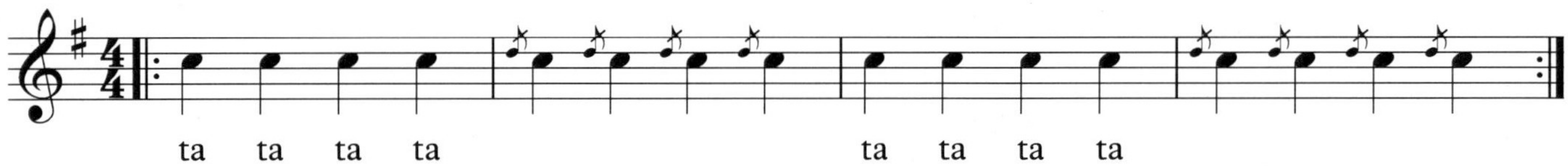

9. As you practice adding cuts to ascending notes, make sure that your cut finger is moving in exact unison with the other fingers being raised to create the new primary note. This will help the cuts sound clearly, without extra bubbles in the sound.

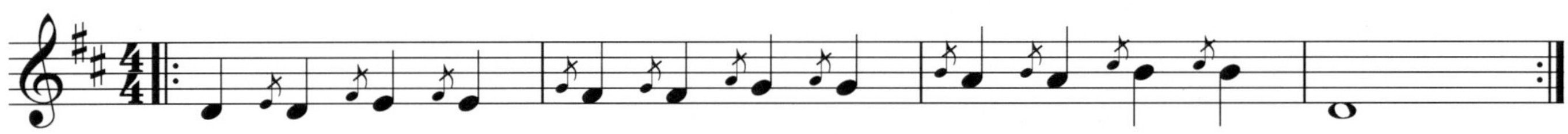

TRACK 34

10.

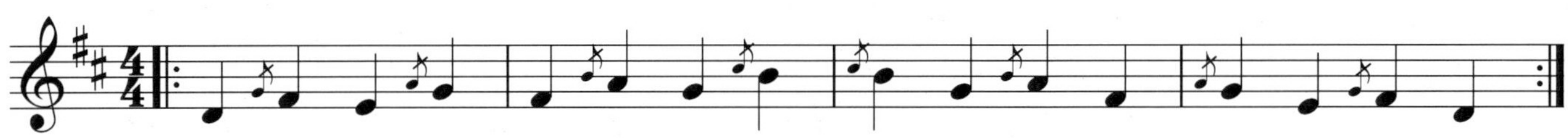

Cuts: Contextual Exercises

As you practice your cuts, remember to slur everything together. Repeated notes without cut symbols can be tongued lightly for now, or if you're ambitious, try adding your own cuts even if they're not marked.

TRACK 35

1. The first four exercises use cuts to separate notes of the same pitch.

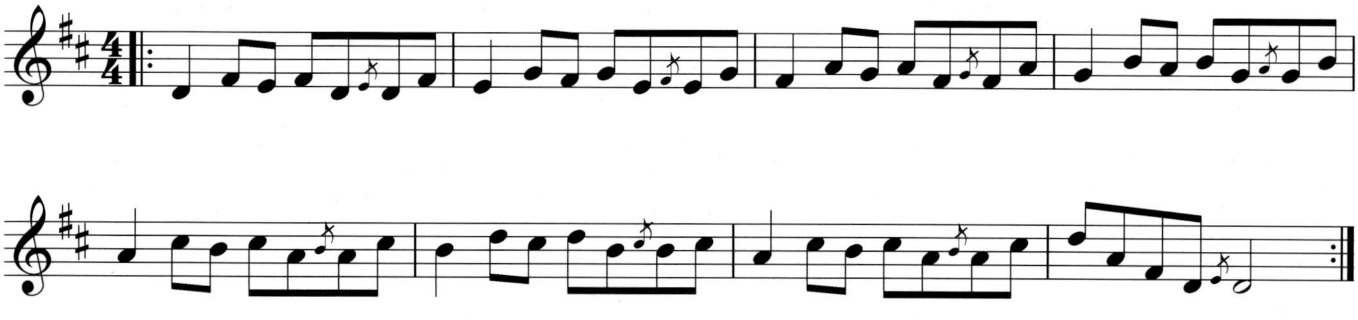

2.

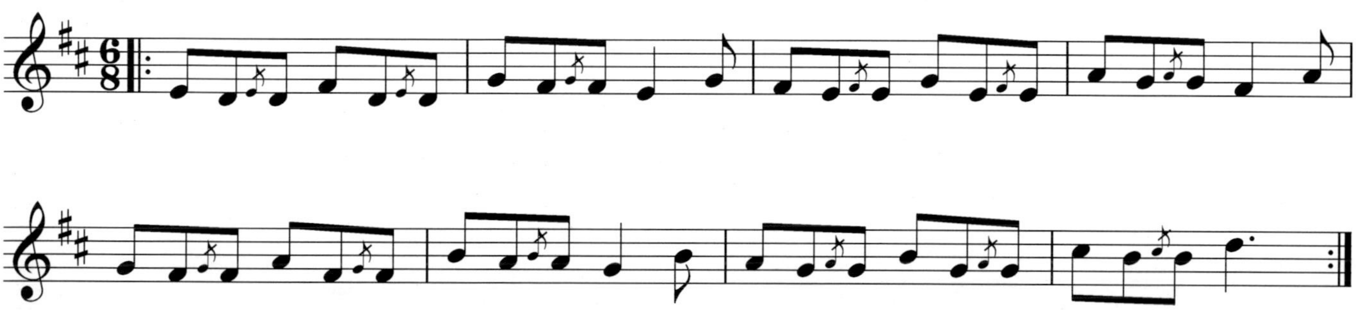

3.

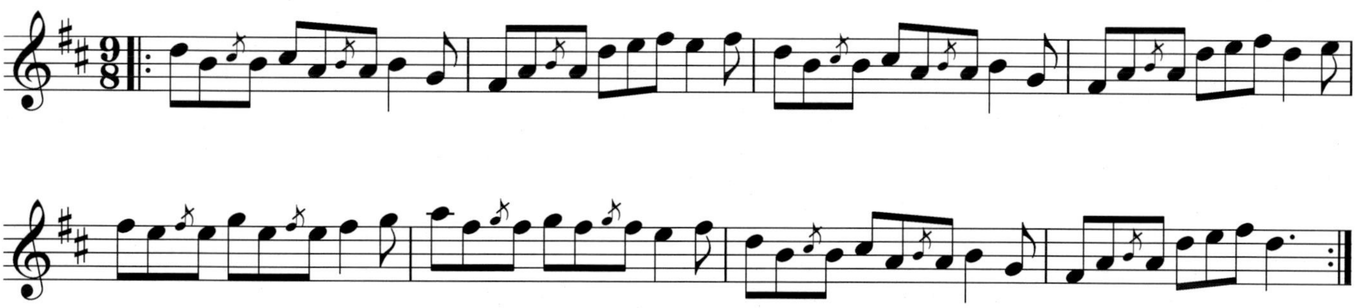

General Tip | Remember, the pitch of cuts does not need to fit into the key signature. If your B cut goes to C♯, you do not need to change it to a C natural to fit G Major or E Minor. If you are playing your cut as a snappy articulation, the specific pitch will not be overtly noticeable.

4. Simple system flutists, remember the fingering for your C natural cuts in measure two.

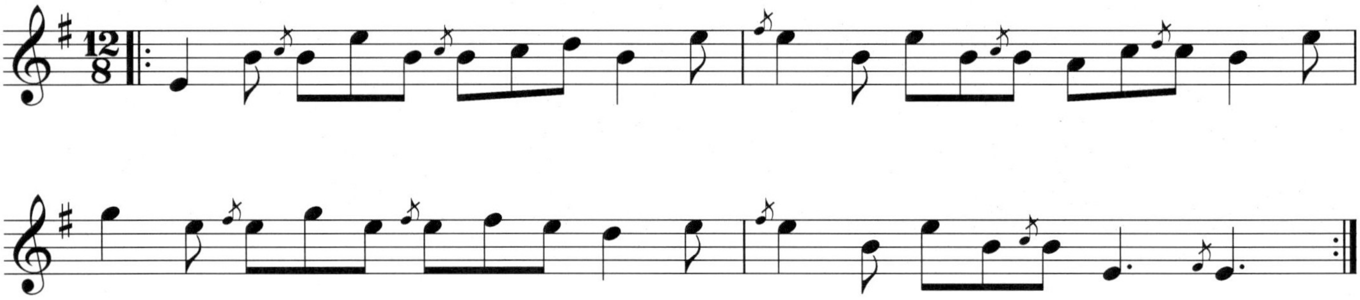

TRACK 36

5. The next four exercises use cuts when ascending either by steps or larger intervals. While you certainly could add cuts to any ascending note, here cuts are confined to rhythmically important notes: downbeats and backbeats.

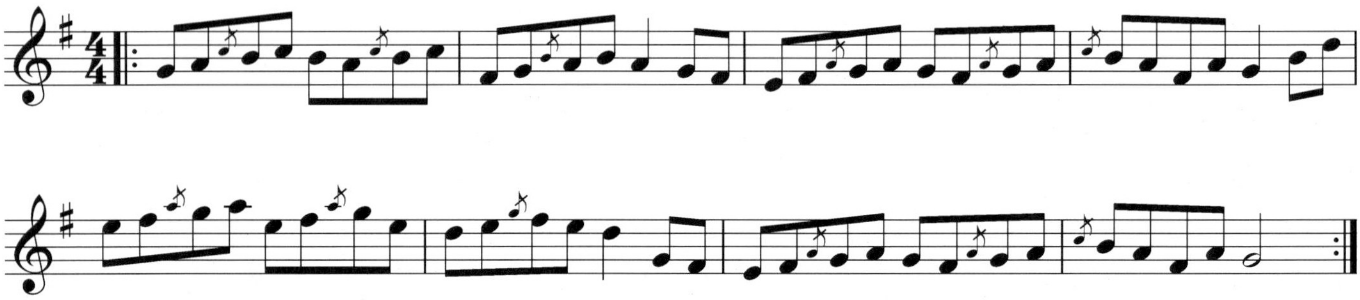

6.

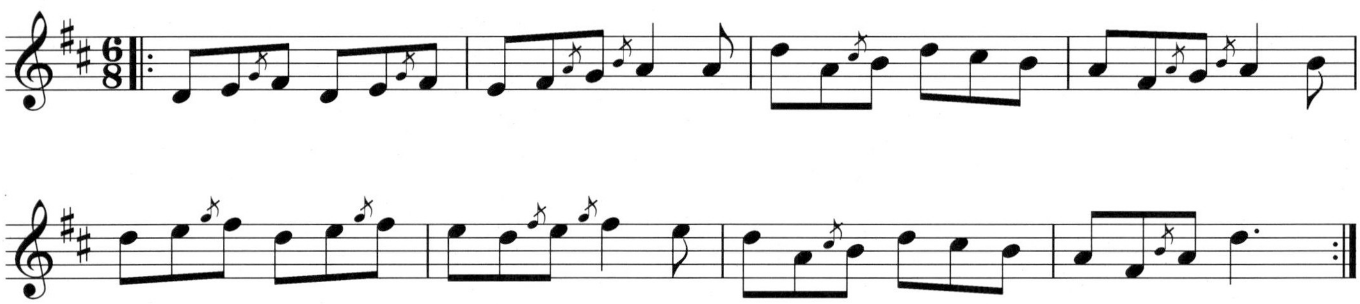

7.

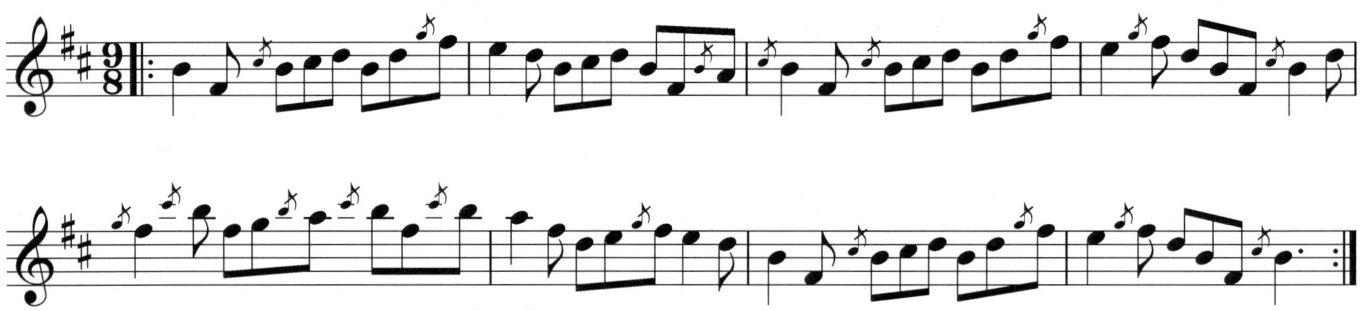

8. Simple system flutists, look out for the C natural cut in the first measure. Remember its particular fingering.

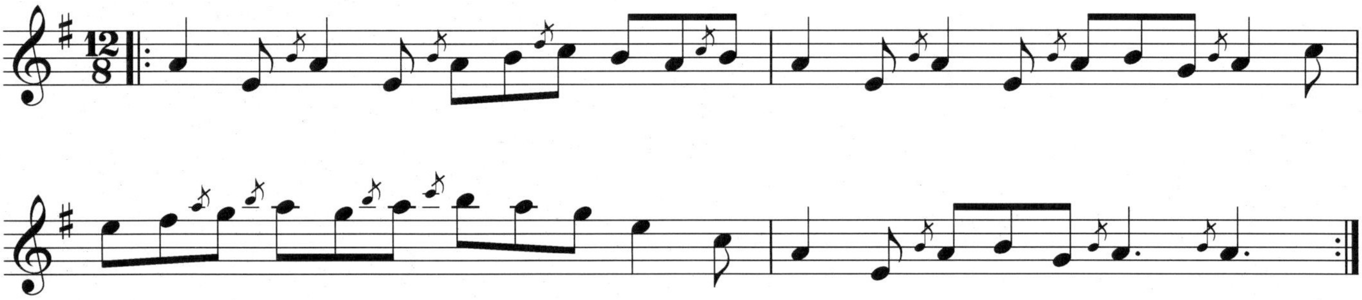

9. The last two exercises use cuts both when separating notes of the same pitch and when ascending.

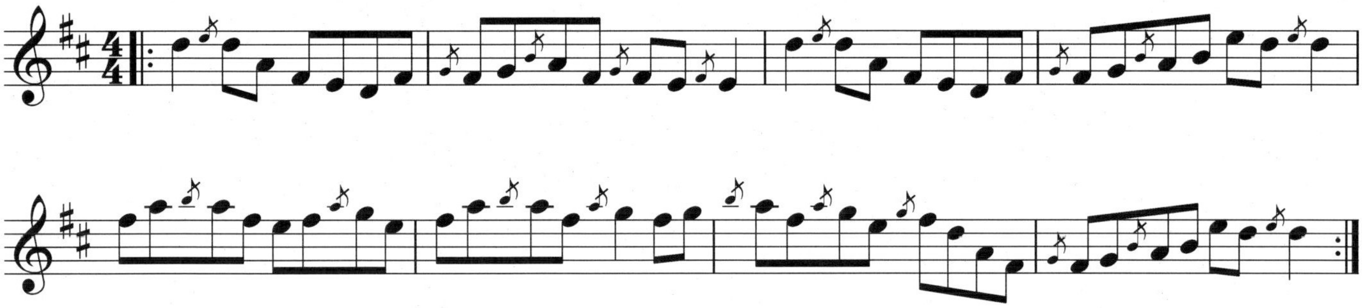

10.

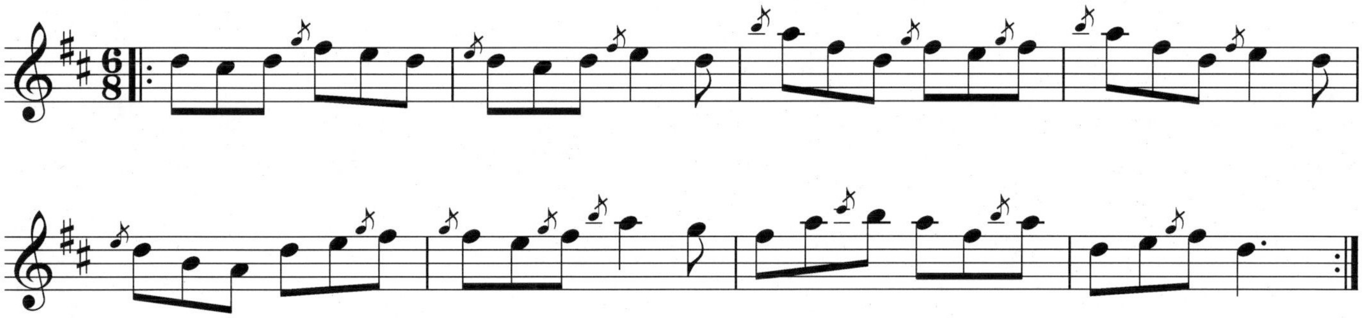

General Tip | By now, you may have noticed that cuts have only been placed on rhythmically important notes. Although cuts can be added to any part of the beat, keeping them on rhythmically important notes is good practice for continuing to emphasize a basic backbeat rhythm.

Cuts: Combined Exercises

Be sure to infuse these exercises with snappy articulation, good backbeat, and appropriate breaths. As you do so, look out for changing time signatures. These exercises are chock-full of ornamentation—more than may be found in many tunes—in order to better train your breath and fingers. Refer to your Symbols Key as needed and add ornaments gradually if you prefer. If breaths are marked in more often than you feel is necessary, you may skip one or two, but be sure not to skip too many or the style will suffer.

SYMBOLS KEY:

Volume I: Backbeat and Breathing	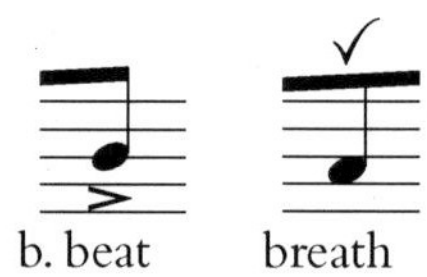
Volume II: Single Ornaments	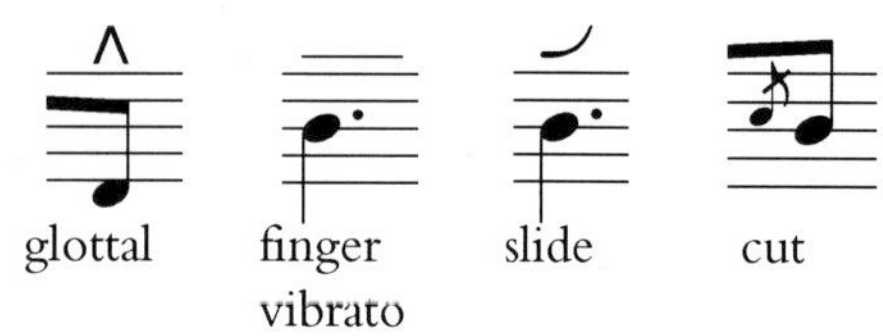

1. Boehm flutists, if your preferred B cut goes up to C♯, that is perfectly fine as long as you play the cut with enough snap.

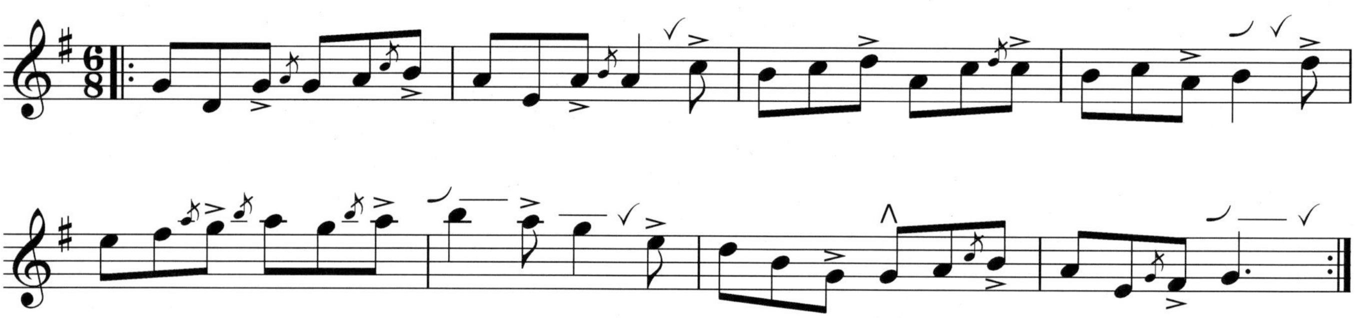

TRACK 37

2. There are multiple options here for rearticulating Ds: glottals and cuts. Cuts can be very effective at the end of a phrase if you are running too low on air to play a good glottal. Also notice the breaths in quick succession in the last two measures. They are placed there in order to vary the structure of the tune and fit in additional ornaments.

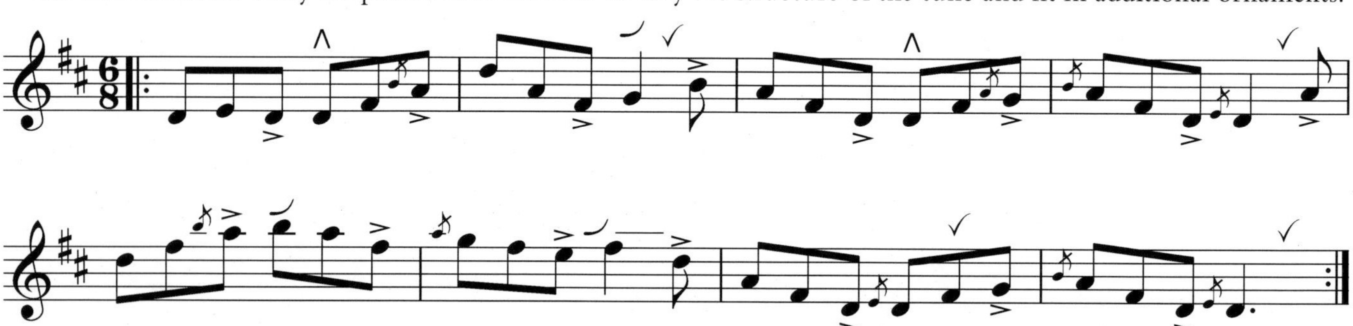

3. Certain descending cuts can actually work beautifully. Moving from E' down to B, with a cut in between, works very nicely (measure three into four).

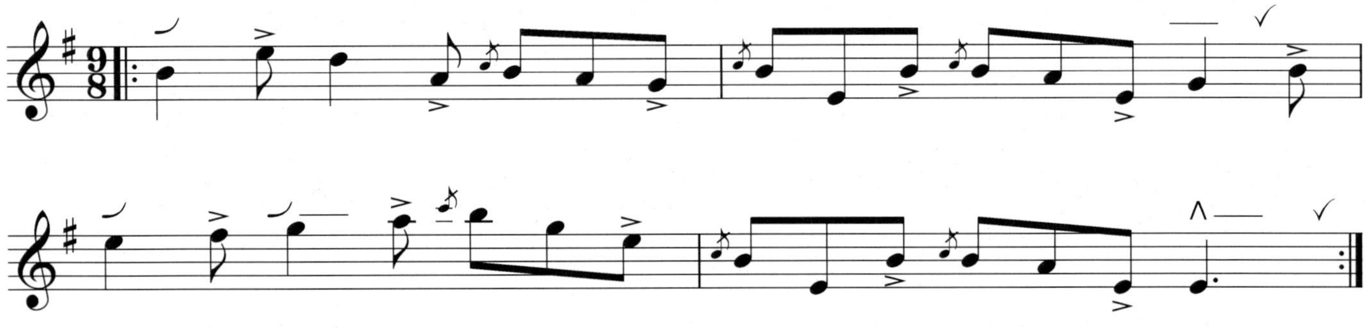

Boehm Tip | Playing so many ornaments on a keyed flute can feel challenging. Keep your fingers close to the keys, and keep your movements short and snappy. For ornament combinations such as slides and finger vibrato, a quick realization of each ornament is all that is needed.

4.

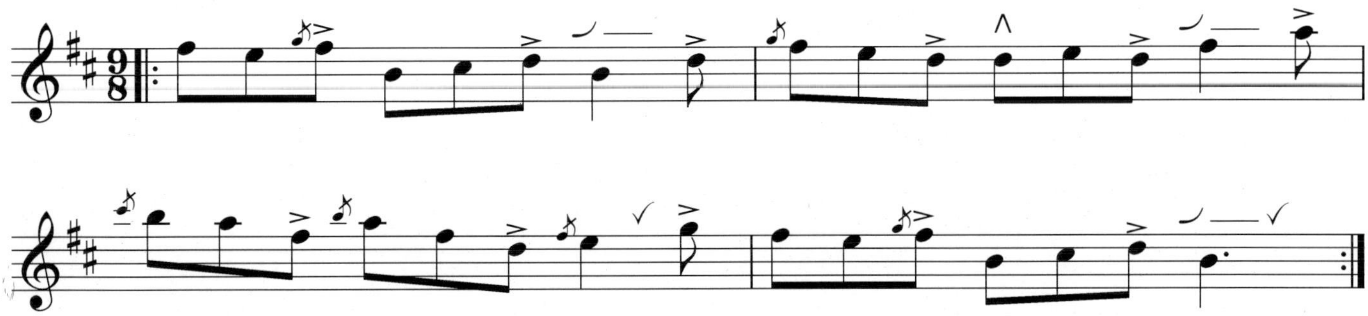

TRACK 38

5. You now have multiple options for rearticulating the repeated As in the last measure. Notice how each one creates a different sound.

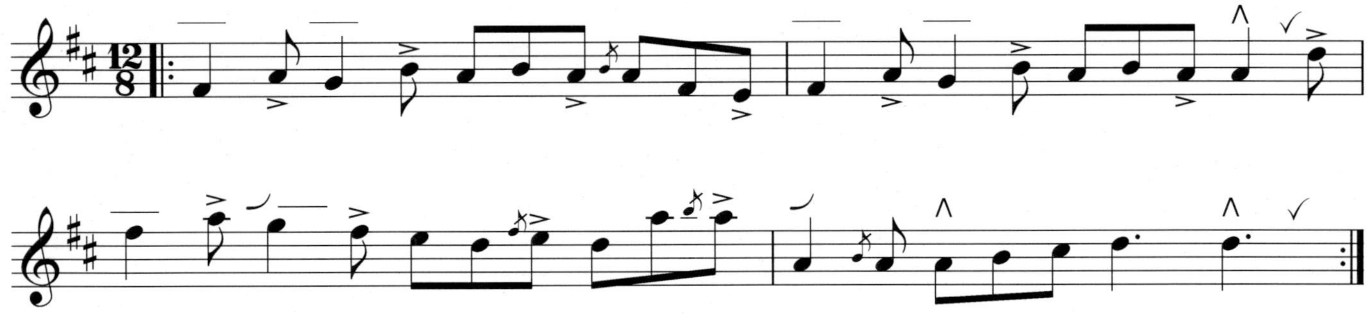

6.

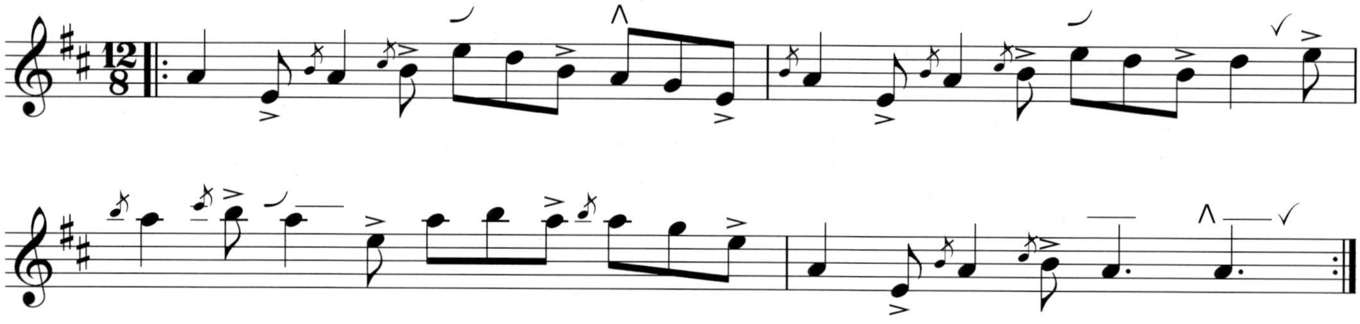

> **Simple System Tip** | Becoming fluent with the unusual fingering of C natural cuts will take some patience. Practice slowly, in small chunks.

7. Watch out for the C natural cut in the fourth measure.

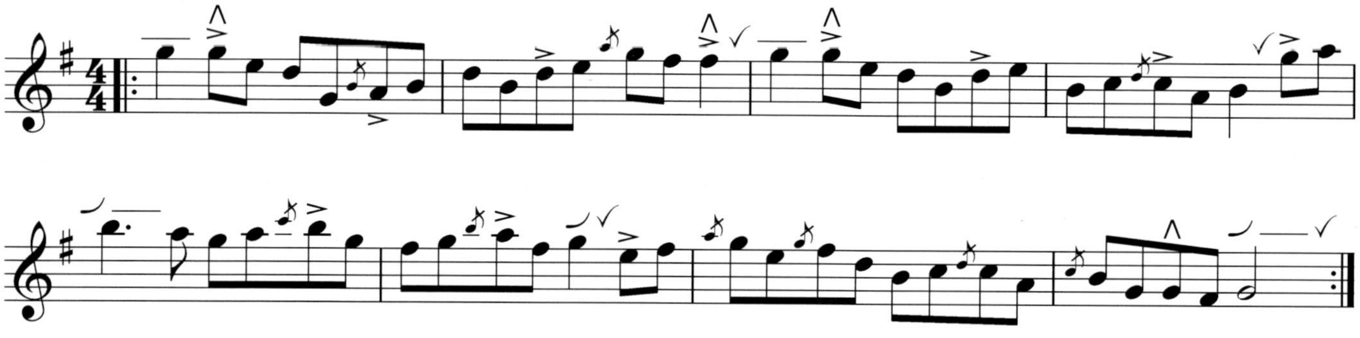

8. Using cuts to give further emphasis to backbeats can be very effective.

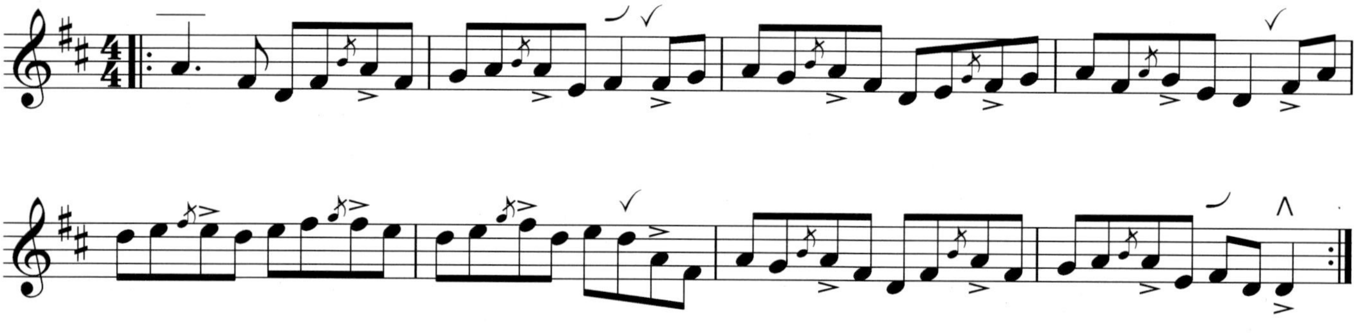

9.

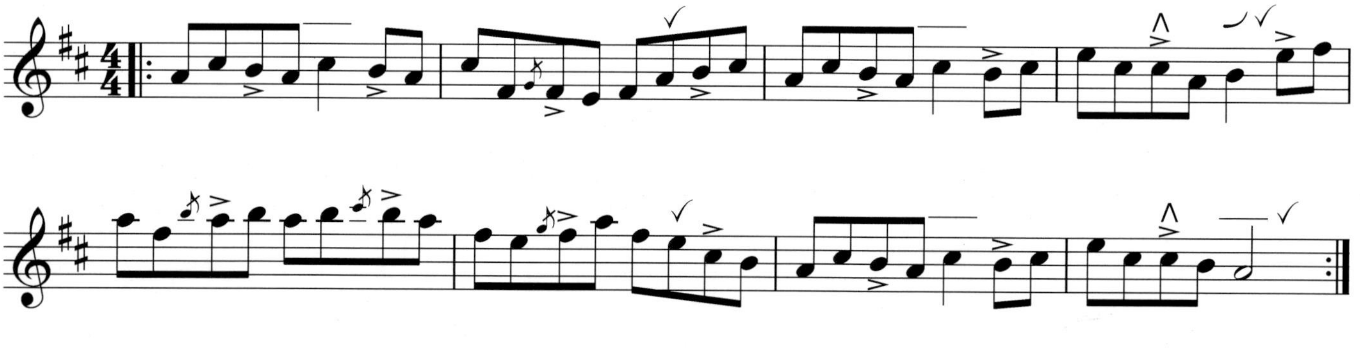

10.

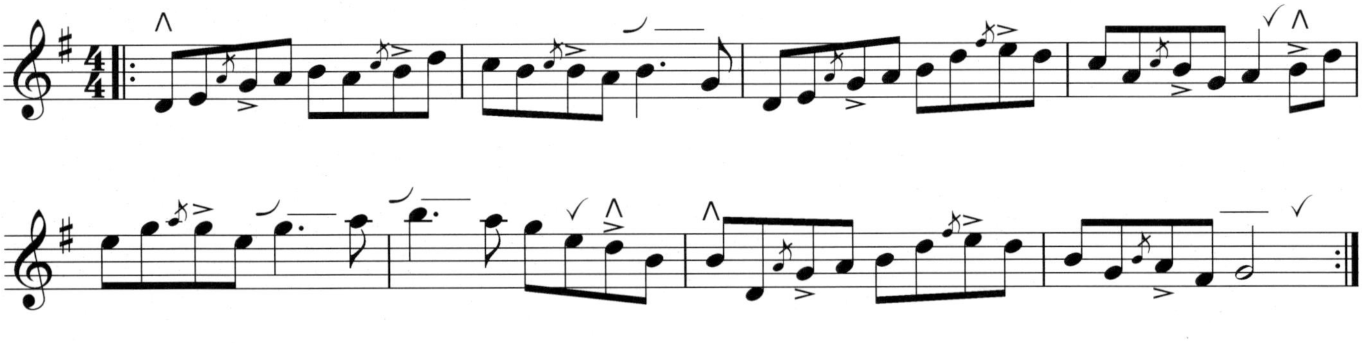

Cuts: Tunes

Now that you feel more comfortable with cuts, we'll begin layering them into our tunes. You may notice that cuts are being used to separate notes of the same pitch, to emphasize downbeats and backbeats, and to lend weight to melodically and rhythmically important notes.

SYMBOLS KEY:

Volume I:
Backbeat
and Breathing

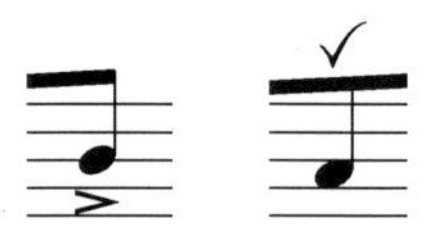

b. beat breath

Volume II:
Single Ornaments

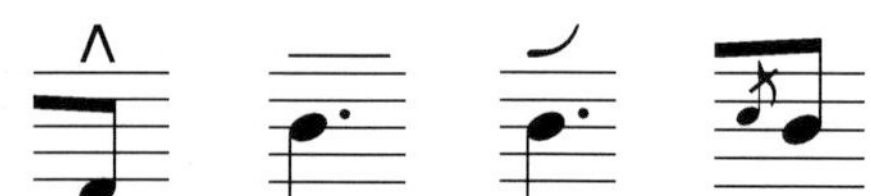

glottal finger vibrato slide cut

Cuts: Boiled Goat's Milk

TRACK 39

Notice that the cuts in the tune are accomplishing three things: providing emphasis to downbeats, amplifying backbeats, and adding pop to the highest point of a phrase (which is also the downbeat). You can certainly add more cuts than the ones added here, but we'll also be adding more ornaments in the coming chapters.

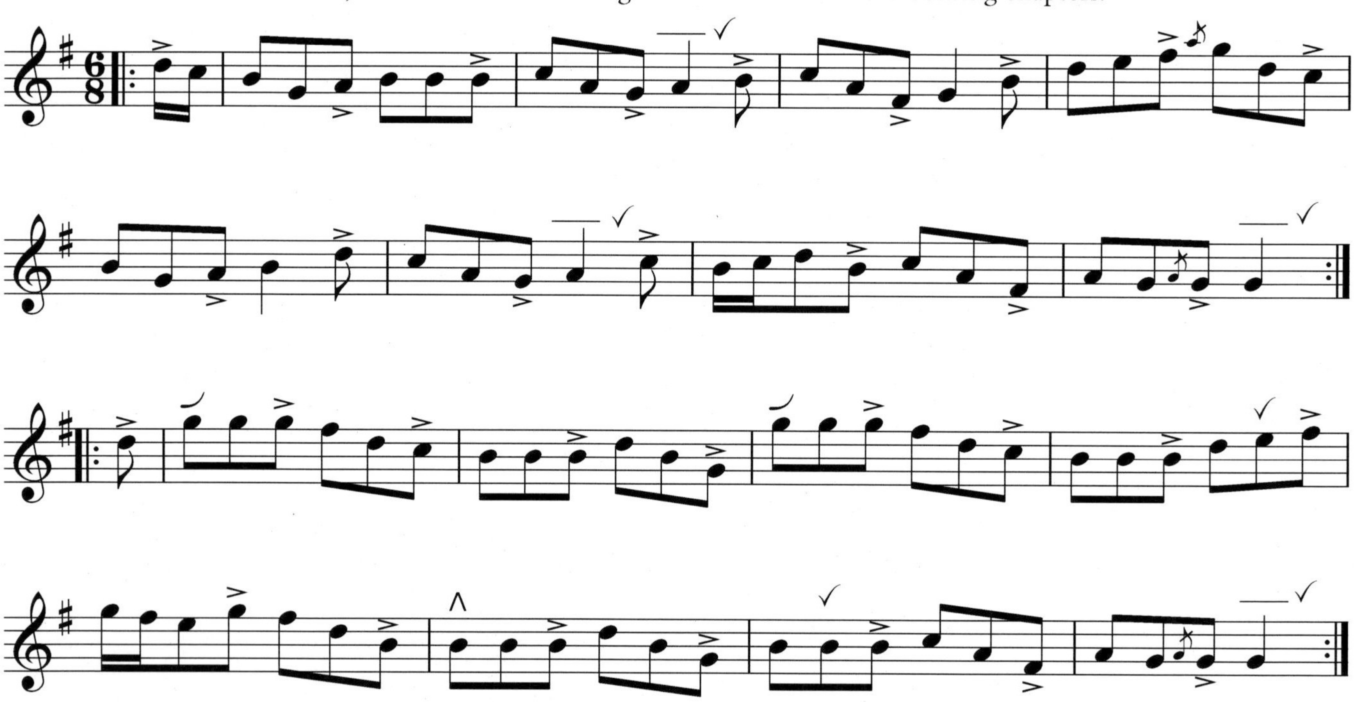

Cuts: Dever the Dancer

Similar to *Boiled Goat's Milk*, this tune adds cuts to emphasize downbeats and backbeats.

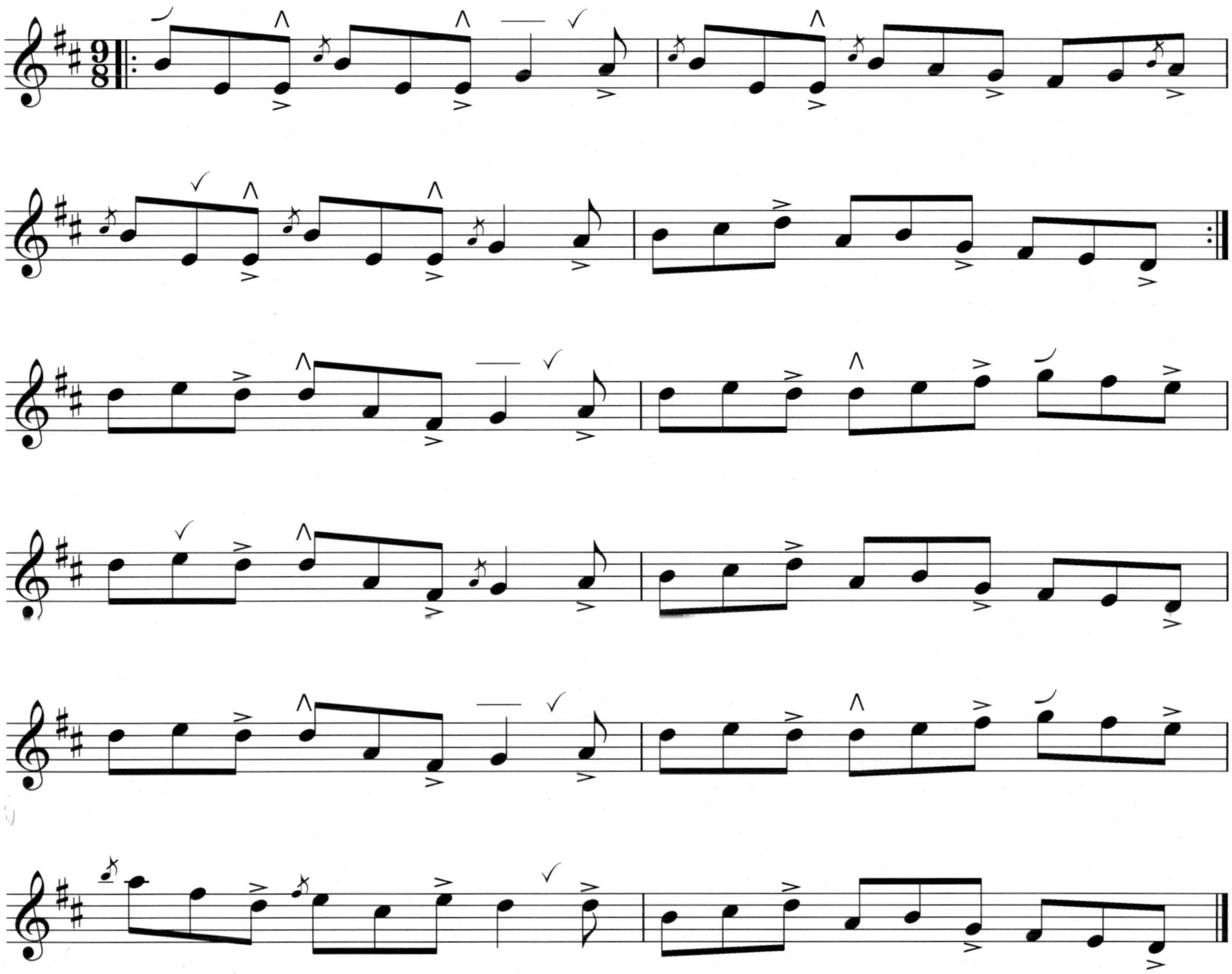

Cuts: The Dingle Regatta

The cuts in this slide are always occurring on downbeats or backbeats, between repeated notes, or when ascending.

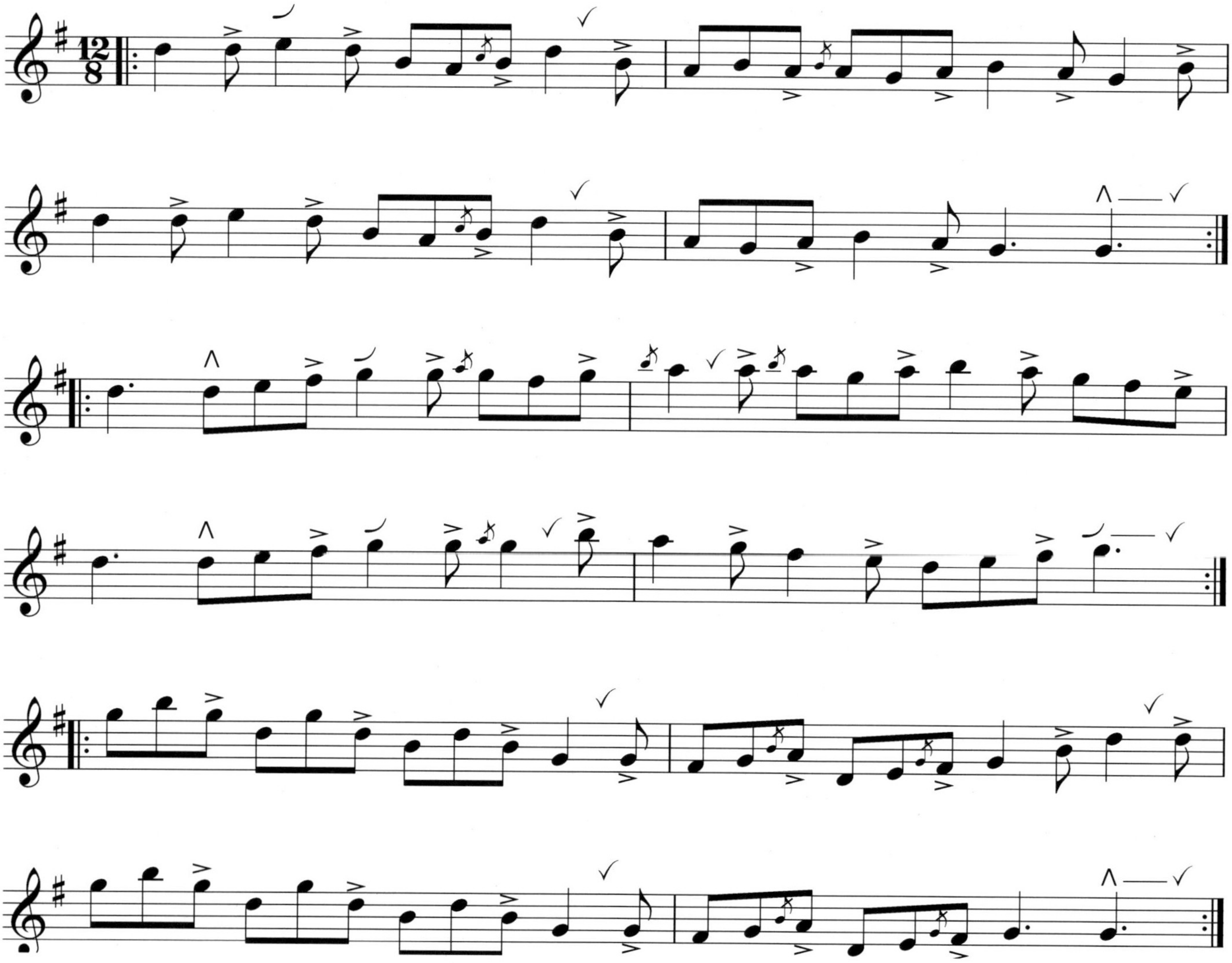

Cuts: My Love is in America

This reel offers the opportunity to include cuts in a line of descending thirds in the penultimate measure of the A and B parts. It's also an example of recycling ornaments when a phrase repeats throughout a tune.

TRACK 40

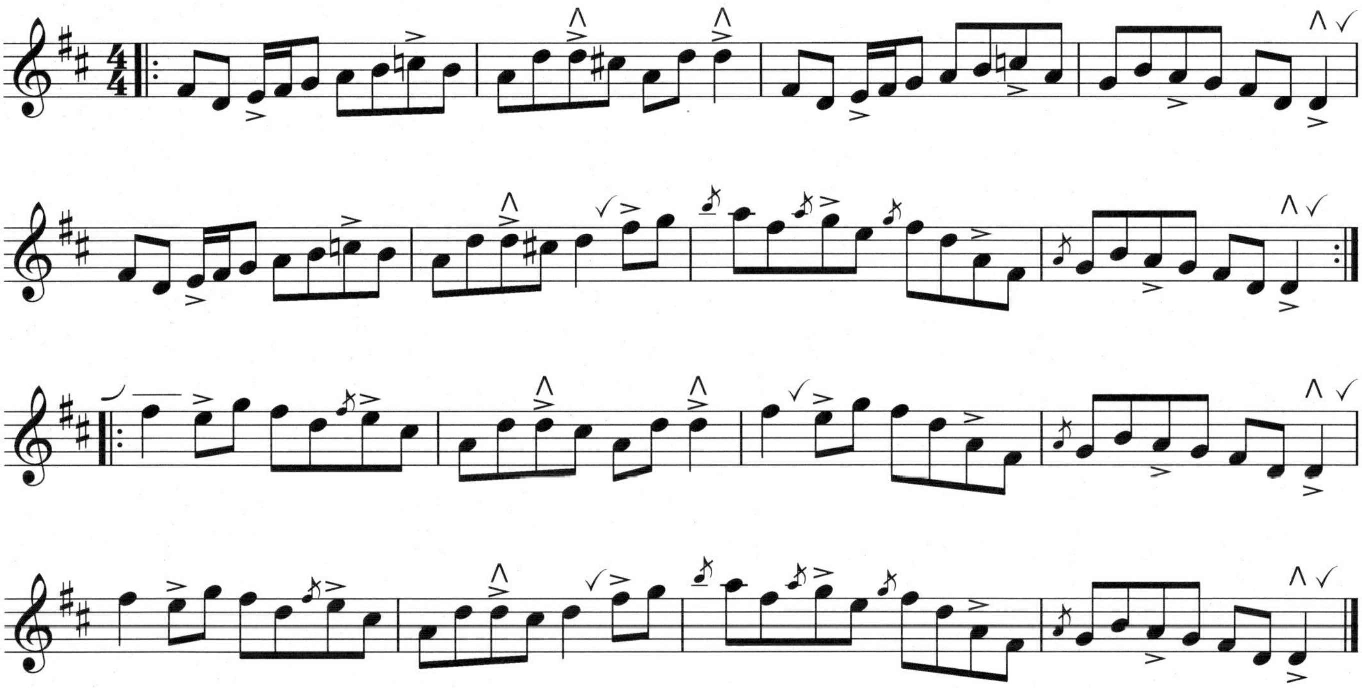

Cuts: The Pretty Blue Seagull

The Pretty Blue Seagull incorporates cuts on downbeats and backbeats. It also uses a cut on the highest note of the entire tune, which occurs in the first measure of the last line.

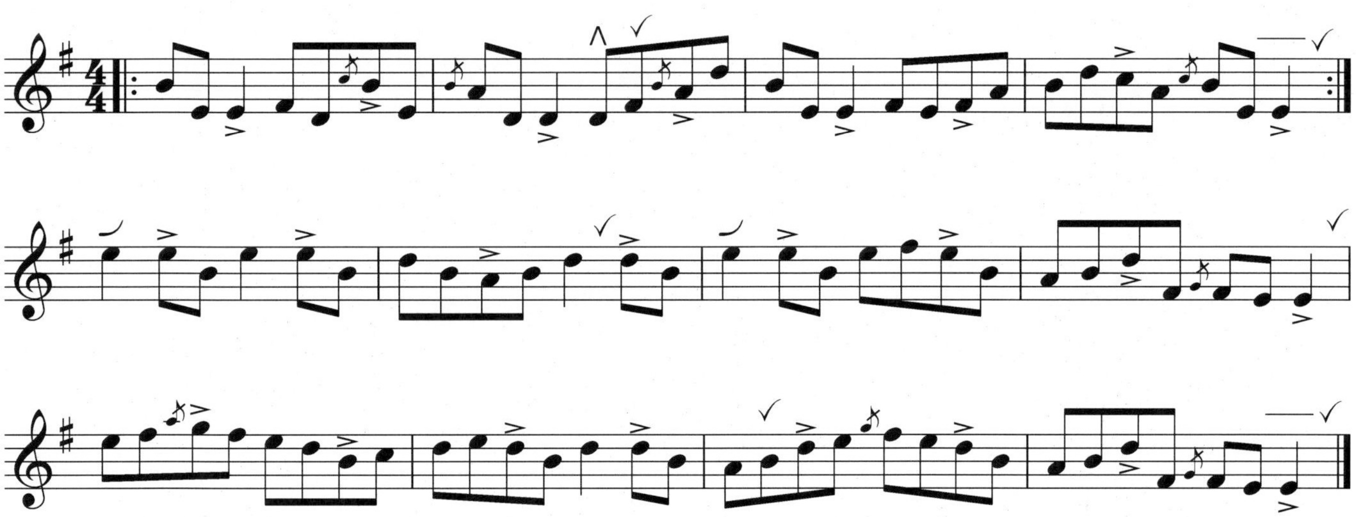

Cuts: The Congress Reel

As in *My Love is in America,* repeated melodic patterns can include the same configuration of cuts.

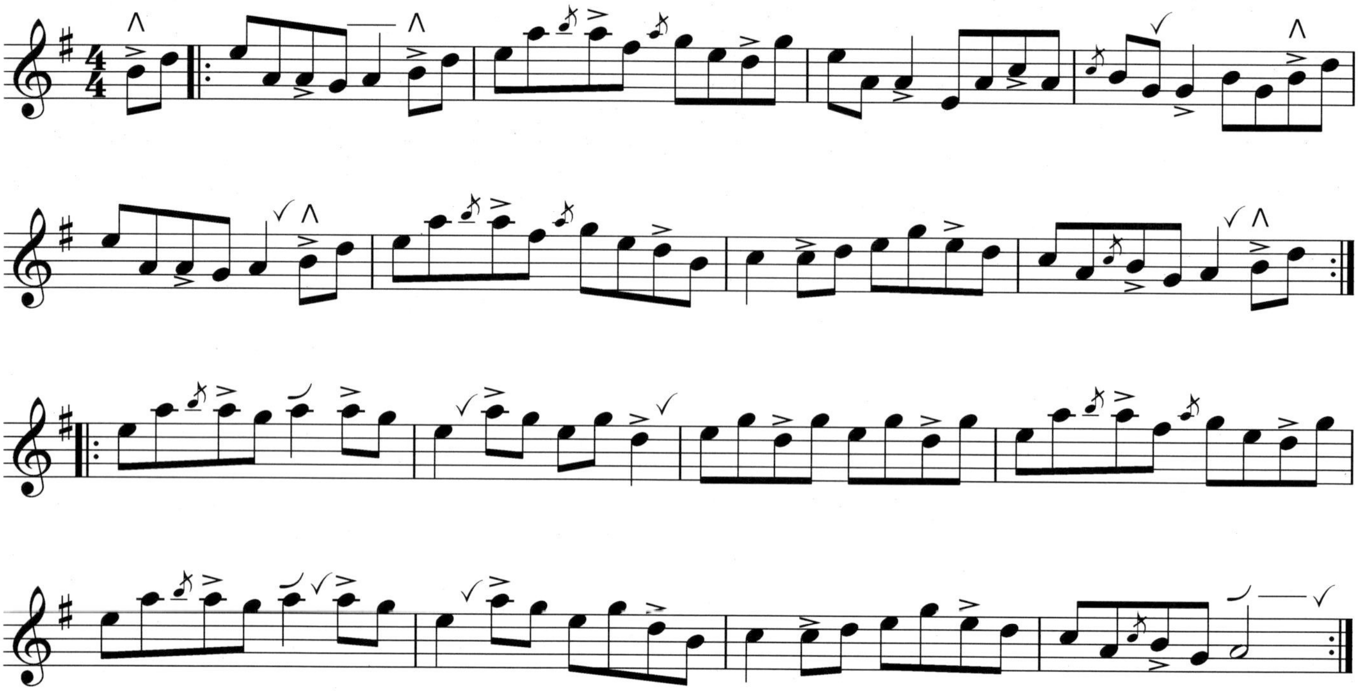

Chapter 5: Taps

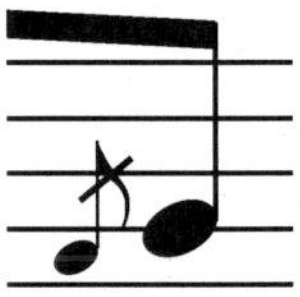

Taps, also called *pats*, *strikes*, or *tips*, are similar to cuts in that they are also a finger articulation used to separate two notes of the same pitch, or to provide rhythmic and melodic emphasis to notes within the tune. Unlike cuts, taps are a lower grace note, and as such, they work very well when descending. Although these ornaments go by so quickly that the exact pitch is largely indistinguishable, it is still possible to hear whether the grace note is lower or higher than the note they modify. Contrasting characters also differentiate taps and cuts: while cuts create a popping, almost disruptive sound, taps are smoother. A musician may therefore choose to use cuts or taps depending on the style and character of the tune, as well as where they fit most ergonomically.

Like cuts, taps are an articulation and should be crisp and percussive in nature. In the previous chapter, we noted that cuts could feel more fluent when ascending, or at least when fingers are being raised in the same direction as the action required for the ornament. Likewise, taps can feel best when descending, or when fingers are being lowered in sympathetic motion to the tap. Taps can also occur in wider or narrower variations by using more than one finger to create the sound. When wider taps are used, it's usually with multiple fingers on the same hand (tapping with fingers on different hands is more difficult to coordinate at speed). Since the distinct sound of a tap is created by a quick action of a finger (or fingers) being lowered and then raised, D/D' cannot be modified with a tap.

Taps Fingering Chart

Taps Fingering Chart:

To play a tap, place all X fingers down and execute a tap by striking and then raising **O**. My own preferences are starred.★

E/E' Tap	Boehm	Simple System
	X X X | X X **O** o o x	X X X | X X **O**

F♯/F♯' Taps	Boehm	Simple System
Option 1 (narrow)★	X X X | **O** X O o o x	X X X | X **O** O
Option 2 (wide)	X X X | **O O** X x o x	X X X | X **O O**

G/G' Taps	Boehm	Simple System
Option 1 (narrow)	X X X | O **O** O o o x	X X X | **O** O O
Option 2★	X X X | **O O** O o o x	X X X | **O O** O

Option 3 (wide)	X X X | O O O o o x	X X X | O O O
A/A' Tap	**Boehm**	**Simple System**
Option 1	X X O | O O O o o x	X X O | O O O
B/B' Tap	**Boehm**	**Simple System**
Option 1 (narrow)*	X O O | O O O o o x	X O O | O O O
Option 2 (wide)	X O O | O O O o o x	X O O | O O O
C/C' Tap	**Boehm**	**Simple System**
Option 1	X O O | O O O o o o	None available
C♯/C♯' Tap	**Boehm**	**Simple System**
Option 1 (narrow)	O O O | O O O o o o	O O O | O O O
Option 2 (wide)*	O O O | O O O o o o	O O O | O O O

Taps: Preliminary Exercises

As you're learning your taps, make sure that they are short and sharp. Taps should not sound like a classical grace note or a slide. Like cuts, taps are meant as an articulation to begin a note. These preliminary exercises are similar to those in the previous chapter, with taps replacing all the cuts. Measures one and three of exercises one through seven should sound rhythmically identical to measures two and four. One of the most common problems with taps is sluggish fingers, or not raising fingers quickly enough. Developing snappy taps is extremely important for advanced ornamentation later, such as rolls and short rolls. Executing good taps requires you to, quite literally, tap the flute.

Transition Tip | If you are playing a brand new simple system flute, taps are where you'll notice just how sharp newly made finger holes can be. It's a rather surprising sensation. Don't shy away from the striking nature of the taps, but stop if it hurts and take a break. Eventually you'll either toughen your fingers, wear the sharp edges smooth, or both.

1. Although these taps are notated as F♯s, they could come out as different notes depending on which tap fingering you've chosen.

TRACK 41

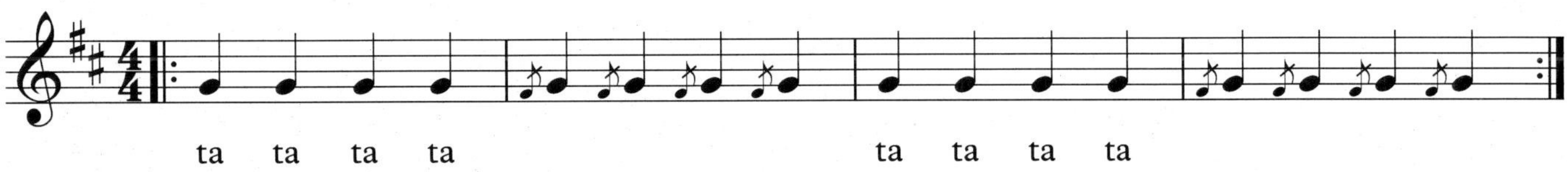

General Tip | It is very common for beginners to have a slow tap. That is, their tap finger stays down too long and creates a long grace note rather than a quick articulation. Unlike cuts, where once raised, the cut finger wants to descend again quickly, tap fingers have to fight gravity and quickly raise again once lowered. Imagine you've accidentally touched a hot stove and are whipping your finger away in reaction. This is an excellent and extremely snappy tap.

Boehm Tip | When approaching taps, a much higher action is required than you've likely ever used before. This means you will have to raise your fingers quite high and bring them down onto your keys in a striking motion (I often raise my fingers high enough to almost completely open my hand). Your keys may be clacking more than you're accustomed to, but this is the nature of playing good taps on a Boehm flute.

2.

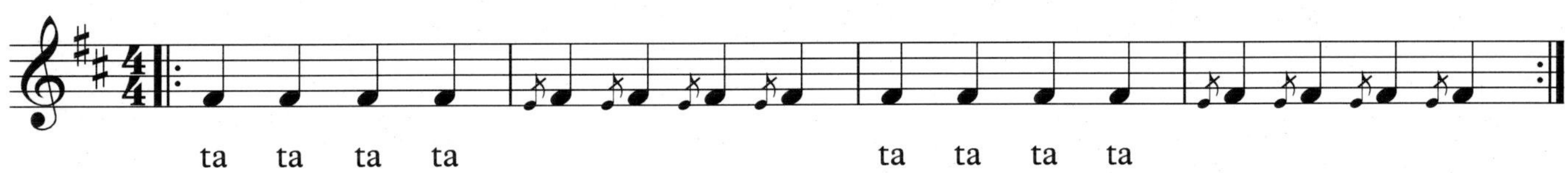

3.

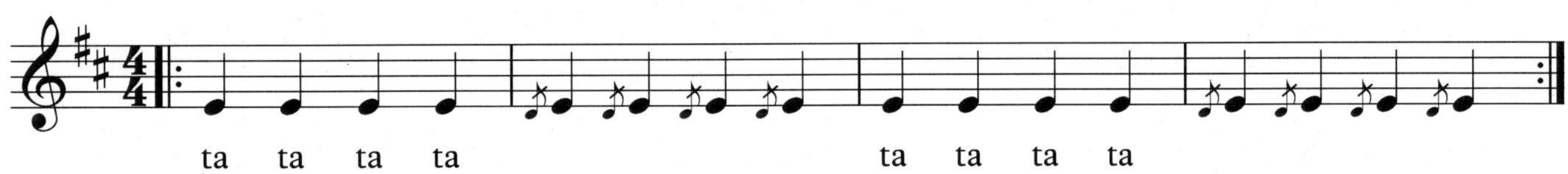

General Tip | Left hand taps can feel slower due to the extended hand position and the fact that this is the primary support point for the flute. While they're in the air, add a slight curl to your left hand tap finger(s); this can increase their speed and counter any sluggishness. Think of your fingers as a cobra suddenly striking.

4.

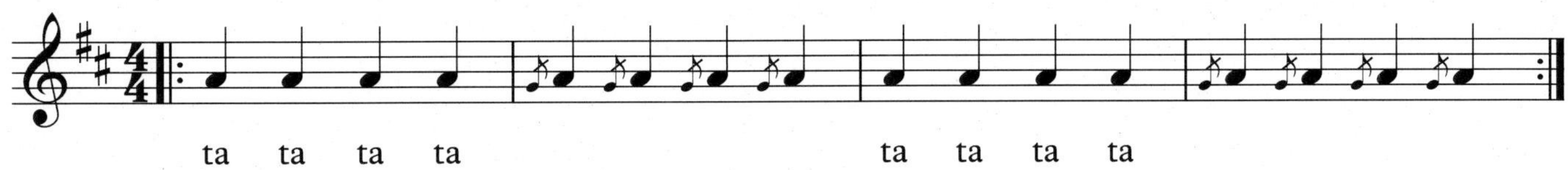

5.

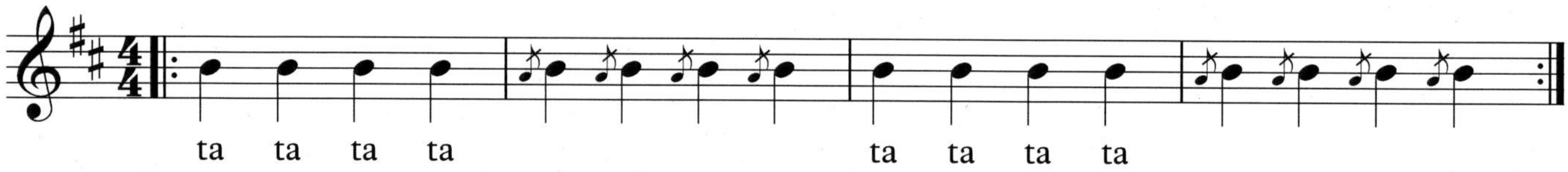

Simple System Tip | Using a single finger for a C♯ tap can be hard for players with smaller hands. Since so much of the pointer finger is wrapped around the flute, it can be difficult to tap this finger with the requisite speed and force. If this is the case for you, consider playing your C♯ taps with multiple fingers, such as your pointer and middle fingers.

6.

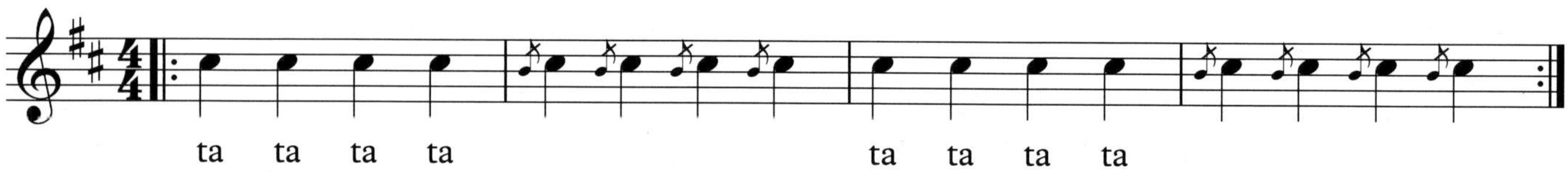

7. This exercise is exclusively for Boehm players. Blessed with a thumb key, Boehm flutes can play C natural taps.

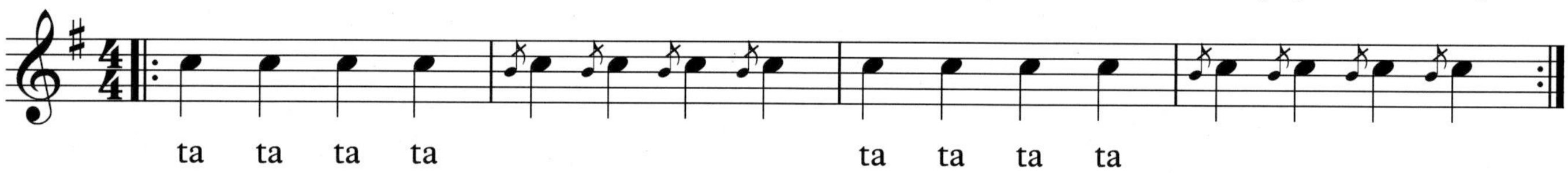

8.

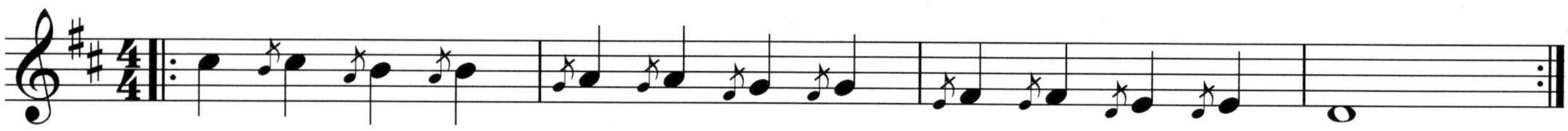

9.

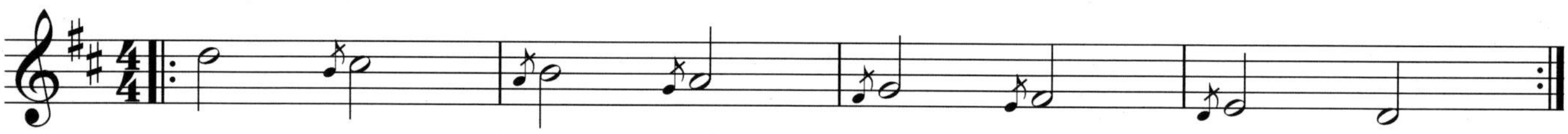

TRACK 42

10.

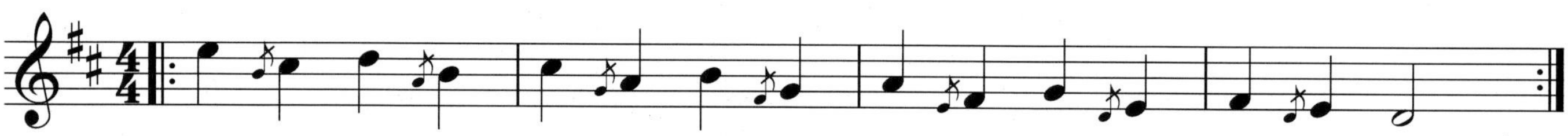

Taps: Contextual Exercises

Now that you've developed snappy taps, let's place these ornaments into more complicated contexts. Be conscientious about maintaining the same speed and accuracy that you cultivated in the preliminary exercises.

General Tip | Keep a strong airstream moving through these exercises so that all your taps are heard clearly. Breathe well and often. Everything should be under one giant slur.

TRACK 43

1. The first four exercises provide a chance to practice taps which separate notes of the same pitch.

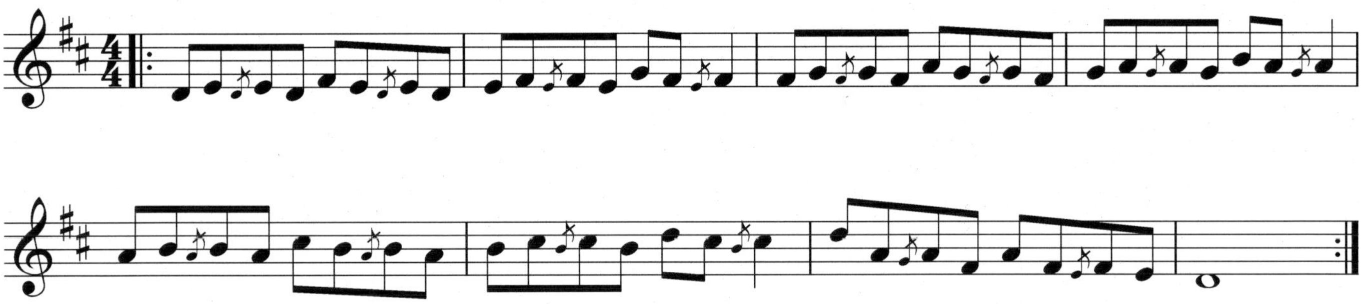

Boehm Tip | C♯ taps can feel unstable to some players. If this is the case, you can recover the stability of the flute by placing your right hand pinkie on its key during the ornament.

2.

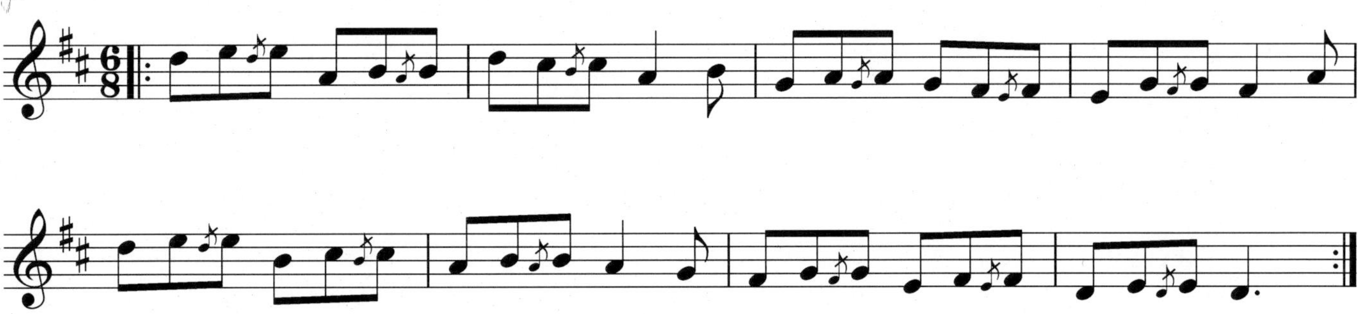

General Tip | It's not uncommon for ornaments to sound slightly different if some fingers are faster than others. Taps executed by the right hand, for instance, may sound clearer and sharper than taps played by a slower left hand, particularly for right-handed players. In contrast, left-handed players may have a different set of slower fingers that need attention. Now is a good opportunity to smooth out those differences.

3.

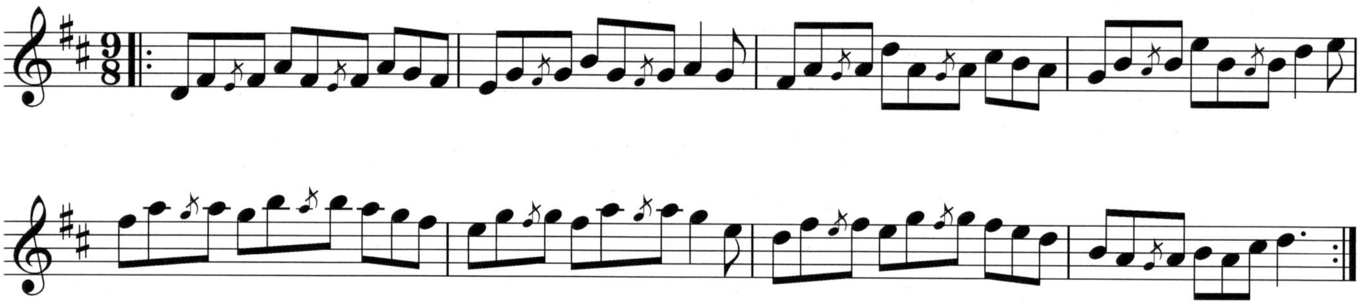

4.

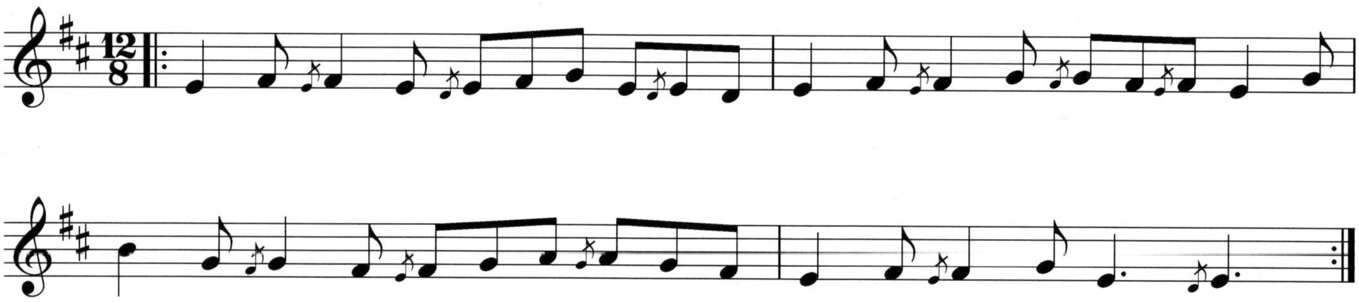

TRACK 44

5. Exercises five through eight focus on descending taps.

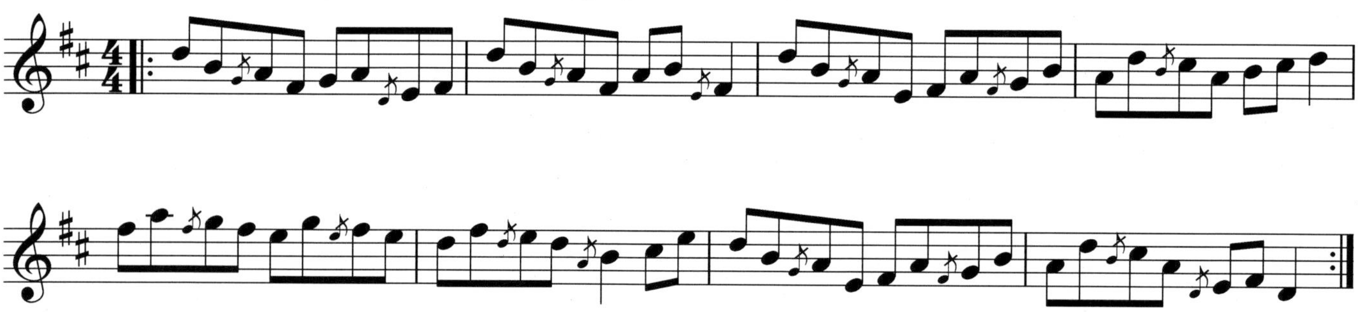

6. Not all tap opportunities are notated in these exercises. If you spot additional possibilities and feel very comfortable with the ornaments already notated, you may experiment with adding more. Keep your taps mostly on downbeats and backbeats for now.

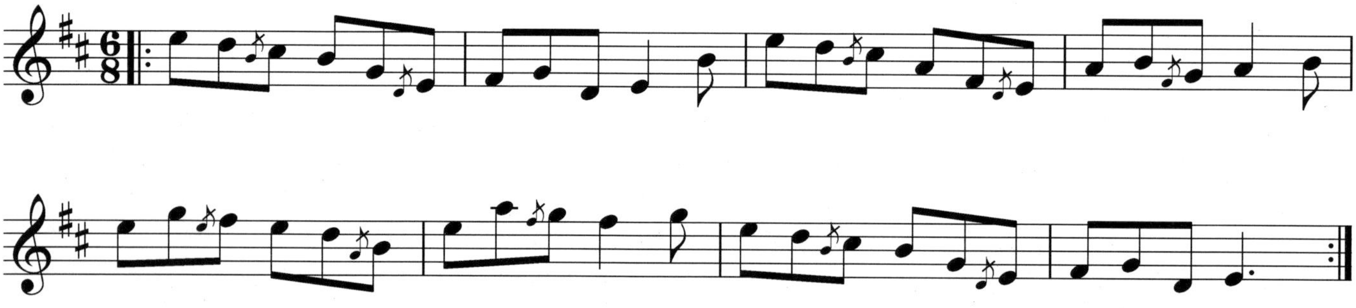

7.

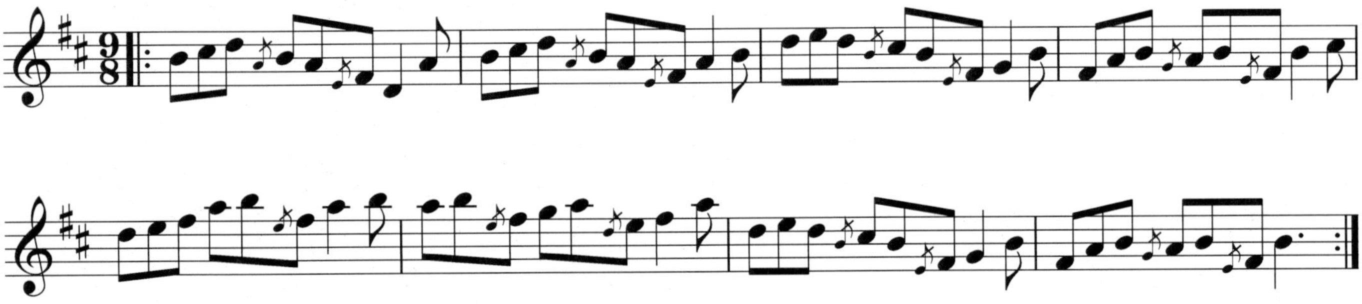

8.

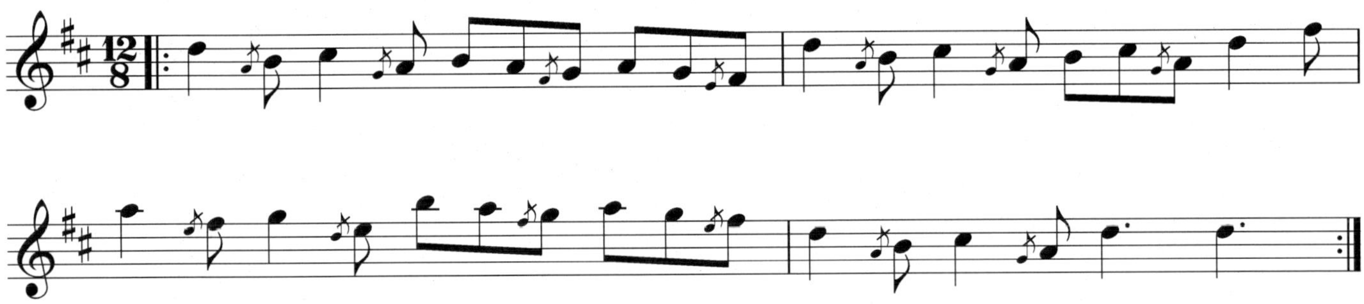

9. The last two exercises use a combination of separating and descending taps. The penultimate measures of these two exercises also have as many taps as possible to give your fingers a good workout. Do your ears like this sound or does it seem too busy?

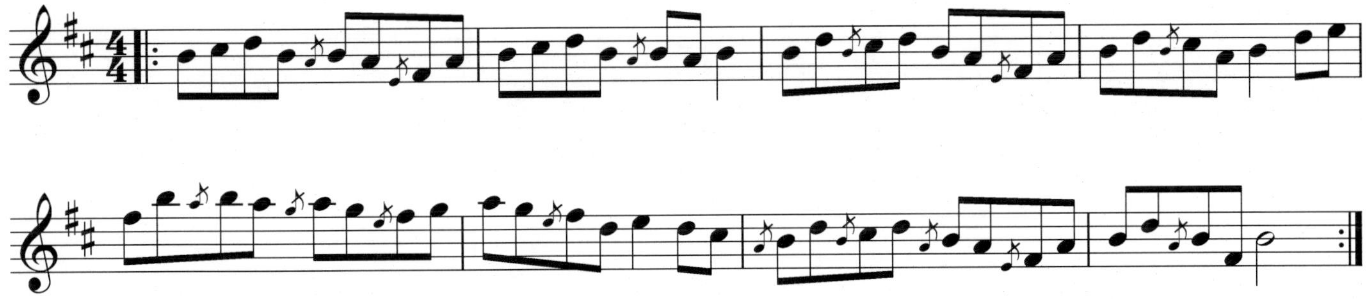

10.

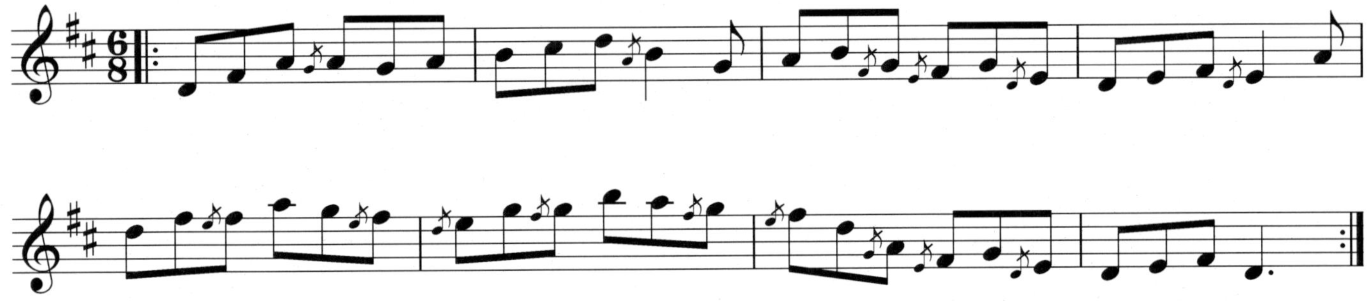

Taps: Combined Exercises

As with previous chapters, feel free to add ornaments gradually as you feel able. It is possible to have *too many* ornaments in a tune, particularly if fingers haven't mastered them yet. Always remember that ornaments are intended to aid the rhythm of the tune. If they are not accomplishing this, then it might be necessary to drop some out. A good way to work up to full ornamentation is to choose one ornament per measure and add those in. Then try two ornaments per measure, then three ornaments, and so on.

Discerning eyes may also notice that some exercises no longer contain all the ornaments. This is a positive development: you've now learnt so much that there isn't always room to squeeze everything into eight bars.

SYMBOLS KEY:

Volume I: Backbeat and Breathing	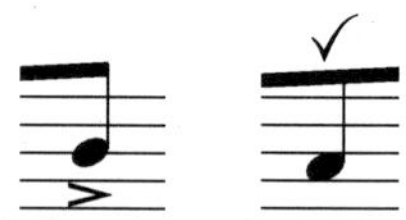 b. beat, breath
Volume II: Single Ornaments	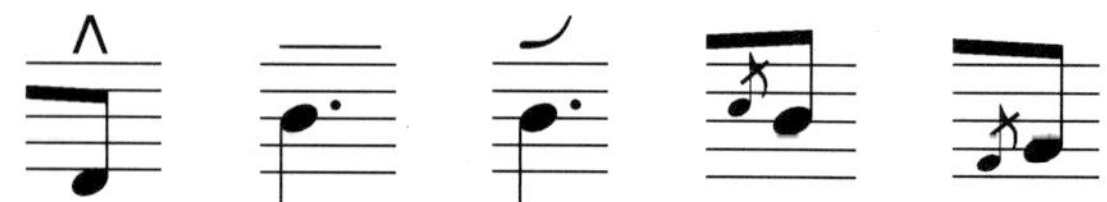 glottal, finger vibrato, slide, cut, tap

1. Look out for the glottal in the penultimate measure. Breaking your airstream before the articulation may be useful in this case.

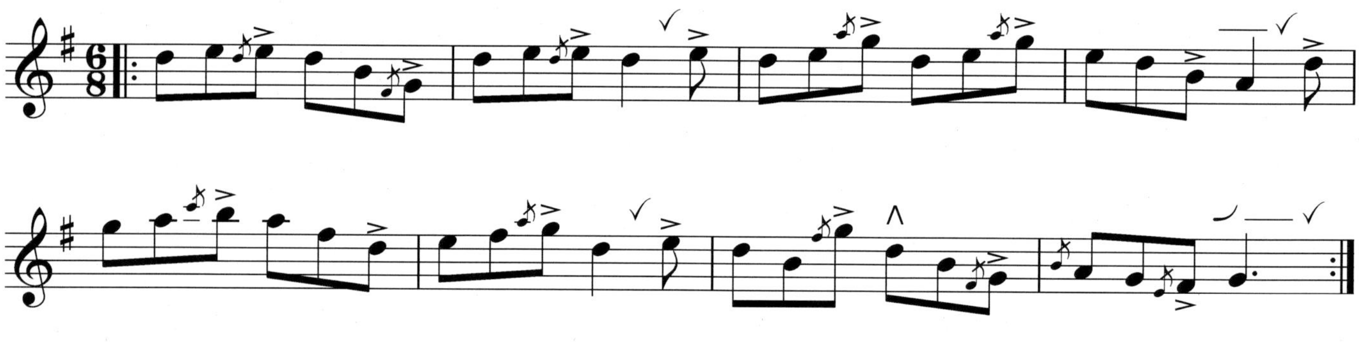

2.

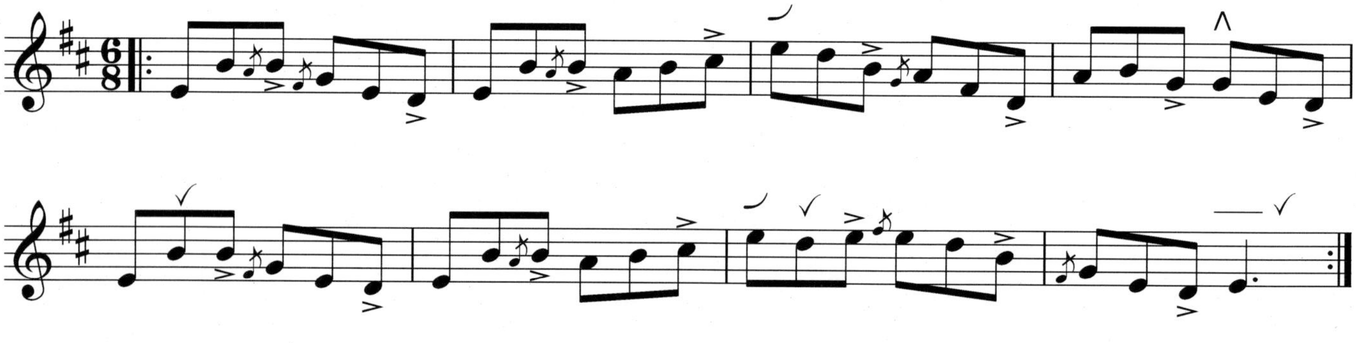

3.

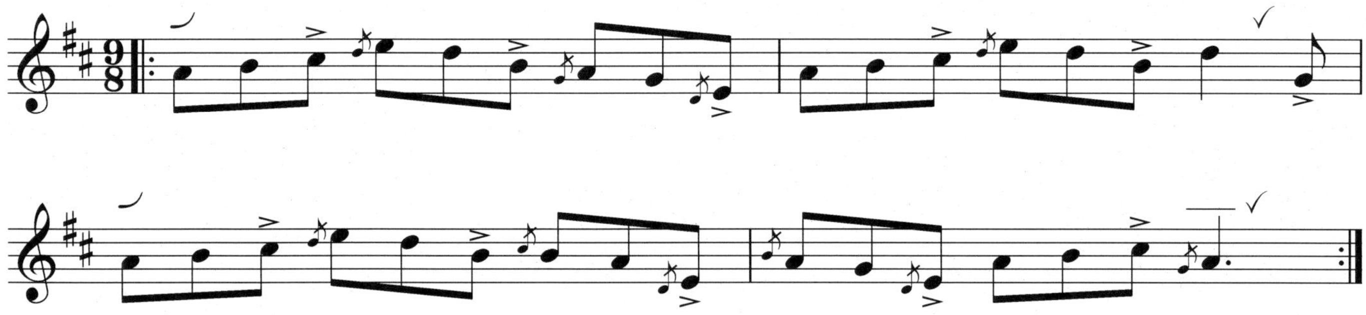

4. Keep a careful eye out for which ornaments are cuts and which are taps.

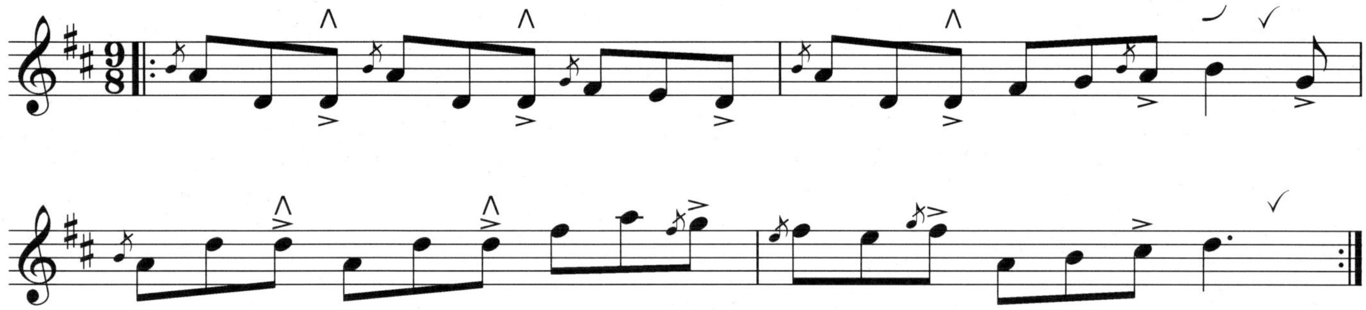

5. You now have multiple ways to rearticulate the repeated Gs in the second and fourth measures.

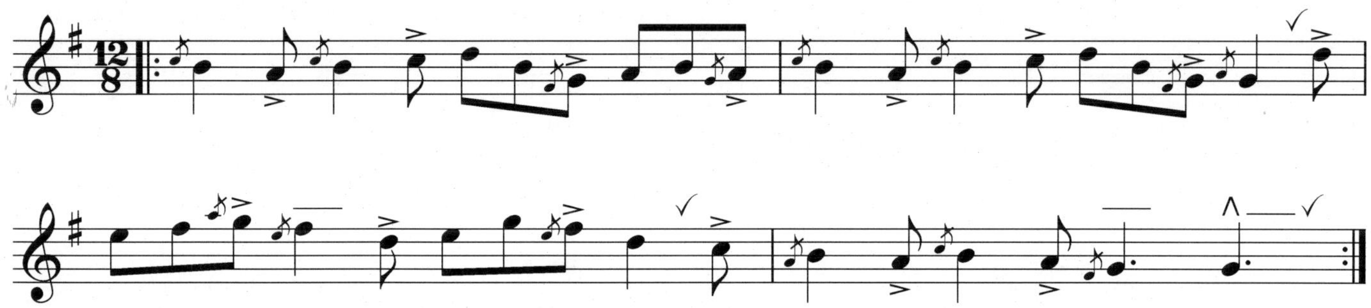

6.

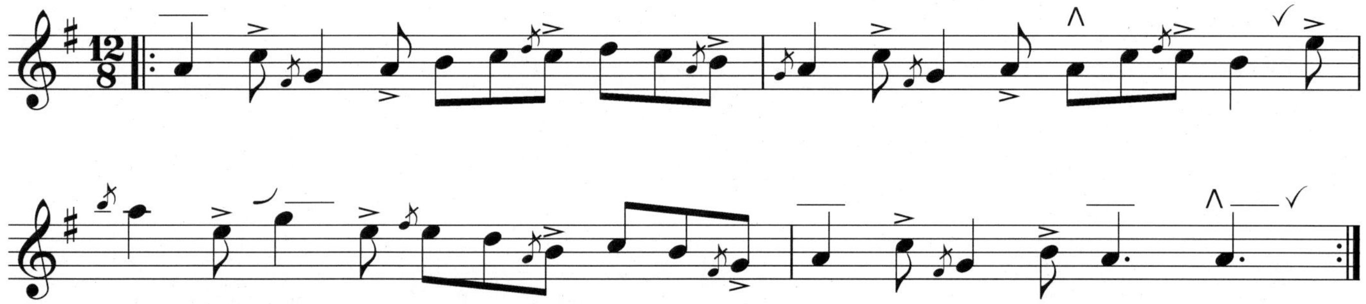

7. Dropping eighth notes out to breathe while remembering all of your ornaments is a particular challenge of Irish traditional flute playing.

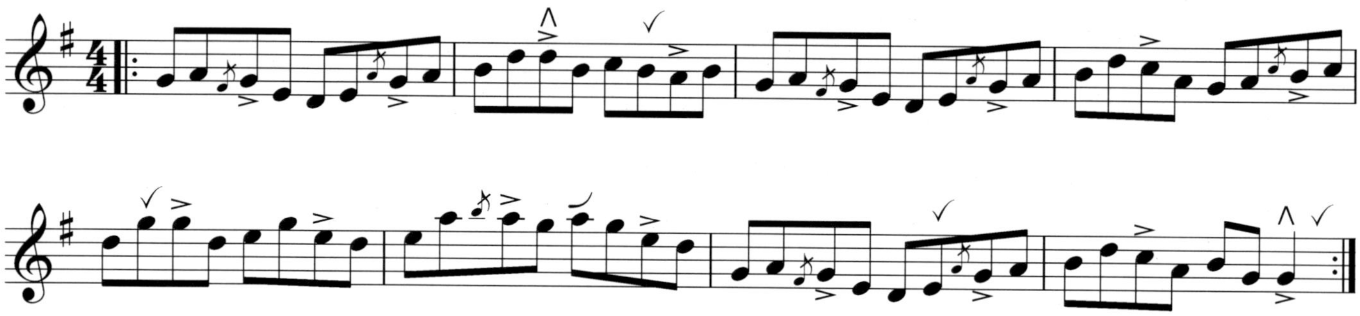

General Tip | The next exercise is the first time you'll have seen an ornament on a rhythmically weak note (the very last B in the first measure). While it is occasionally advisable to avoid placing ornaments in places such as these, sometimes it also works beautifully within the structure of a tune. In this case, a tap works very well as it is the subtlest of our available "separating" ornaments. Both glottals and cuts have the potential to be more disruptive and could draw too much attention to this weak beat. A tap, especially if sufficient emphasis is given to the backbeat just prior, is therefore a good choice.

TRACK 45

8. In measures one, three, and seven, experiment with playing the backbeat B stronger than the tap immediately following it. Taps sound great in minor tunes such as these, especially in contrast to the single cut in measure five to make the high register pop. There is also a cut in the last measure, a necessary change since it is an ascending line.

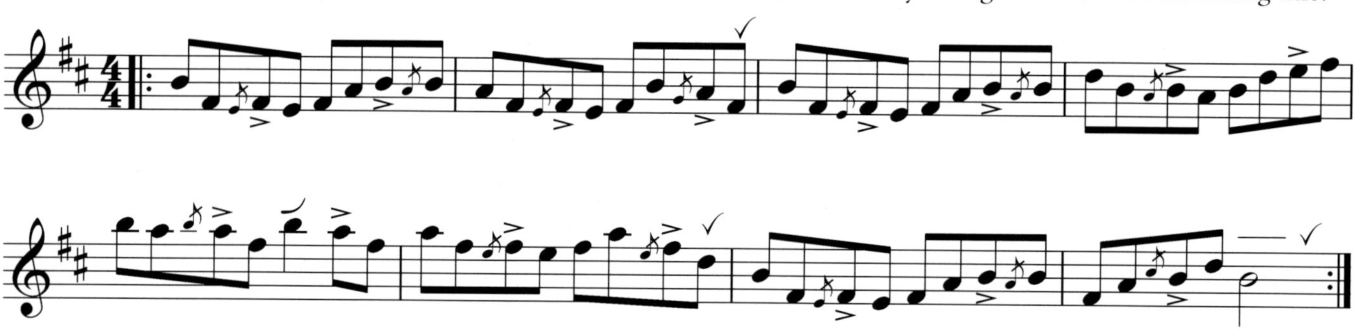

TRACK 46

9. In contrast, using cuts in a major key can give the tune a lot of energy.

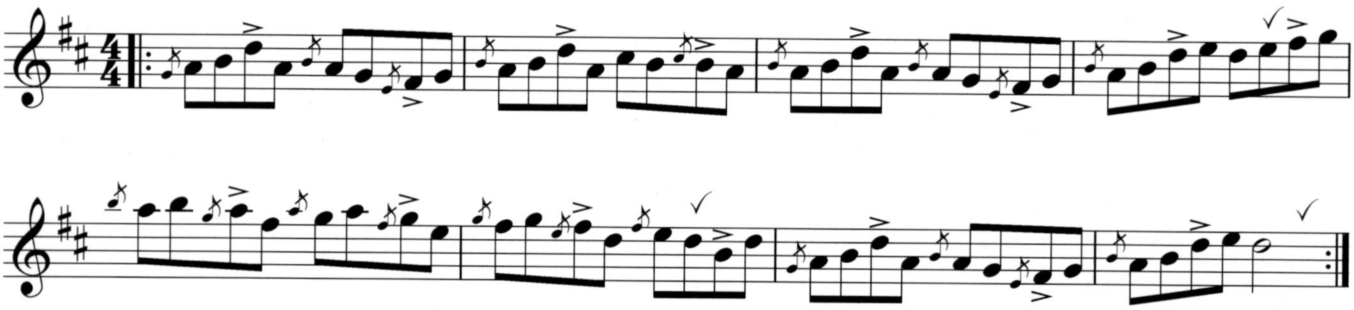

TRACK 47

10. Compare the cuts in this minor tune to the taps in exercise eight. They create a very different sound.

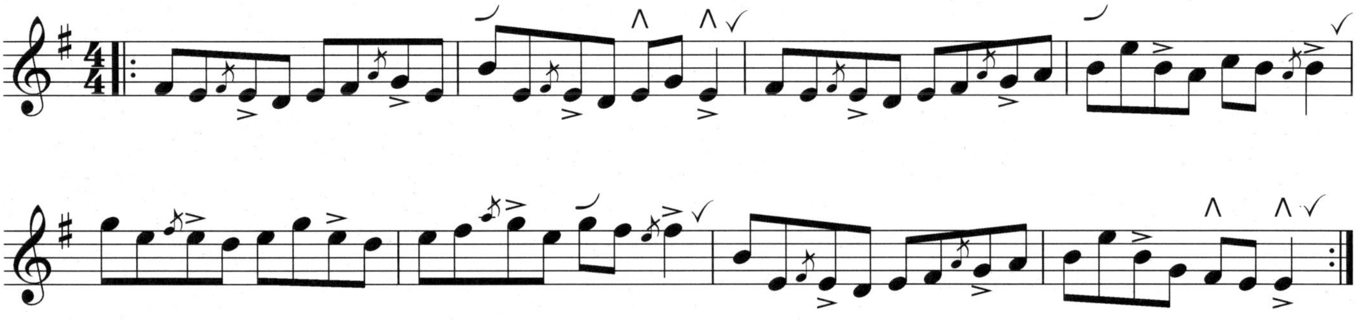

Taps: Tunes

In contrast to our combined exercises, it will feel like we're adding little to our tunes in each chapter. Ornaments are being added sparsely because we're leaving space for many more techniques to come. If you feel up to it, please feel free to add more ornaments as you see fit.

SYMBOLS KEY:

Volume I: Backbeat and Breathing	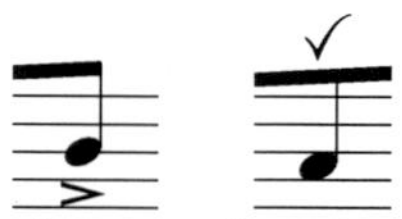 b. beat, breath
Volume II: Single Ornaments	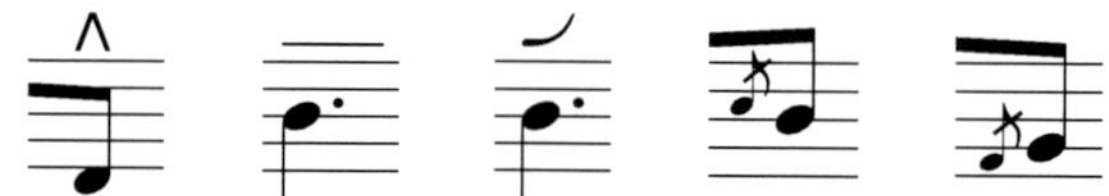 glottal, finger vibrato, slide, cut, tap

Taps: Boiled Goat's Milk

You may notice that both cuts and taps are now available to separate repeated Gs at the end of the A and B parts. Taps are also added to the backbeats of some descending lines.

TRACK 48

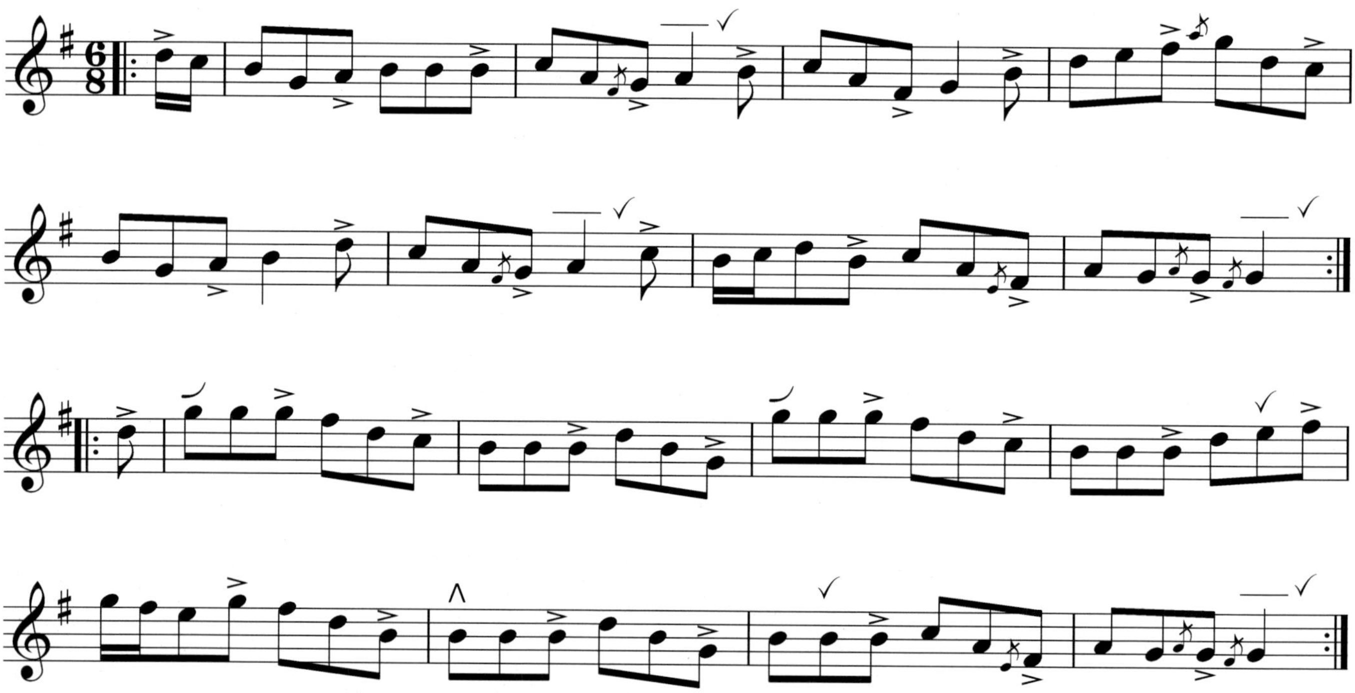

Taps: Dever the Dancer

Taps are added to downbeats and backbeats of descending lines in *Dever the Dancer.*

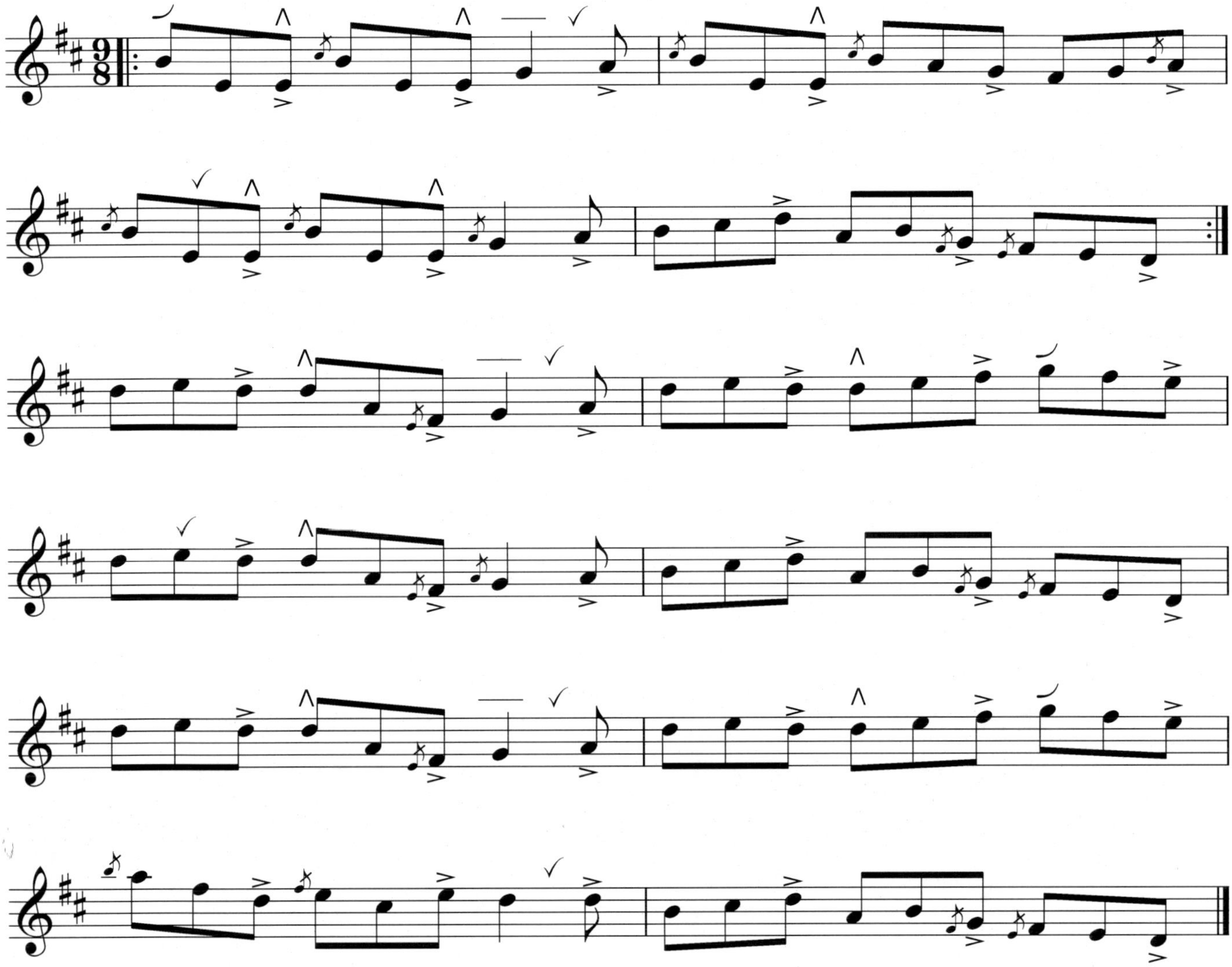

Taps: The Dingle Regatta

You'll find taps added to the B and C parts of *The Dingle Regatta.*

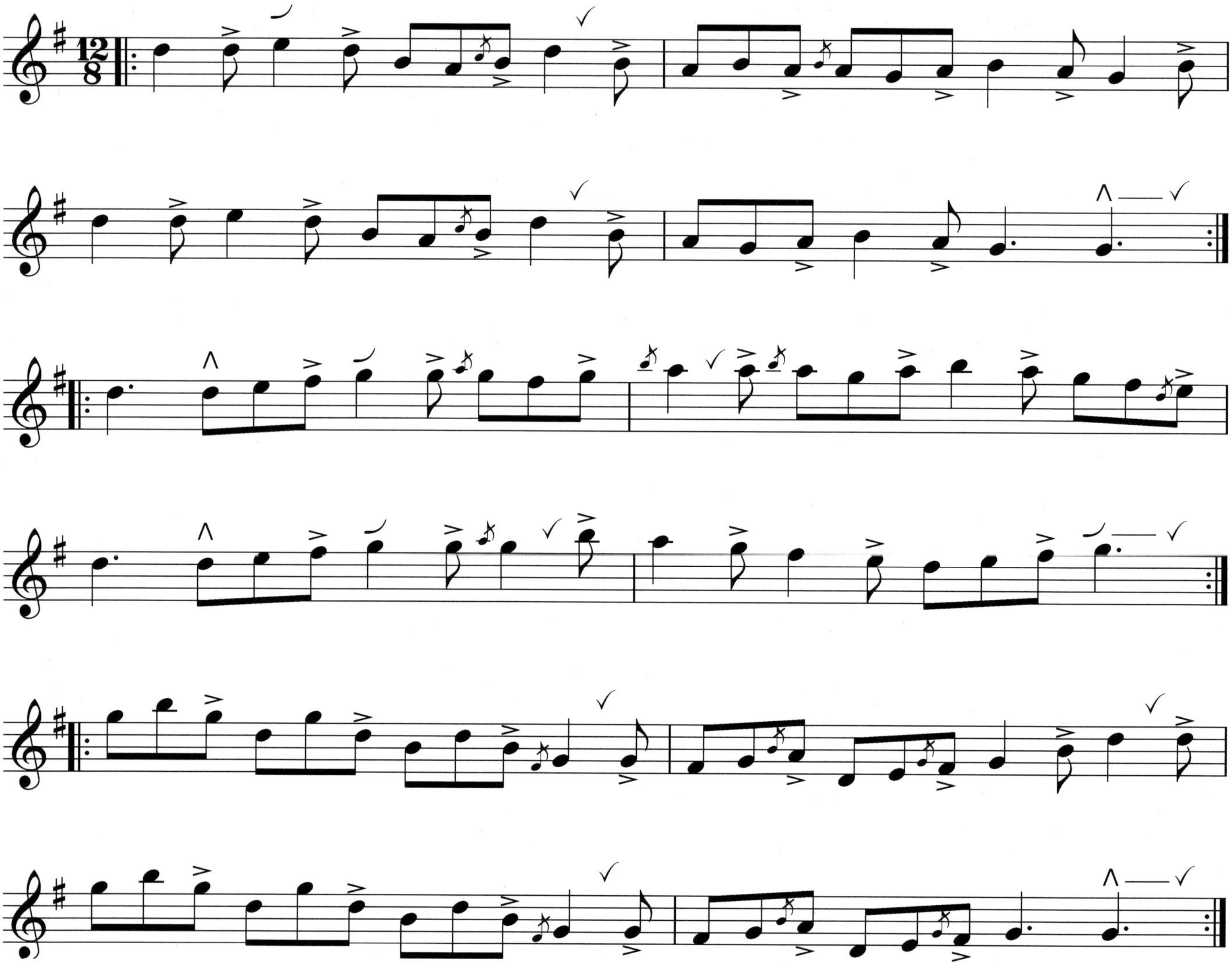

Taps: My Love is in America

A quick alternation of cuts and taps is seen in the final measures of the last three lines.

TRACK 49

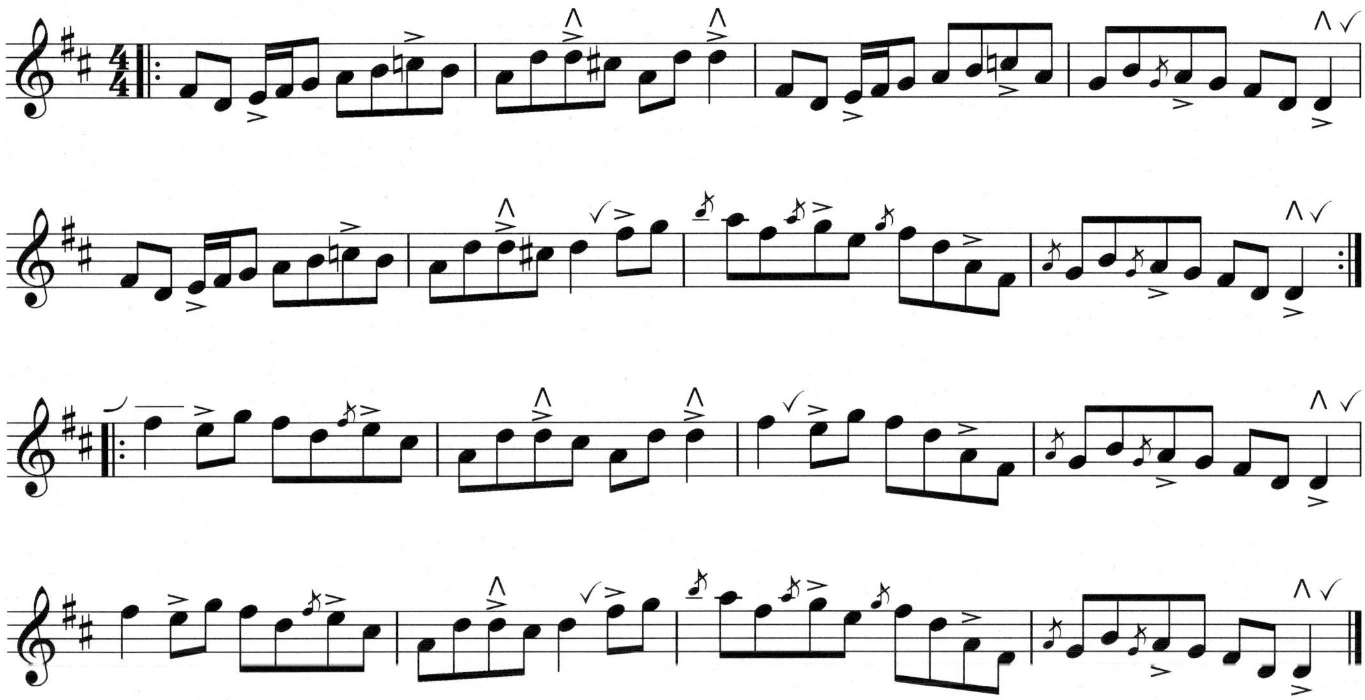

Taps: The Pretty Blue Seagull

With a smoother, mellower sound, taps are a great way to articulate repeated notes in minor tunes. There are many repeated Es in this tune waiting for combined ornaments in Volume III. If you are inspired, you could add taps between these Es as well.

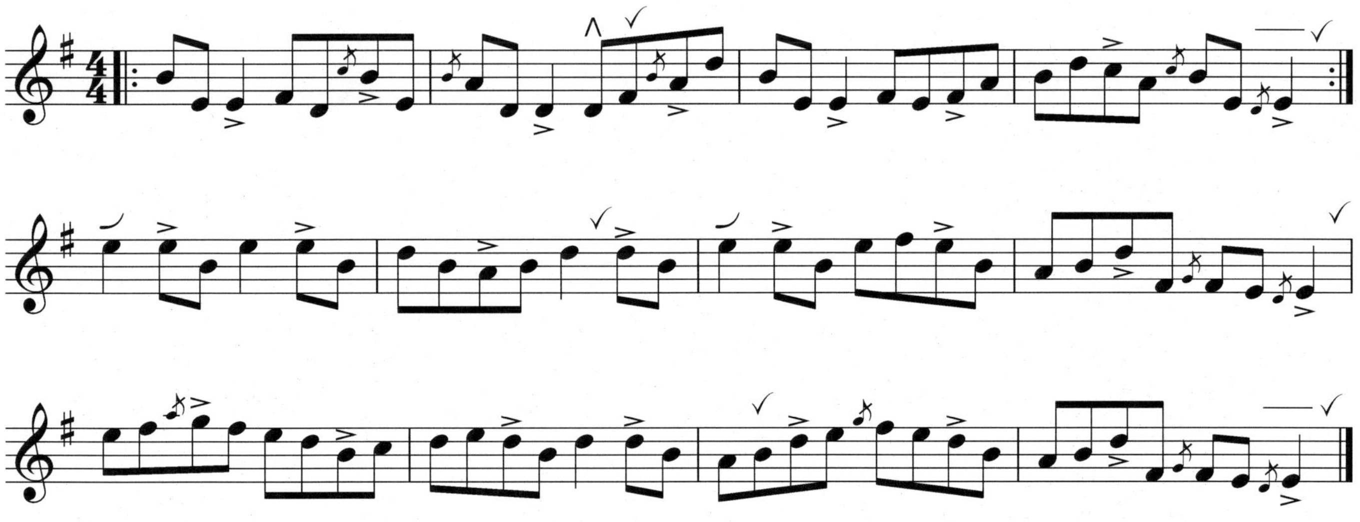

Taps: The Congress Reel

The Congress Reel is filled with repeated notes requiring ornaments to separate them. Adding taps to repeated notes not already separated by cuts or glottals is fair game.

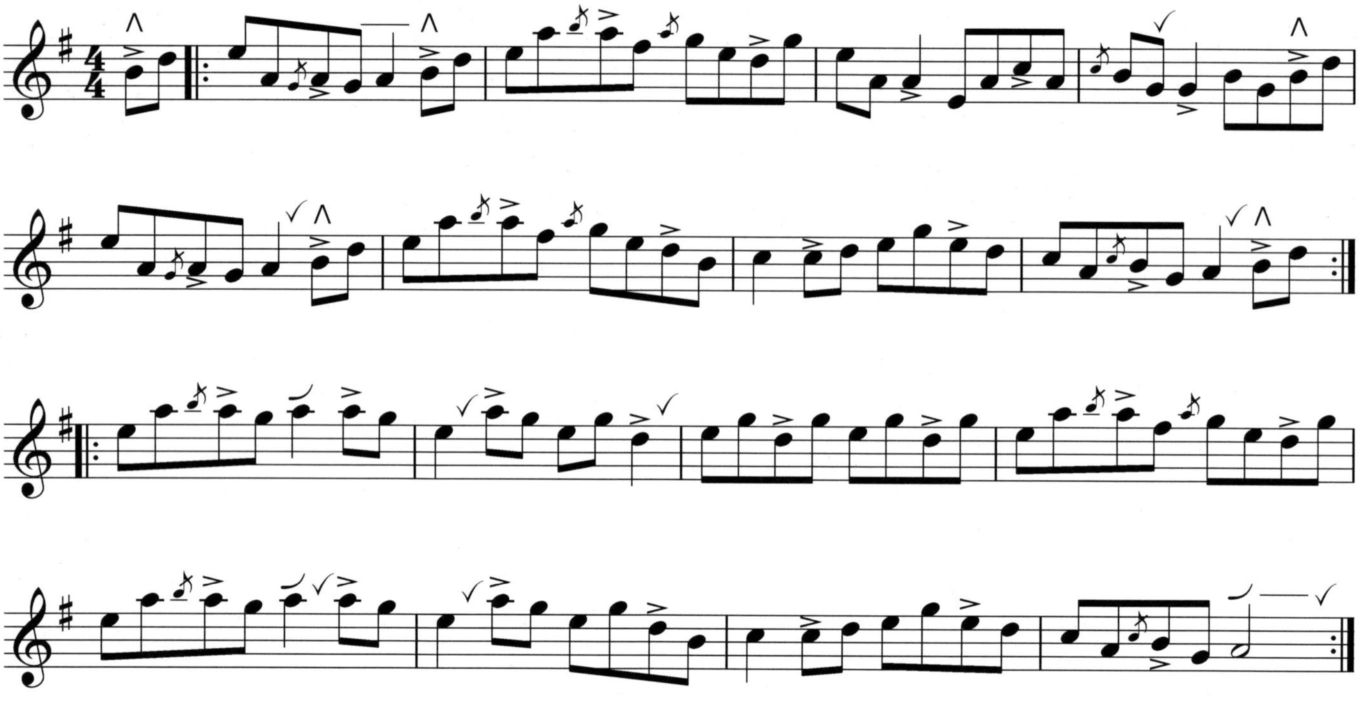

Chapter 6: Bounces

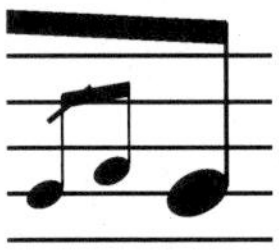

Bounces are exactly what they sound like: they are created by striking a finger down, bouncing it back up, and then quickly bringing it down again. Bounces do not occupy their own rhythmic space or replace notes within a tune, but instead are similar to a set of two grace notes modifying a primary note. Bounces are played extremely quickly, often with the first two notes of a bounce occurring right before the beat and the primary note resolution occurring on the beat. When executed correctly, a bounce creates a bubbling sound.

Since bounces are created by rapidly adding a finger (or fingers), they are commonly used when descending. Many players use bounces in stepwise descending motion. When a tune moves from a G to an F♯, for instance, they'll bounce onto the F♯. It is also possible to bounce between descending thirds. This is easier when the added fingers are on the same hand; coordinating bounces between fingers on different hands can be significantly more challenging. C♯ to A, B to G, G to E, and F♯ to D are therefore great opportunities to bounce on descending thirds. Since bounces require adding fingers, it is generally not possible to bounce onto a C natural or C♯ (although Boehm players could execute a C♯ to C natural bounce if they wanted to). Bounces do not require particular fingerings and there is subsequently no fingering chart in this chapter, but there are two or three fingering tricks for Boehm flute that will be addressed as they come up.

Bounces: Preliminary Exercises

To play successful bounces, your fingers need to be extremely quick. Relaxing your fingers, beginning with a high action, and allowing the motion to come from your hand will help your bounce finger move fast enough. We'll learn the technique in the right hand first before moving on to the left.

> **General Tip** | Bounces work best by first, raising finger(s) high in preparation for striking the first note of the ornament, and second, keeping finger(s) as low as possible while completing the rest of the figure. Keep your bounces as close to the following downbeat as possible.

1.

TRACK 50

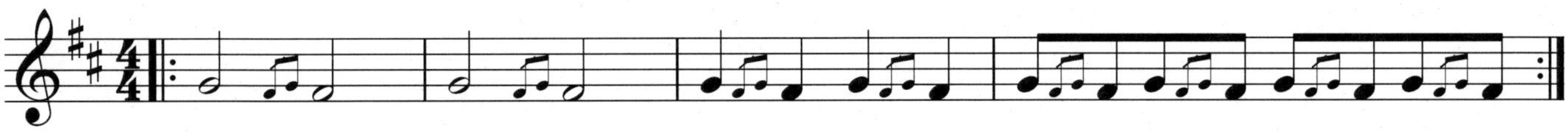

Boehm Tip | For F♯ to E bounces, Boehm players should use their middle finger F♯:

XXX | OXOo
o x

2.

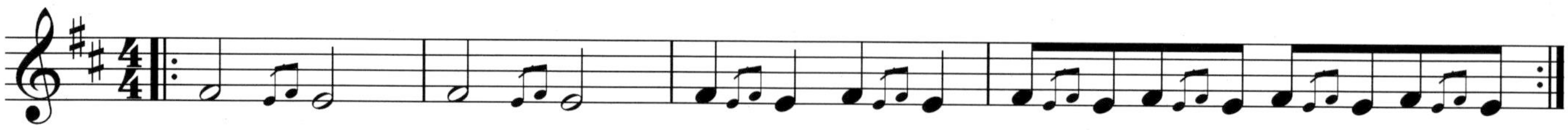

Simple System Tip | E to D bounces in the bottom octave are a paradox: while keeping your finger as relaxed and light as possible, you need a firm embouchure and a strong airstream. Otherwise, your low D will not speak clearly and your bounce will be lost.

3.

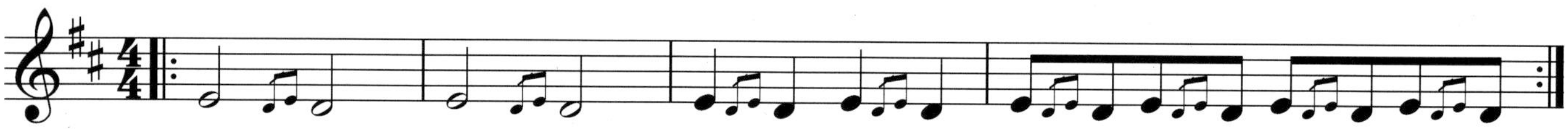

General Tip | As previously discussed in *Cuts* and *Taps*, creating ornaments with the left fingers may feel very different to your comparatively unrestrained right hand. Due to the stretched position of the left hand and the fact that it is the primary support point for the flute, your left hand may feel slightly slower and left hand ornaments may therefore need a little more attention.

4. Start as slow as you need to and stay as relaxed as possible.

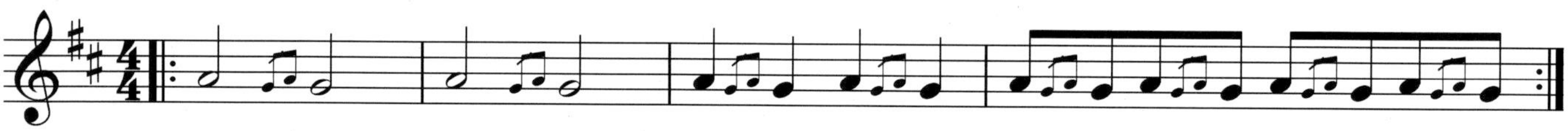

5. If you are using a piper's grip in the right hand but not the left, your bounces may feel slightly different when played by curved fingers. The challenge will be making sure all bounces sound similar.

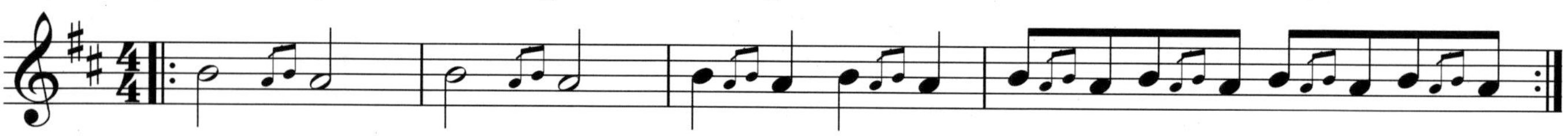

Boehm Tip | If your C♯ to B bounces feel a little too slow or awkward, you can also try quickly tapping the first trill key once you've arrived on the B. This can sound quite different if it's not done well, so listen carefully to your other bounces and see if you can match the sound.

6.

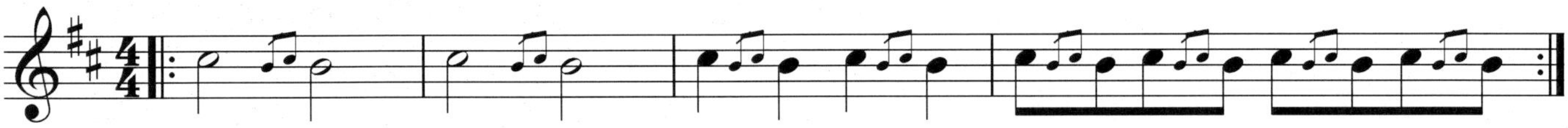

7. This is a good opportunity to listen to all of your bounces and begin smoothing out any differences in their sound.

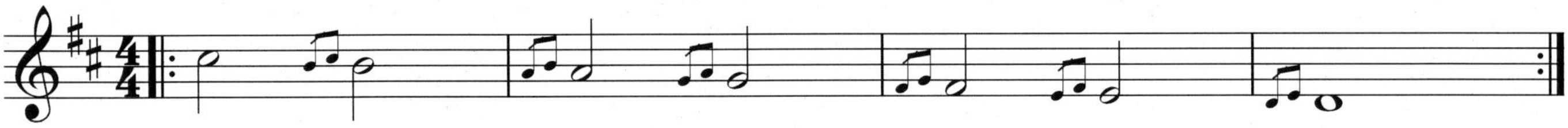

Boehm Tip | F♯ to D bounces work best when using a ring finger F♯ without the pinkie. This makes quick work of bouncing onto the D. This fingering works for both octaves.

XXX | OOXo
ox

TRACK 51

8. The right hand can play descending third bounces from G to E and F♯ to D.

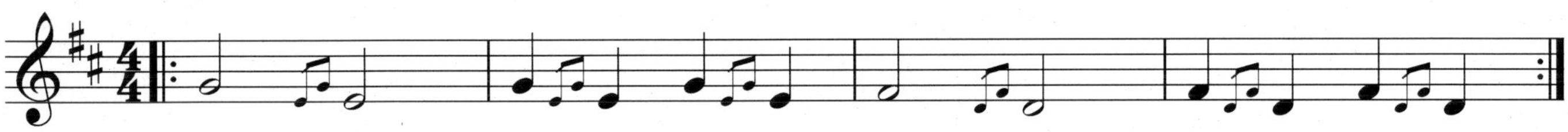

General Tip | If C♯ to A bounces also feel tricky, it is possible to bounce with just the middle finger instead. The pointer finger should come down (and stay down) while the middle finger bounces.

9. The left hand can play descending third bounces from C♯ to A and B to G. Like other left hand bounces, these may initially feel slower and may therefore require some extra attention.

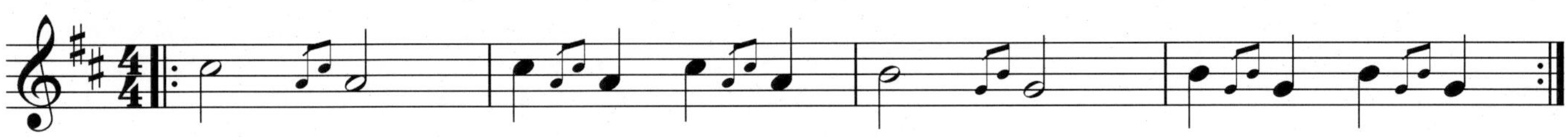

10.

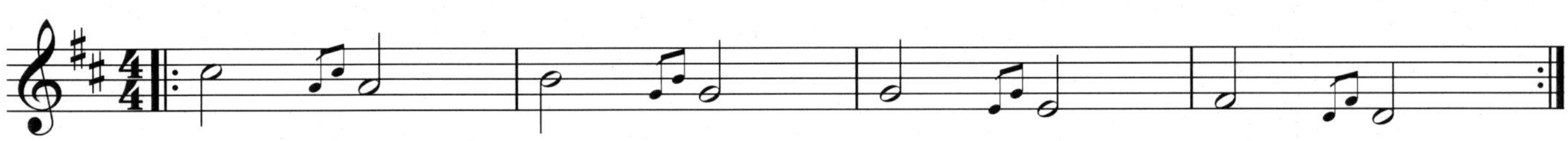

Bounces: Contextual Exercises

Notice that we're still adding ornaments primarily to downbeats and backbeats. Start these exercises slowly and make sure your bounces sound like a fast bubble, not slower grace notes.

Simple System Tip | If you seem to be missing descending third bounces, double check whether you are keeping your fingers spaced accurately above the finger holes. Doing so will allow you to hit your bounces with immediate precision, without any cracks marring the sound.

1. Keep your eyes peeled for both stepwise and descending third bounces.

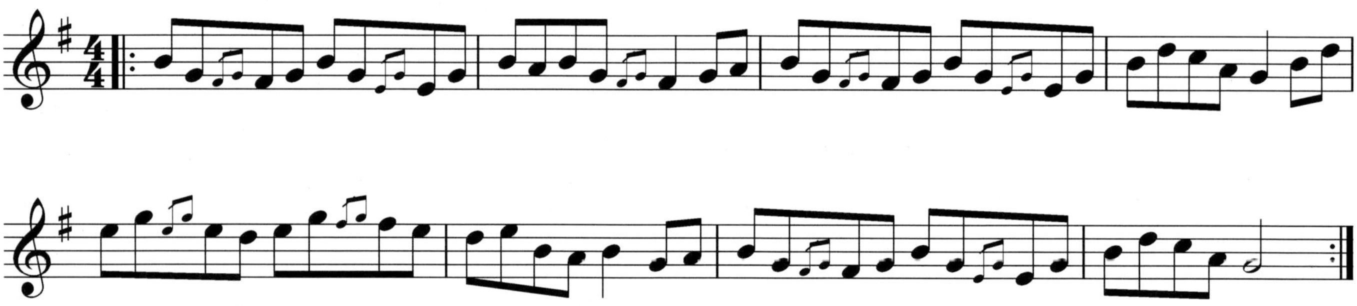

Boehm Tip | Remember to use your middle finger F♯ when bouncing to E, and your ring finger F♯ (without pinkie) when bouncing to D. This means flipping back and forth between the two F♯s fairly frequently when using these bounces.

2. You may notice that this exercise has both F♯ to E and F♯ to D bounces.

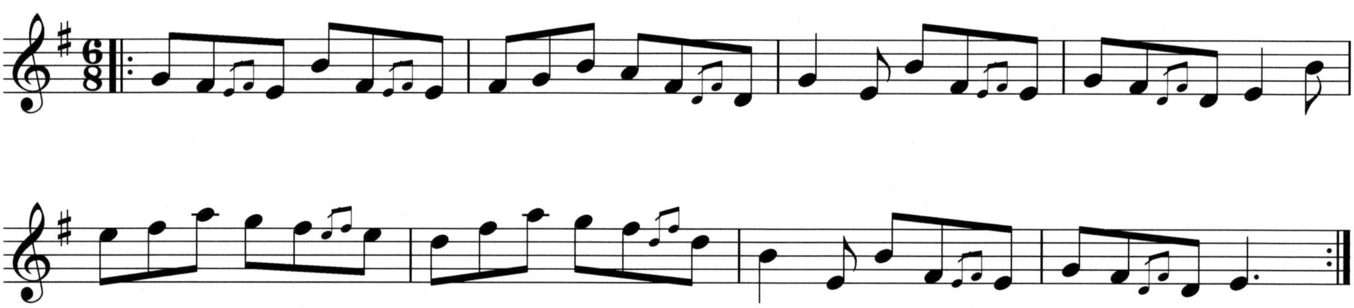

General Tip | Upper octave E' to D' bounces can use the same fingering as the lower register. Another option is raising the pointer finger of the left hand on the first D' and keeping that finger up for the remainder of the ornament.

Simple System Tip | Some flutists may notice that their "ring finger bounces," that is, A to G and E to D bounces, initially feel slower than other ornaments. This is often due to the stretched position of these fingers, which can create tension and make it difficult to relax enough to play with the necessary speed. There is also the concern of covering these far-reaching holes accurately. As is often the case, slow and relaxed practice is key, as well as the acknowledgement that these particular bounces may just need a little more attention and affection than some of the others.

3.

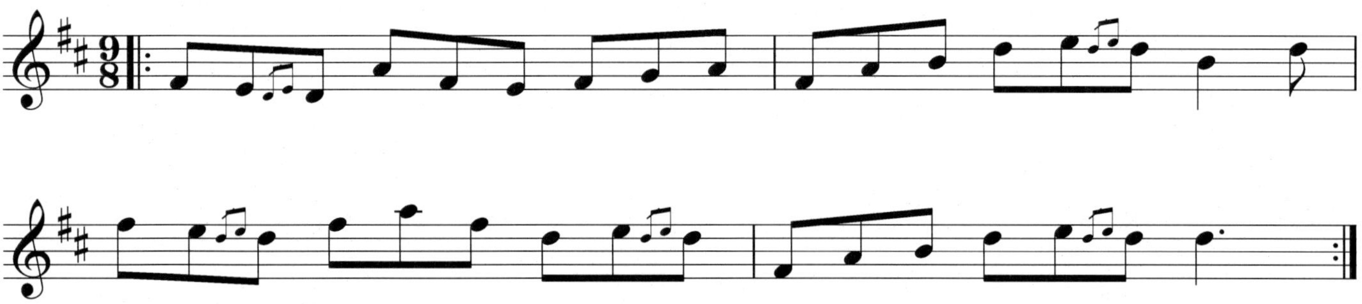

4. You can certainly add another bounce between the A and G in the last measure, but it could also be helpful to breathe there too.

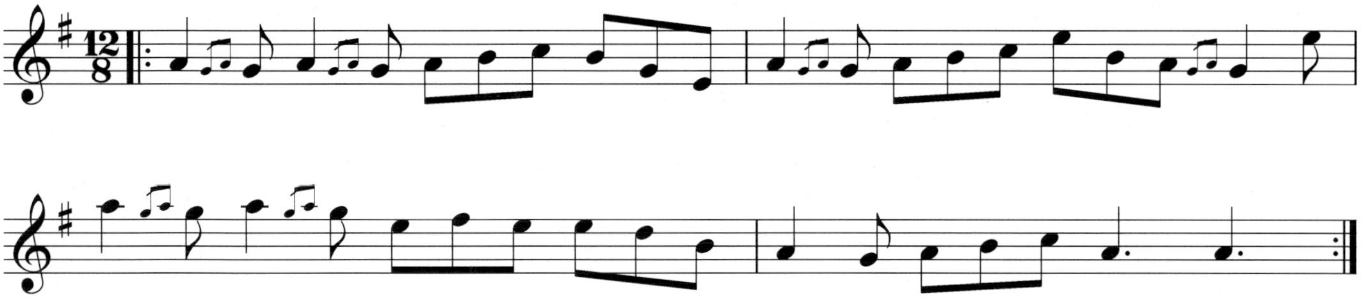

General Tip | Great breath support makes for great bounces. Keep your air moving.

5. Keep an eye out for both B to A and B to G bounces.

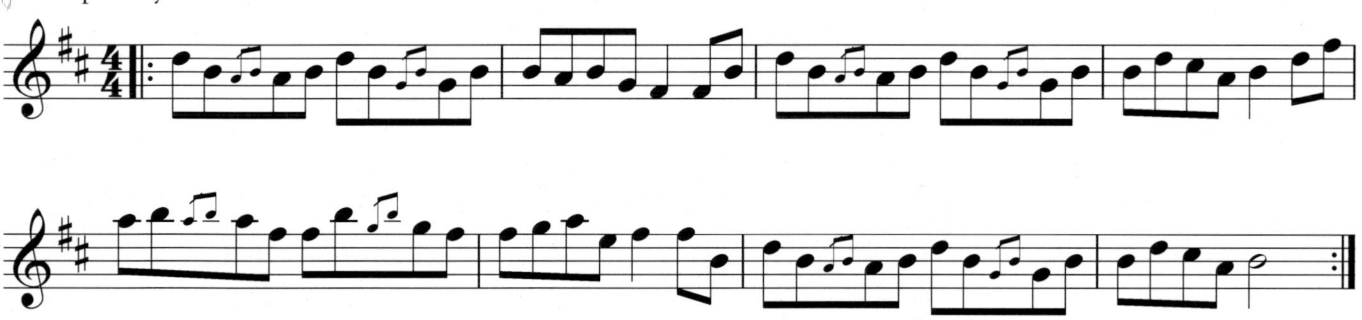

6. Notice that this exercise has both C♯ to B and C♯ to A bounces.

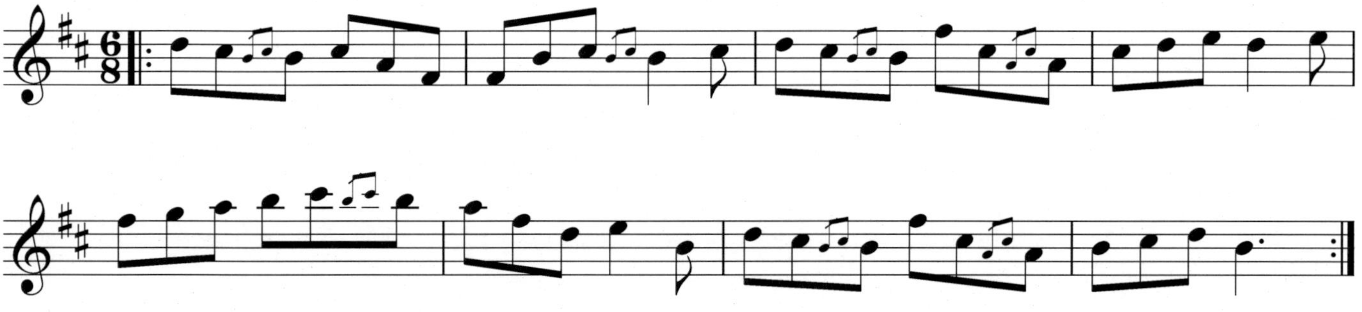

TRACK 52

7. Here is a great ring finger bounce challenge. Keep a strong airstream moving and pulse onto the bounces. Since these ornaments are all on backbeats, your pulses will fit perfectly into the compound meter of the tune. This is one of the appeals of adding ornaments to downbeats and backbeats.

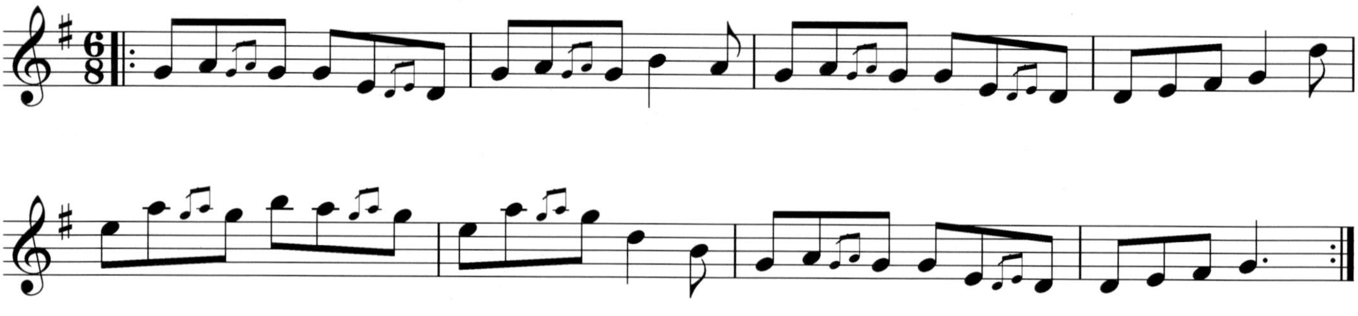

8.

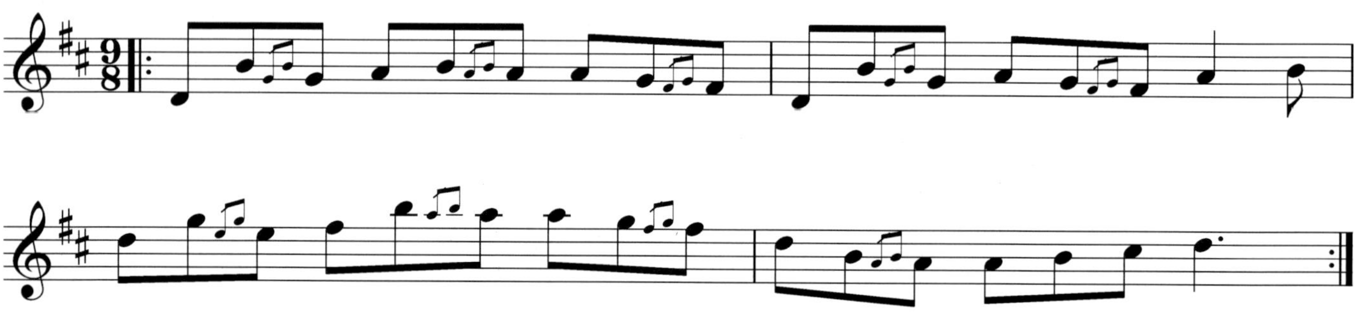

9.

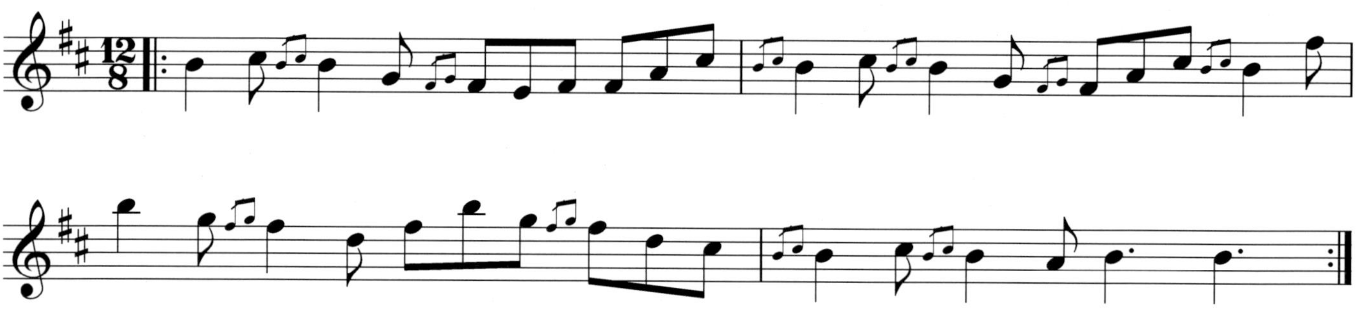

Boehm Tip | As discussed in *Fingerings and Technique* in Volume I, motion between D and F♯ is one of the few places where using a ring finger F♯ is preferable to a middle finger F♯. However, sometimes certain phrases require you to choose and stick with one F♯ over the other, even if that fingering feels less fluent. In exercise ten, for instance, measure four contains a D', F♯', and then an F♯' to E' bounce. Some flutists may prefer playing the D' to F♯' with a ring finger F♯, but the bounce requires a middle finger F♯. In this instance, there is no time to flip between the two F♯s and it is necessary to choose the fingering that will work for the entire phrase. Since a D to middle finger F♯ is inconvenient but doable, but a ring finger F♯ to E bounce is impossible, we must therefore use a middle finger F♯ to satisfy the requirements of the phrase.

TRACK 53

10. You may have noticed that there is no bounce between the B and A in measure six. While it is certainly possible to add a bounce there, it is also on a weak beat. If a player wishes to add that bounce, they will want to make sure they have very fleet fingers so as not to interfere with the rhythm of the tune.

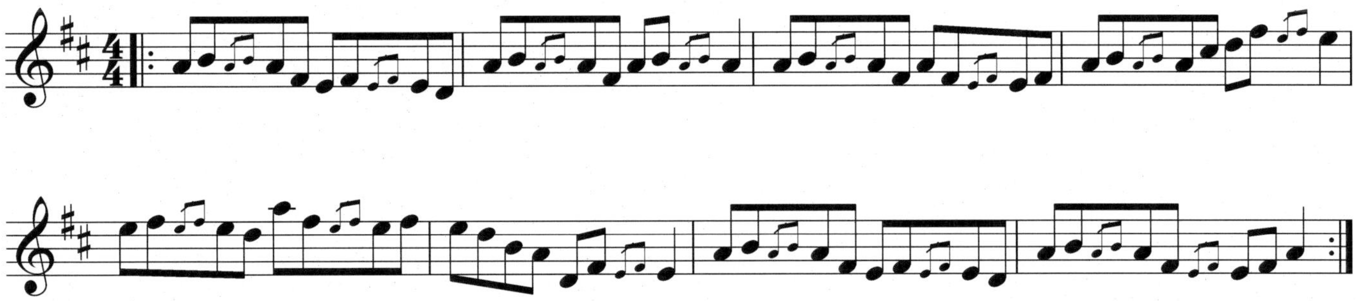

Bounces: Combined Exercises

As mentioned in previous chapters, there are now enough ornaments that you may not see all of them in each exercise. As always, start slowly and add ornaments gradually if you need to. If you feel confident with what is already notated, you may experiment with adding more ornaments as long as they don't interfere with the overall rhythm.

SYMBOLS KEY:

Volume I: Backbeat and Breathing	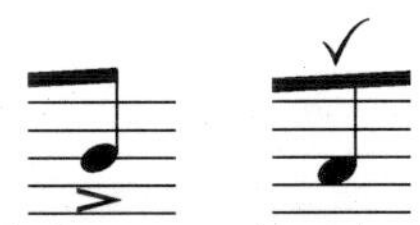 b. beat, breath
Volume II: Single Ornaments	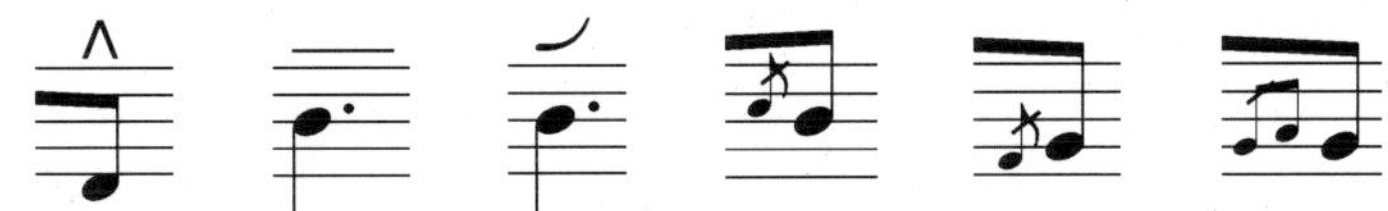 glottal, finger vibrato, slide, cut, tap, bounce

1. Notice that there are bounces added to both descending steps and thirds.

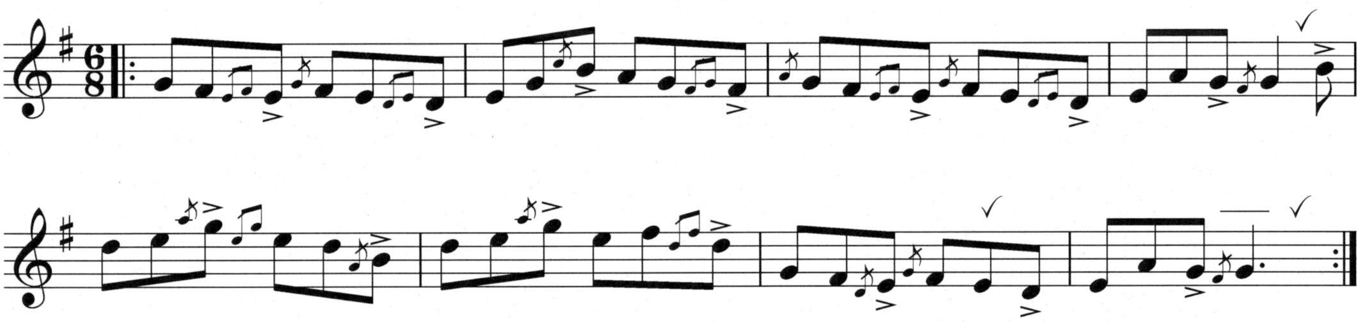

2. Ornaments can be "recycled" on repeated phrases. The G, B, and E in measures three and seven use the same configuration of cuts and taps.

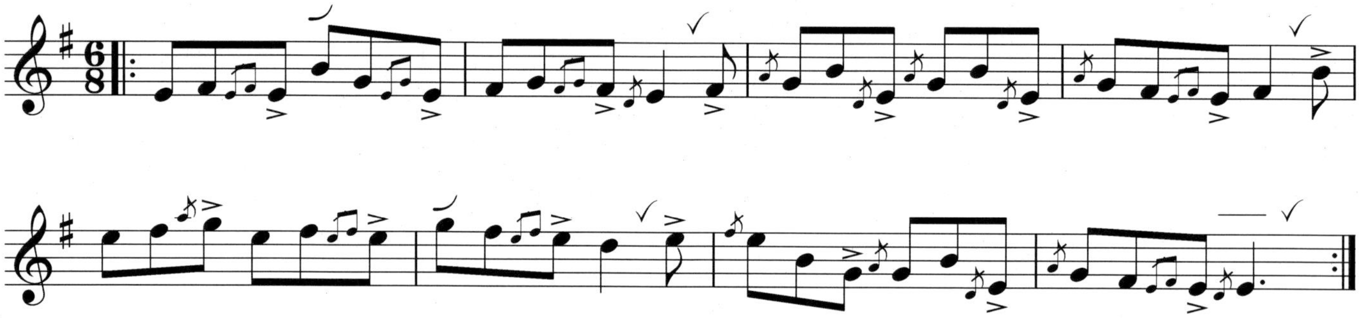

Simple System Tip | Remember your unusual fingering for C natural cuts:

O X X | X O X

or

O X X | O X X

3. If you do choose to take the breath on the C in measure four, you can forgo the cut when you come back in.

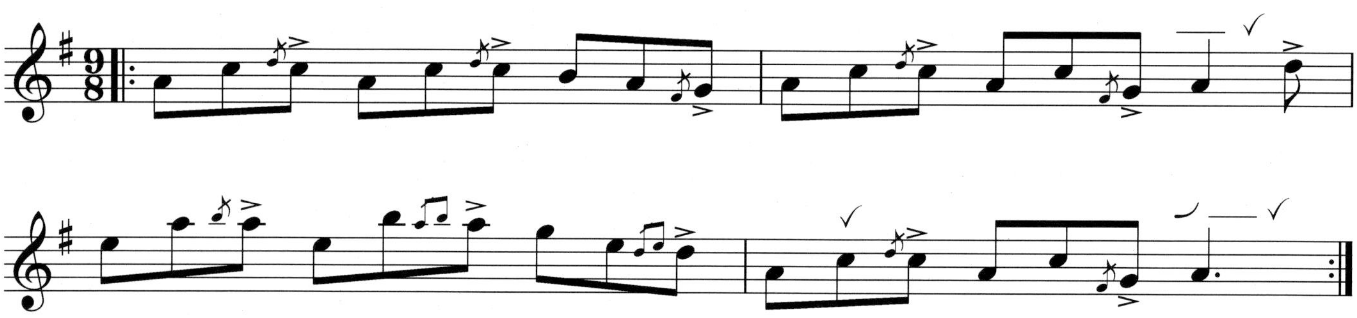

TRACK 54

4. Cuts immediately following glottals can break to a higher pitch than usual. This is perfectly fine. Actually, I think this effect sounds great and I use it fairly often.

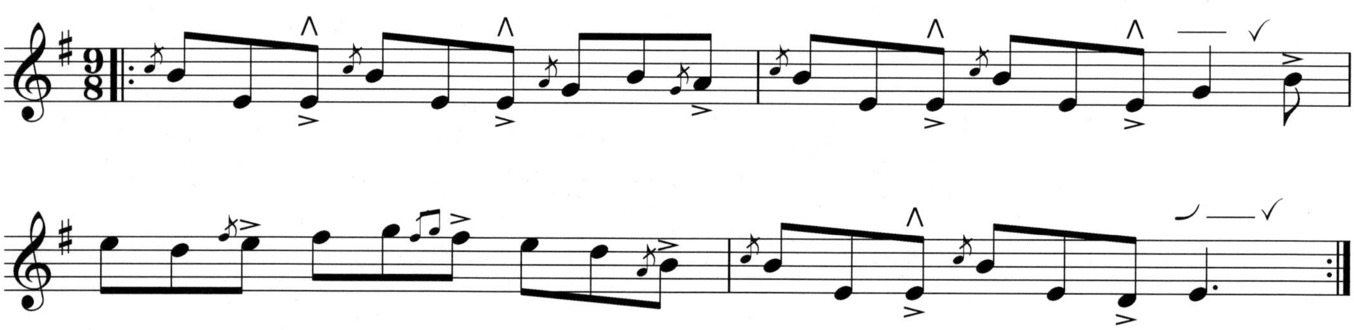

5. Be sure to take a big enough breath in the third measure in order to have air for your very last glottal.

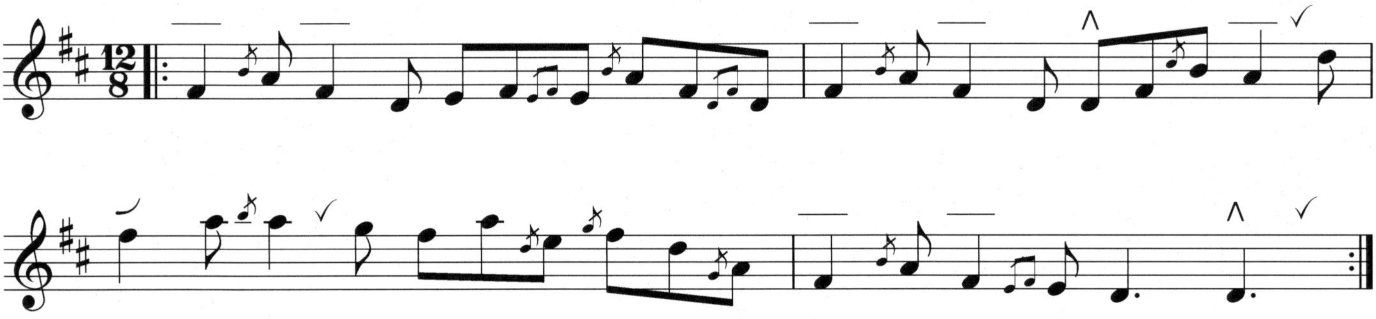

General Tip | There's a lot going on now. Are you remembering your backbeat? It is still (and will always be) the canvas that supports everything you do.

6.

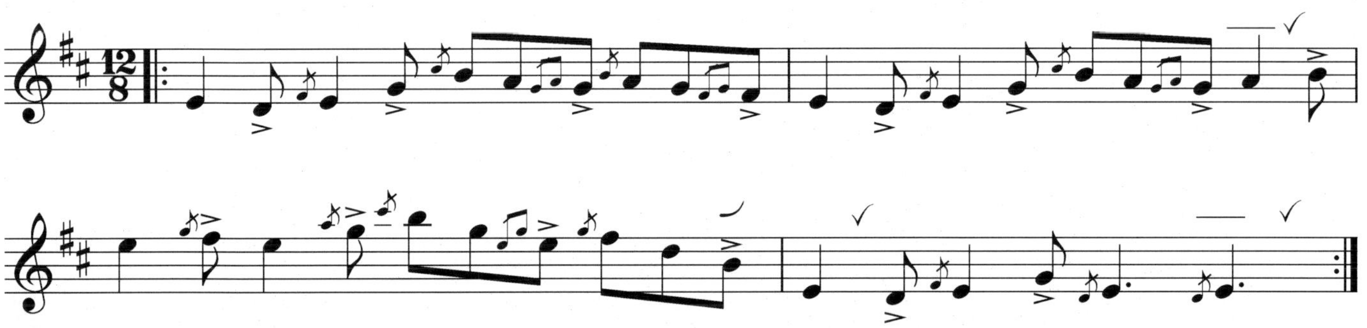

7.

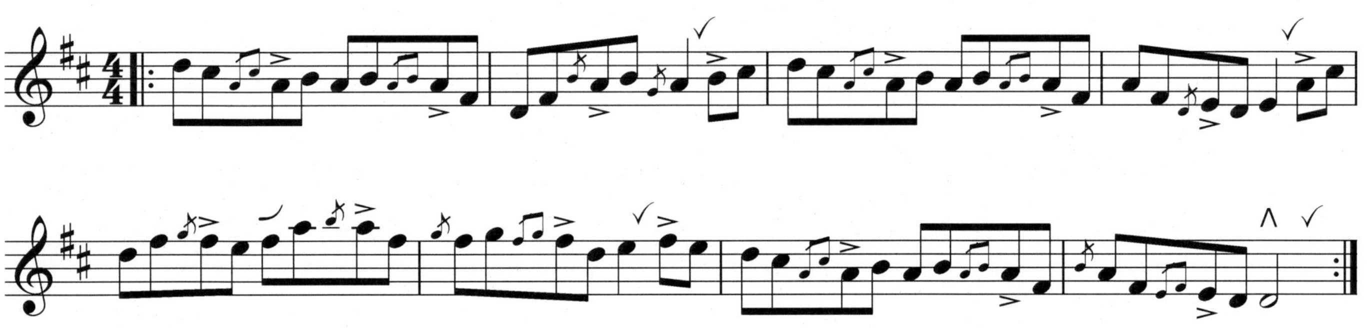

8.

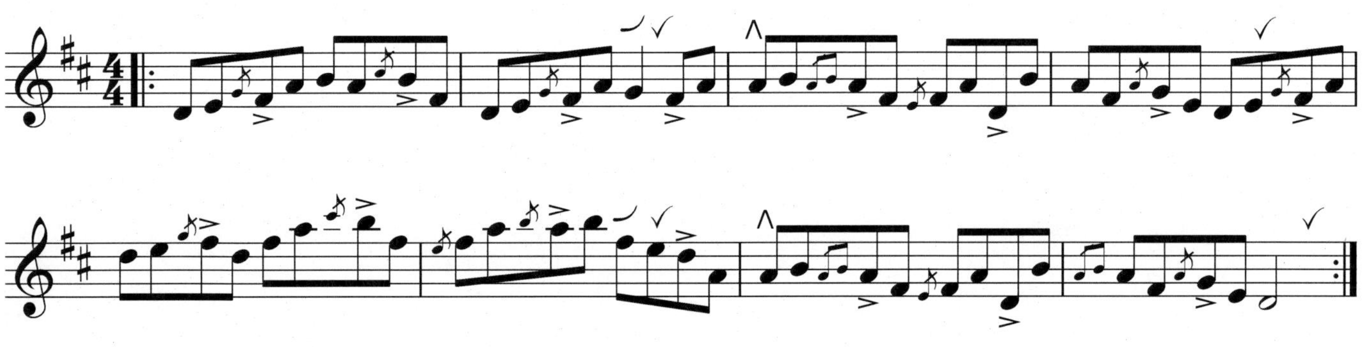

TRACK 55

9. A long G provides contrast to the running eighth notes around it. Glottals create emphasis just before the end of each phrase.

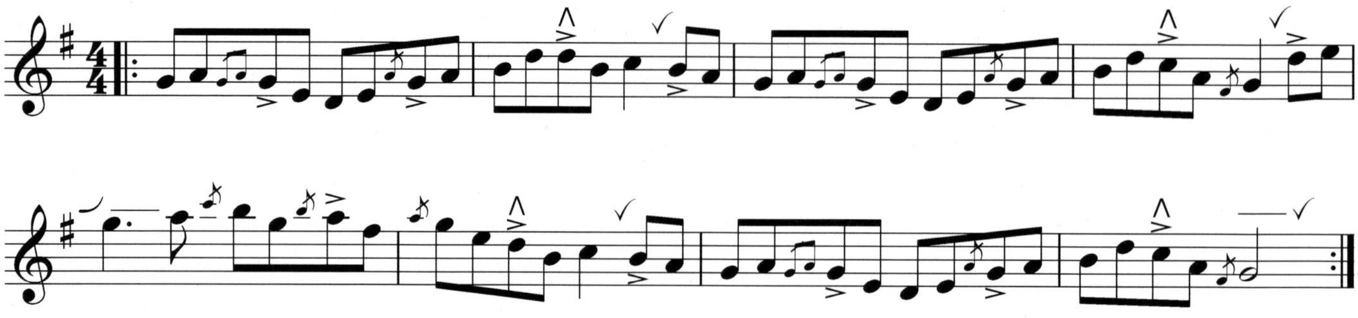

TRACK 56

10. A melody with running eighths will need to drop rhythmically weak notes to make way for breaths. Using a combination of the two potential breathing spots in reel rhythm creates a nice variation to the sound of the tune.

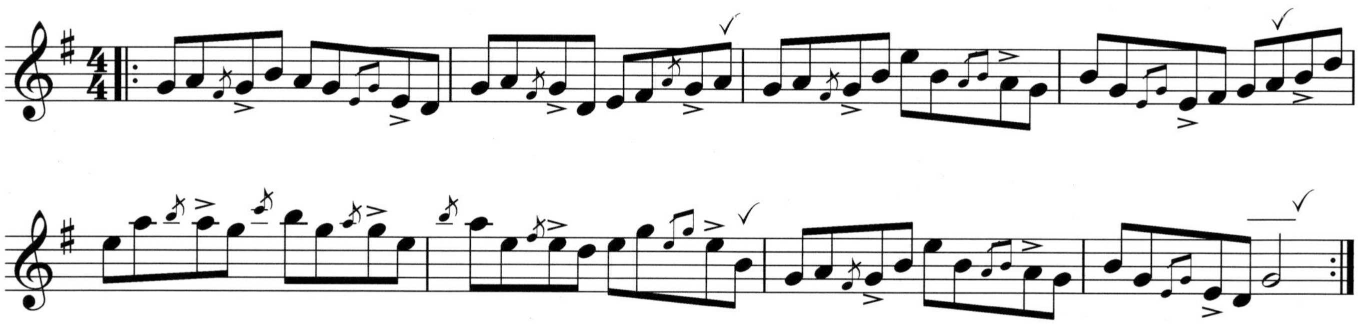

Bounces: Tunes

As we work through these tunes, you may notice that there are just a few bounces scattered here and there. With bounces working best on descending steps and thirds, and taps also working in descending motion, some tunes do have fewer opportunities for bounces. As you learn more and more ornaments, it will become clear that not all of them will (or should) fit into every tune. Ornaments can be left out or played less frequently due to the structure of a tune or a musician's personal preference. Our goal is to someday know these ornaments well enough that we can *choose* to add as many or as few as we'd like.

SYMBOLS KEY:

Volume I: Backbeat and Breathing

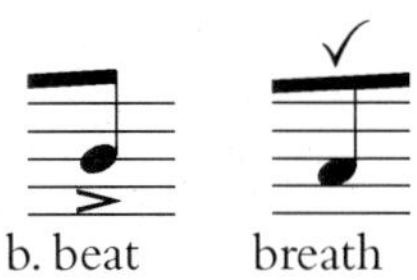

Volume II: Single Ornaments

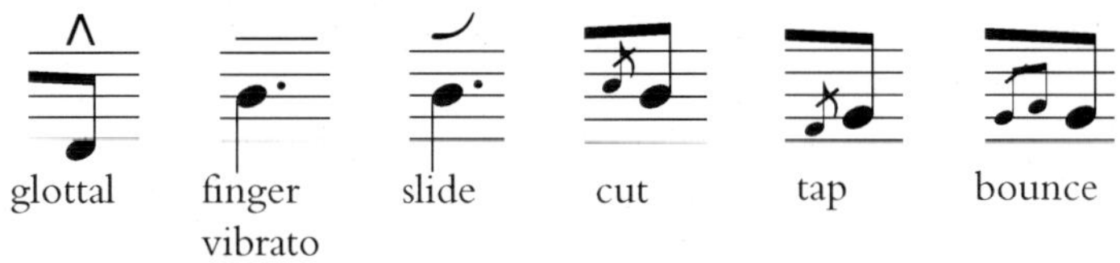

Bounces: Boiled Goat's Milk

Bounces work very nicely in the descending lines in the B part of *Boiled Goat's Milk*.

TRACK 57

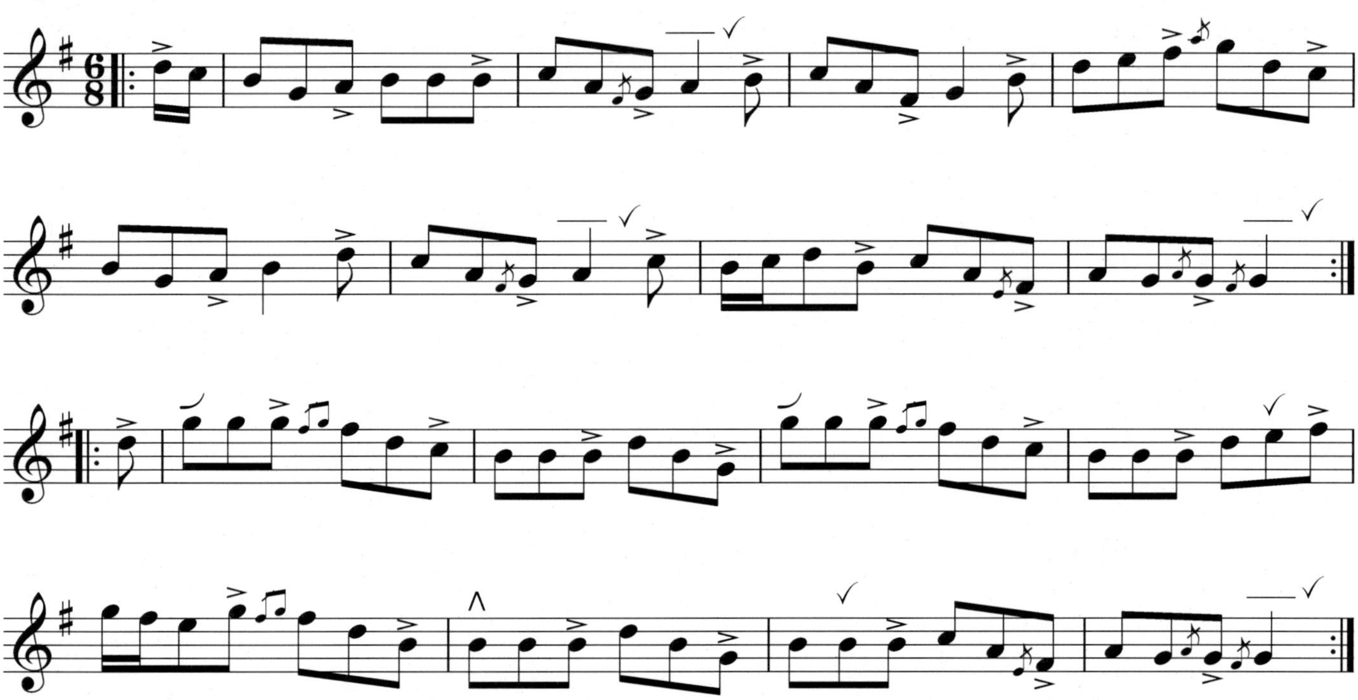

Bounces: Dever the Dancer

Dever the Dancer has additional opportunities for E' to D' bounces that are not notated. Although we are saving those spots for more advanced ornaments in Volume III, you are welcome to add those bounces now. You may also notice that this is the first recording of *Dever the Dancer* to appear since the beginning of the book. Compare this page to its sparsely ornamented version in *Glottals* (page 14, track 10). This comparison provides an accelerated demonstration of how much a tune can change with the addition of ornamentation.

TRACK 58

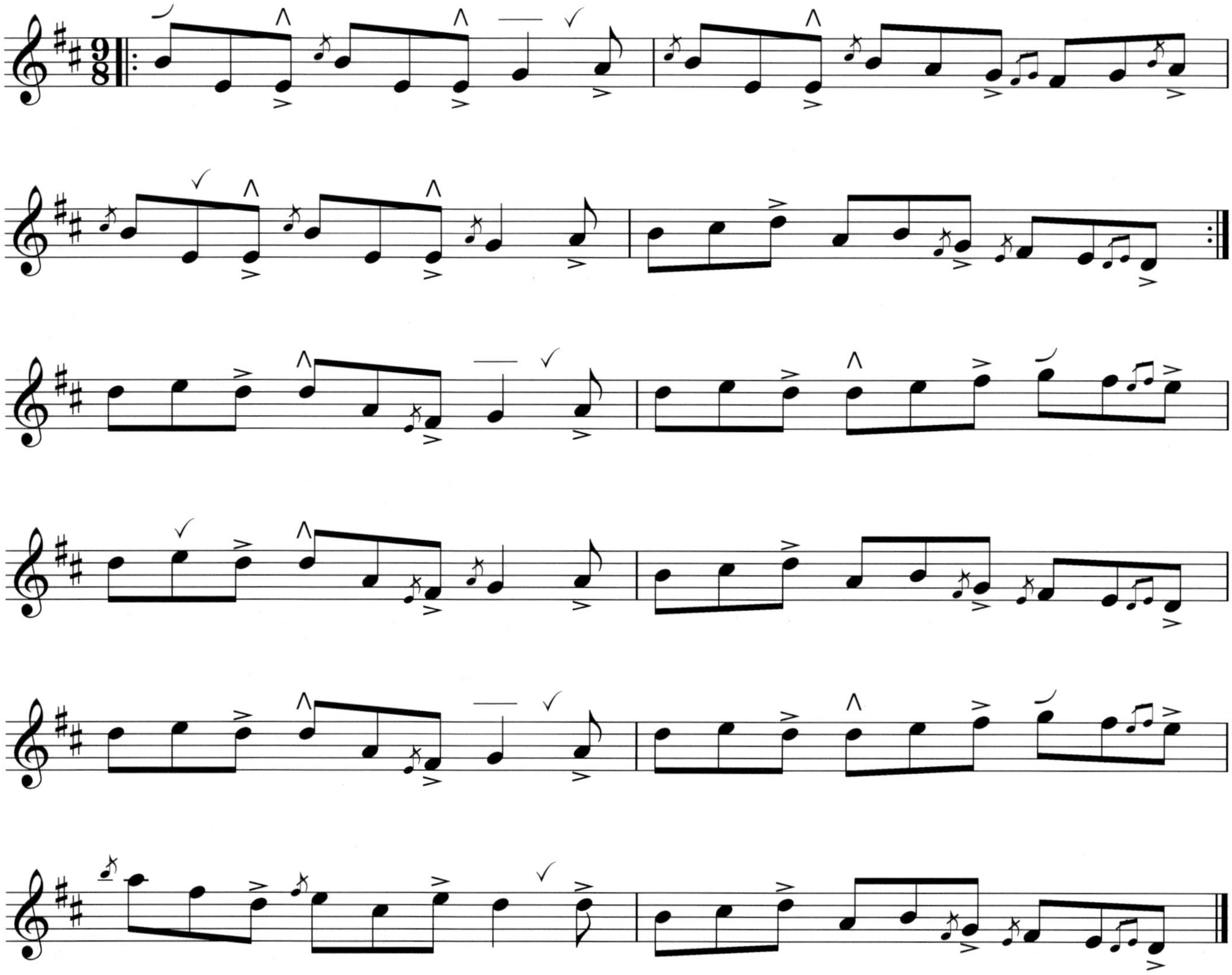

Bounces: The Dingle Regatta

In *The Dingle Regatta*, there are just a few bounces added to accent the highest phrase of the B part.

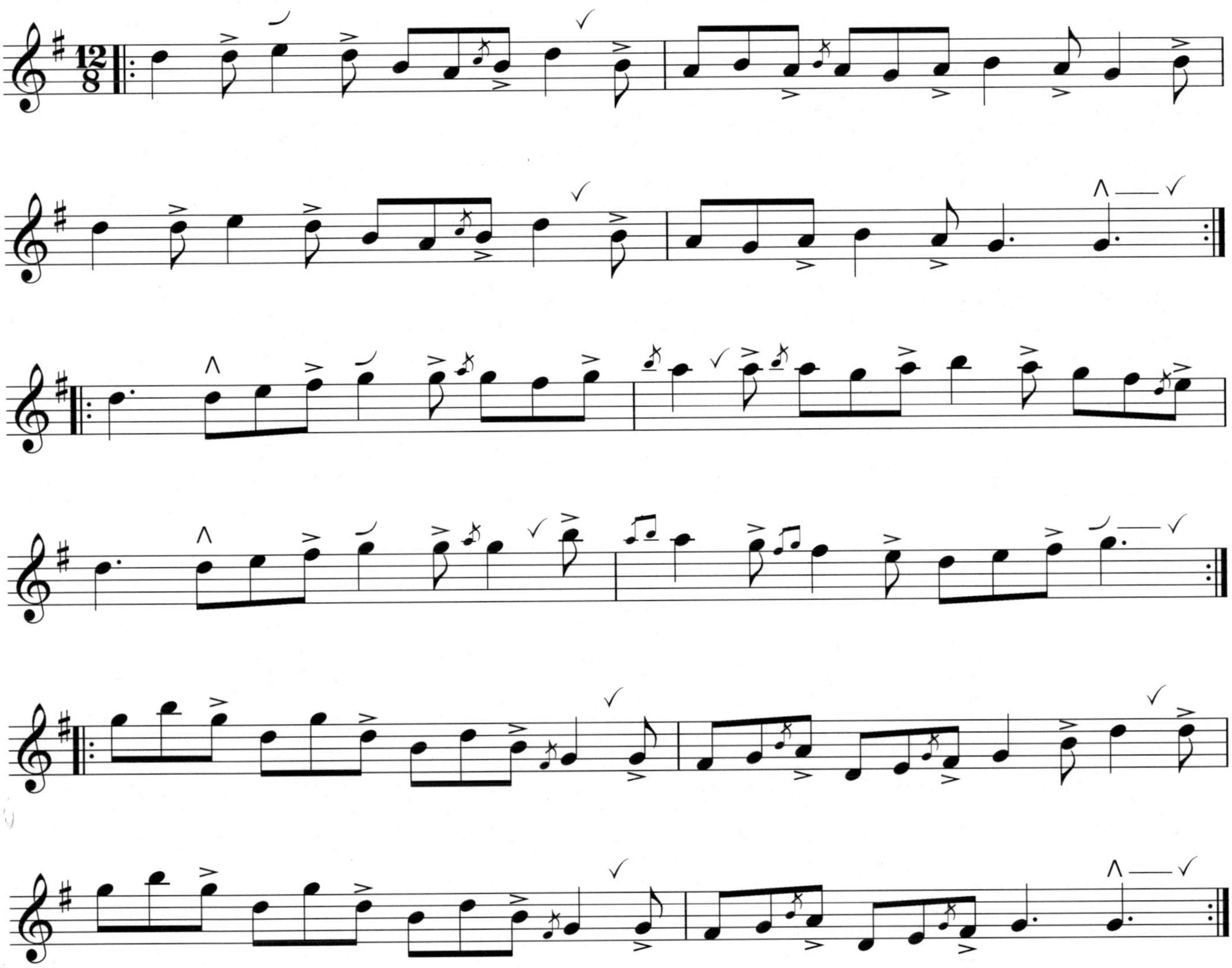

Bounces: My Love is in America

The structure of *My Love is in America* offers opportunities for bounces at the end of each phrase, as well as in the beginning of the B part.

TRACK 59

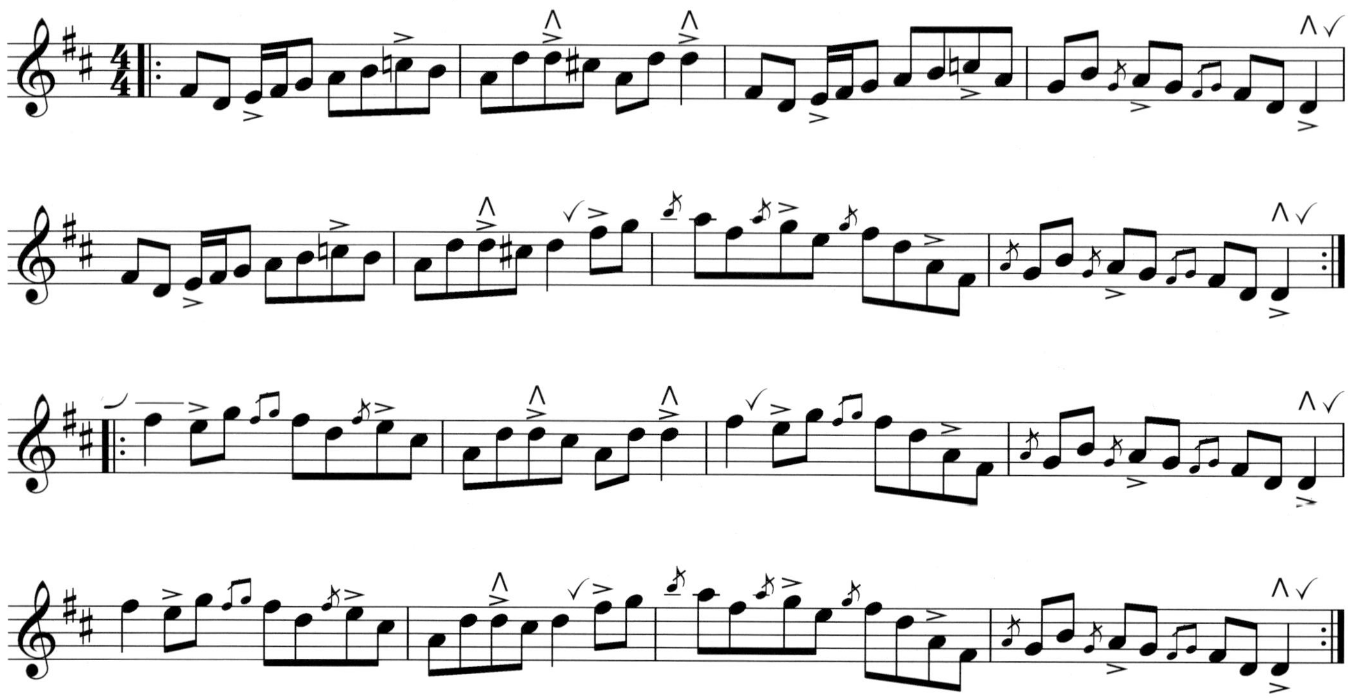

Bounces: The Pretty Blue Seagull

This reel offers several chances to use E to D bounces, particularly since it is not possible to add taps to Ds.

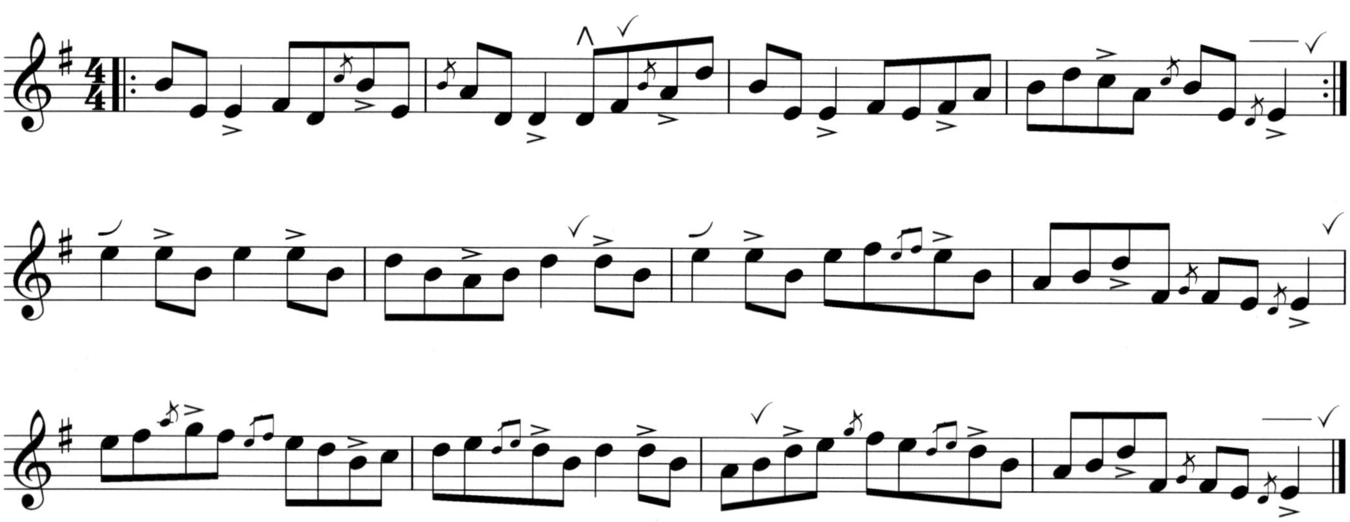

Bounces: The Congress Reel

The Congress Reel has many G to E descending thirds, offering plenty of opportunities for G to E bounces.

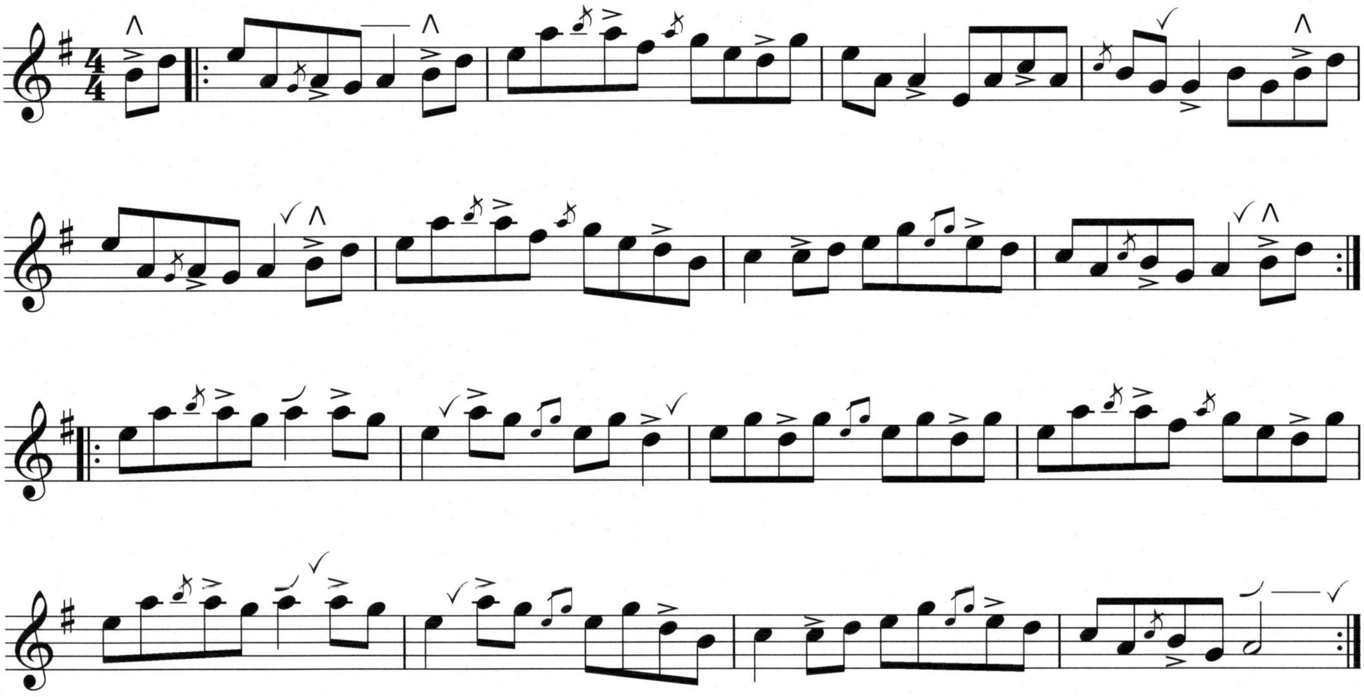

Chapter 7: BCD' Triplet

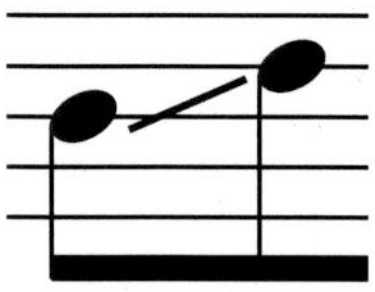

The *BCD' triplet*, also called the *BCD bounce*, links ascending B to D' eighth notes already in the melody by adding a C natural grace note in between them. The BCD' triplet is very different than a melodic link, however, due to the percussive nature of the ornament. The sound is created through strong breath support, as well as through the cross fingering between B and C natural and the effect of the three simultaneously added fingers between C natural and D'. In order to achieve this sound, it is necessary on both the Boehm and simple system flutes to use the C natural in the following fingering chart. It is worth noting that like previous ornaments, the diatonic pitch is less important than the rhythmic effect. If playing in the key of D, for example (which contains a C♯ in the key signature), a flutist may often keep the C natural in the triplet. This is because a BC♯D' triplet may not have the same percussive quality. If a flutist does make the change, it may be in a slower tune when the presence of the C natural would be more noticeable and perhaps unwelcome.

Triplet refers more to the three notes involved rather than the rhythm of the ornament. Unlike other first tier ornaments, which do not occupy rhythmic space, the C natural of the BCD' triplet encroaches slightly on the B already within the tune. The BCD' triplet sounds very much like two sixteenths and an eighth, with the sixteenths occurring on the B and C and the eighth occurring on the D':

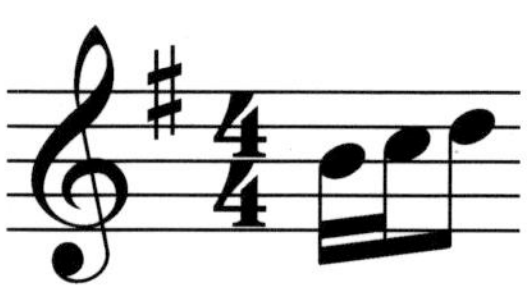

This is true whether in reels or compound meter tunes, although emphasis may shift slightly depending on where the ornament falls in relation to downbeats and backbeats. Some flutists may play a more accelerated version of this, hovering somewhere between sixteenth and thirty-second notes on their Bs and Cs. The key is primarily to keep the ornament snappy and percussive, with quick fingers and strong breath support.

BCD' Triplet Fingering Chart:

This fingering chart walks you through each note of the BCD' triplet. For simple system flutists, there is no change from the standard fingerings of each of these notes. To play the ornament, start on B and play each note in quick succession within a single breath.

	Boehm	Simple System
B	X O O	O O O o o x	X O O	O O O
C natural	O X X	O O O o o x	O X X	O O O
D'	O X X	X X X o o x	O X X	X X X

BCD' Triplet: Preliminary Exercises

These preliminary exercises focus on mastering a fast motion between B, C, and D', as well as placing the ornament in different meters. BCD' triplets will sound slightly different depending on whether they begin on rhythmically strong or weak beats.

Boehm Tip | Spend some time familiarizing yourself with this new C natural fingering:

OXX | OOOo
oX

You will be using this fingering only in BCD' triplets, and your usual C natural fingering for everything else.

Simple System Tip | Simultaneously closing all three fingers of the right hand can be a particular challenge. Keeping these fingers perfectly spaced above the holes will be instrumental in playing this ornament well. If you are unsure that your spacing is correct, play a D, "freeze" your fingers into this correct spacing, and raise them accordingly. This is the spacing you should have when you begin the ornament. If this still feels problematic, revisit *Spacing* in Volume I.

TRACK 60

1. This exercise is intended to help you practice adding a quick C natural grace note between B and D'. The BCD' triplet is denoted by the line linking the B and D'.

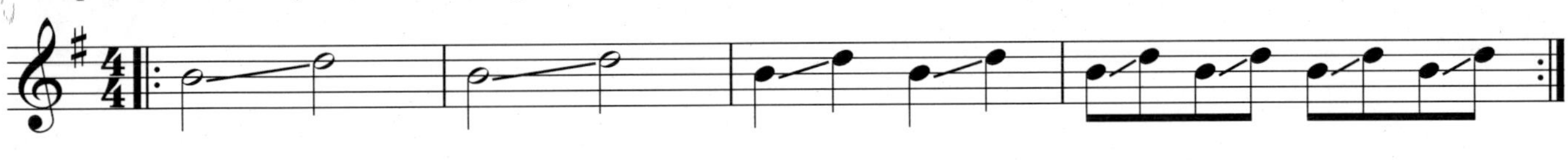

General Tip | Whether a BCD' triplet starts on a strong or weak beat will influence how you move your breath within the ornament. The tendency is to move the breath very strongly, ending emphatically on D'. This works very well if starting on a weak beat, because then the D' ends on a strong beat (either a downbeat or backbeat) with a big breath pulse. If starting on a strong beat, however, this means D' will fall on a weak beat and there is danger of adding too much emphasis to this note. Be careful of this subtle but important distinction as you begin working with the BCD' triplet.

2. In this exercise, the triplet starts on weak beats, the D' falls on backbeats, and you are free to follow your breath all the way through the ornament.

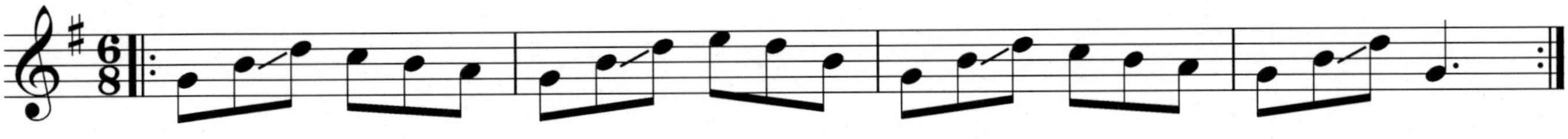

3. As in the previous exercise, feel free to lean on the D's here since they fall on backbeats. Boehm flutists, this is good practice for flipping back and forth between your C natural fingerings.

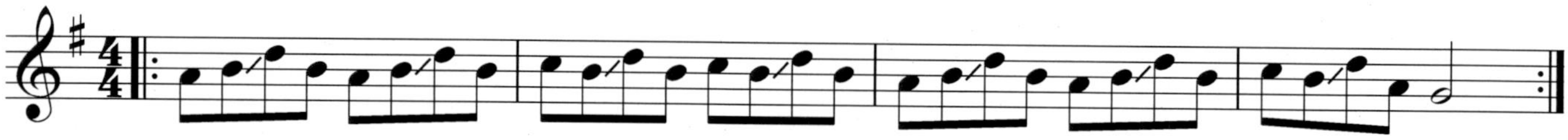

TRACK 61

4. Here the BCD' triplet begins on downbeats and ends on weak beats. Don't lean on the D' too heavily.

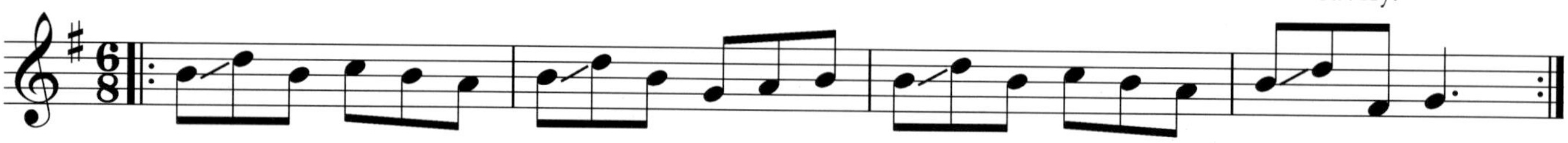

5. A similar concept to exercise four, this reel rhythm also has BCD' triplets ending on weak beats. Don't lean on the D' too heavily.

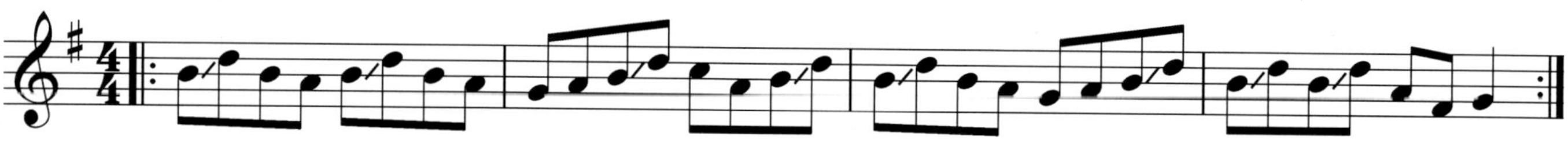

BCD' Triplet: Contextual Exercises

As you move through these exercises, pay particular attention to whether ornaments are ending on rhythmically strong or weak beats and use your breath accordingly.

1. These BCD' triplets start on downbeats and end on weak beats.

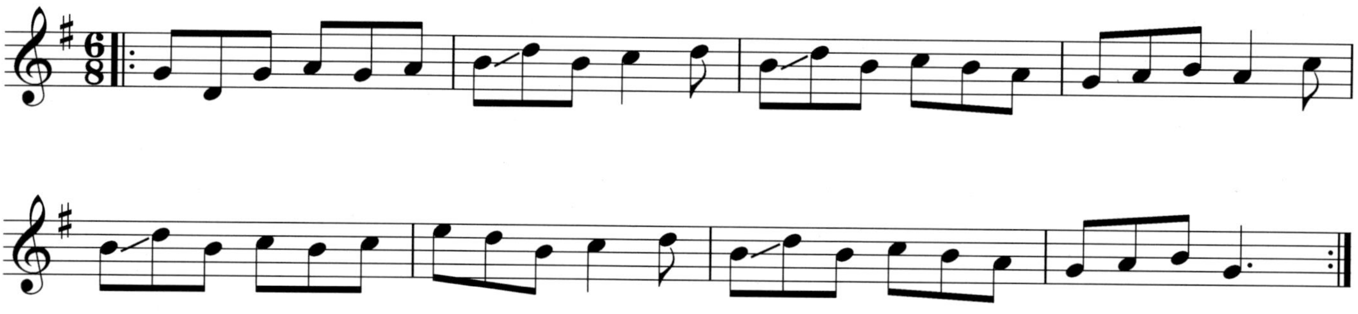

2. This slip jig rhythm contains BCD' triplets which start on weak beats and end on backbeats.

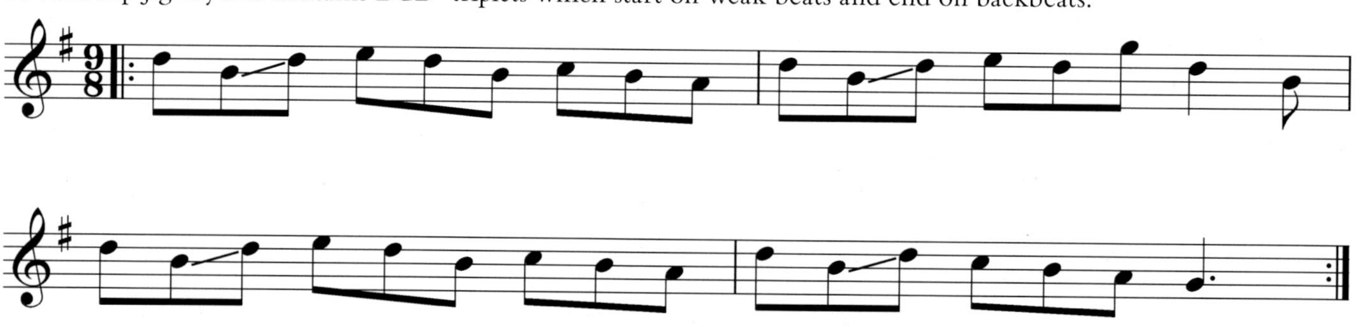

TRACK 62

3. This slide rhythm contains both strong and weak beat BCD' triplets.

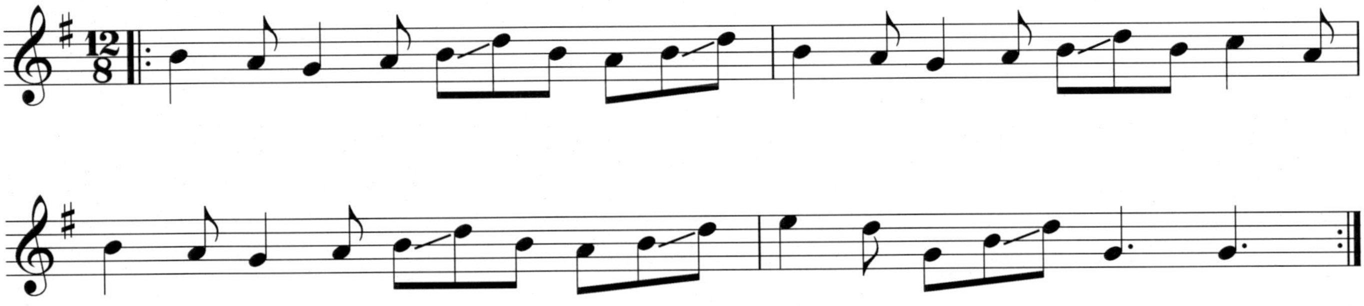

4. In reel rhythm, it is possible to start BCD' triplets on both downbeats and backbeats.

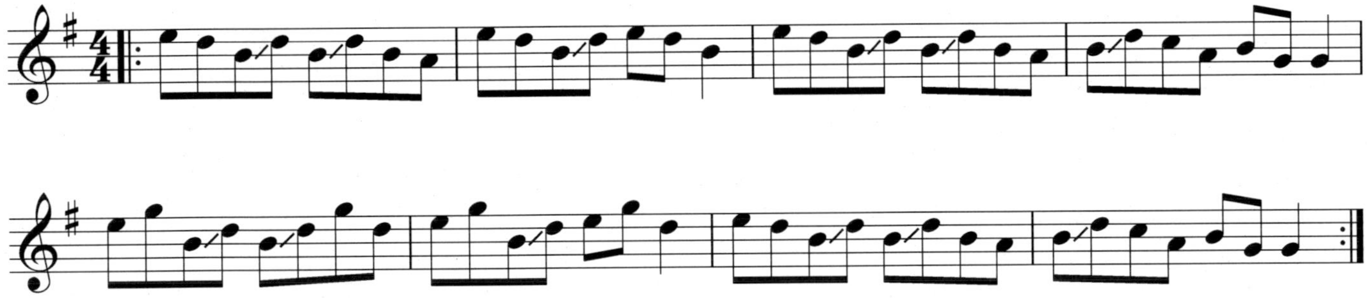

TRACK 63

5. Reel rhythm also offers the possibility of ending on backbeats.

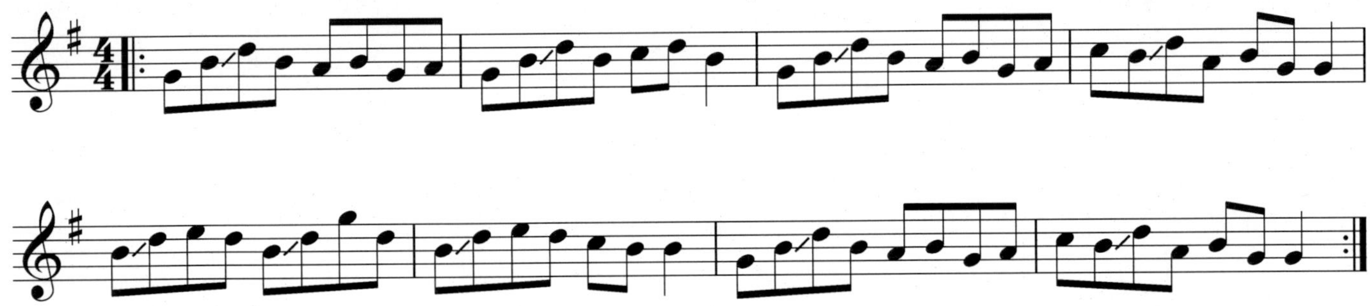

BCD' Triplet: Combined Exercises

You have just learned the last of the single ornaments and now have nine different ways of adding to tunes. As in previous chapters, move through these exercises slowly and add ornaments and techniques gradually. Always remember that if it ever feels like there is too much going on, it is perfectly acceptable to return to just your backbeat in order to regroup.

SYMBOLS KEY:

Volume I: Backbeat and Breathing

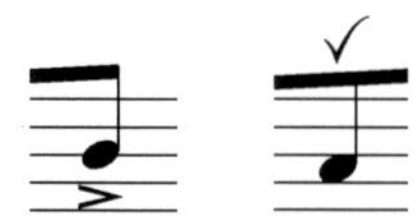

b. beat · breath

Volume II: Single Ornaments

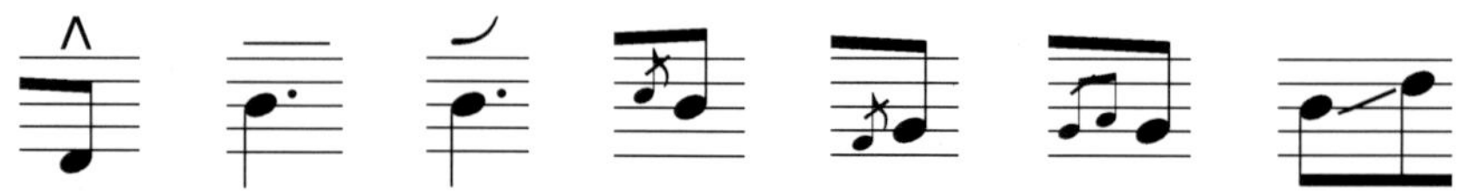

glottal · finger vibrato · slide · cut · tap · bounce · BCD' triplet

1.

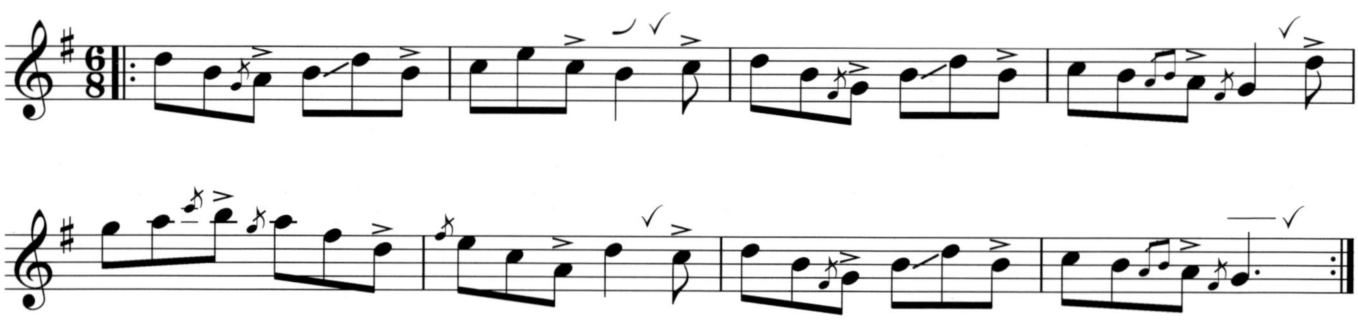

2. Notice the slides on these descending Bs. While it is certainly possible to tap on these notes instead, sliding creates a very different sound.

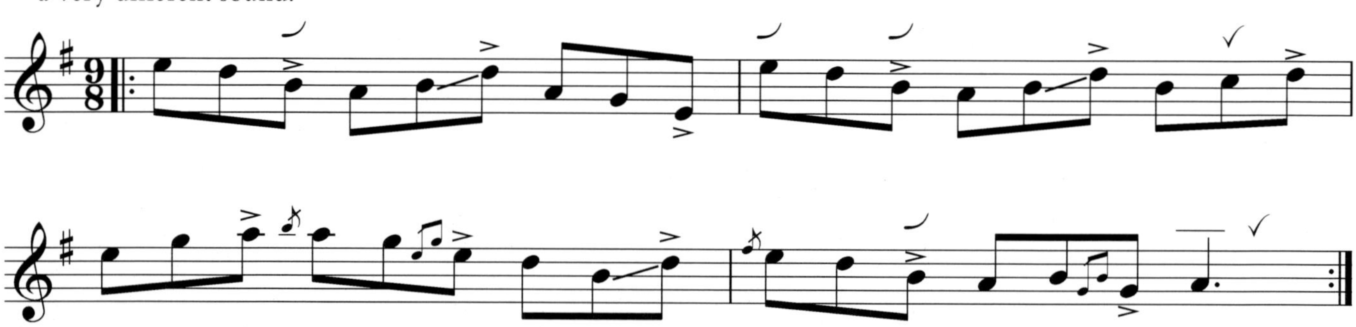

General Tip | You may notice there are no BCD' triplets between Bs and Ds occupying quarter-eighth note rhythms. This is because BCD' triplets work best when placed between two eighth notes.

TRACK 64

3. Using glottals to begin BCD' triplets gives them an additional punch. You may also notice there are B slides and taps back to back in measures one, two, and four. Using a combination of ornaments such as these can provide a more varied sound.

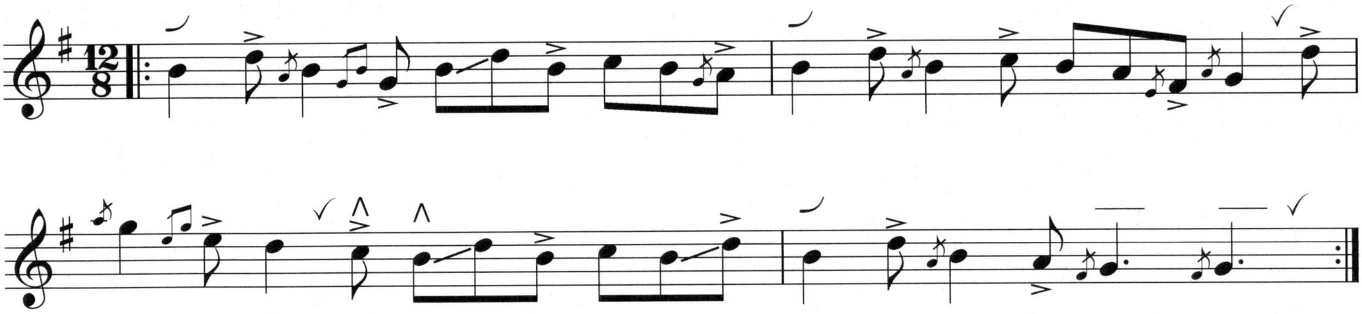

4. Using different ornaments in the high and low registers can create interesting contrast.

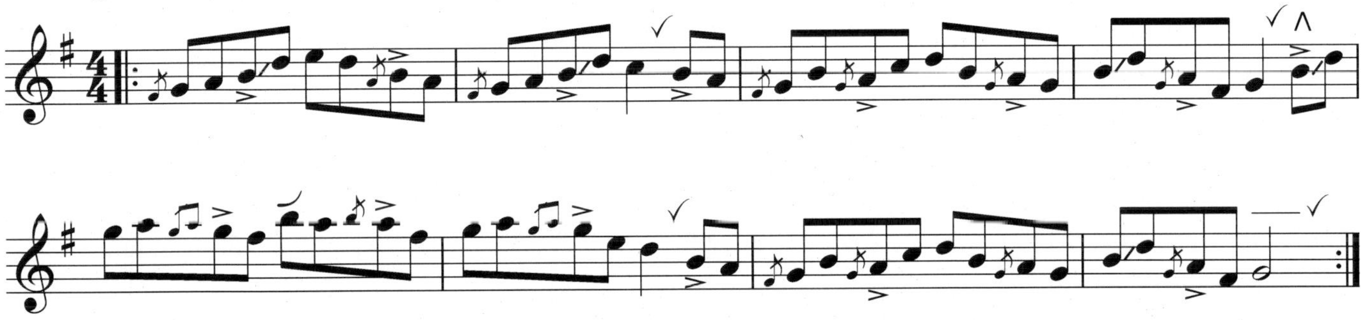

Transition Tip | If you are moving back and forth between Boehm and simple system flutes, you may notice that you are making different choices about which (and how many) ornaments to play on each flute. While all the ornaments are possible on each instrument, you may prefer certain ornaments on one flute but not the other. This is perfectly fine, and you may begin to notice this more often as you learn additional ornamentation.

TRACK 65

5. Although this exercise is in the key of D, with a C♯ in the key signature, the BCD' triplet still works when played fast enough.

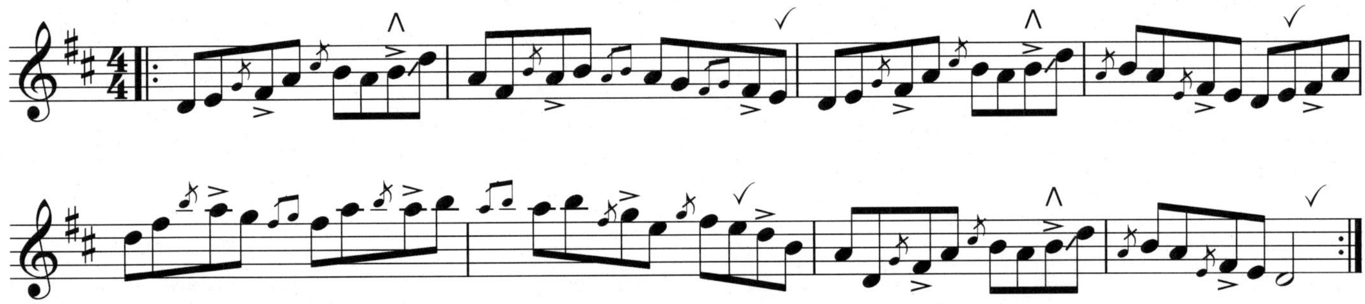

BCD' Triplet: Tunes

You may notice that *Dever the Dancer* and *My Love is in America* are missing from this section. This is due to the fact that these tunes do not have B to D' ascending third eighth notes, and therefore do not use the BCD' triplet. As you progress through the series, you will be learning more advanced ornaments that sometimes have increasingly specific requirements for how and where they are added to tunes. It will therefore happen that not every tune can use every ornament or technique. We will also see this happening occasionally in Volume III.

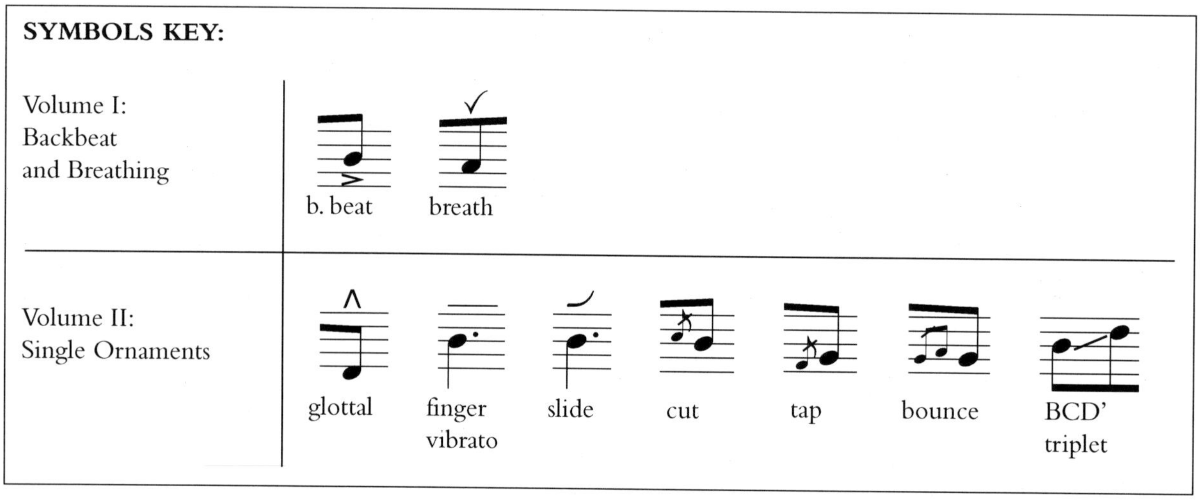

BCD' Triplet: Boiled Goat's Milk

If this looks the same as the last chapter, you're correct. *Boiled Goat's Milk* has its own BCD' triplet option in the body of the tune in measure seven. If you'd like to play this as written, perfectly in time without any extra breath pulse, you certainly can. However, if you'd like to turn it into a BCD' triplet, simply speed up the figure slightly and move your breath faster.

TRACK 66

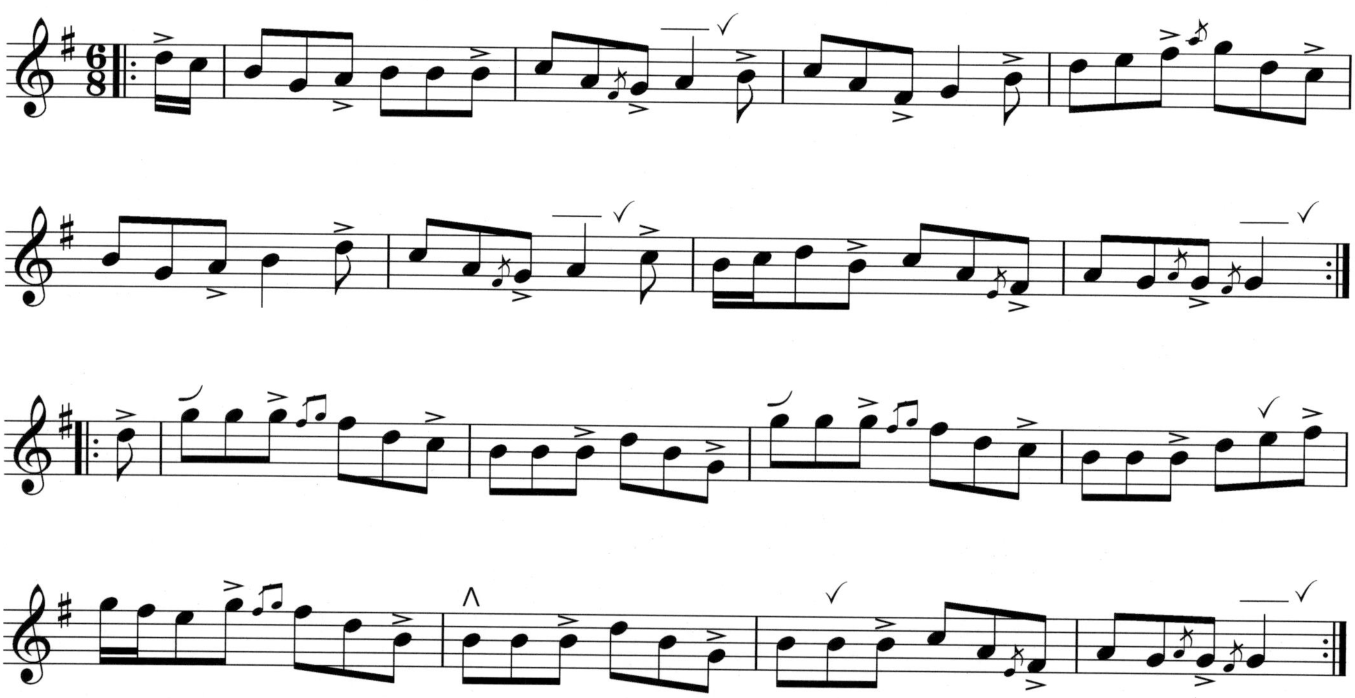

BCD' Triplet: The Dingle Regatta

There are lovely opportunities for BCD' triplets in the C part of *The Dingle Regatta.* This is the first time a recording of this tune appears since the beginning of the book. Compare this version to page 15, track 11 in *Glottals.* This comparison will demonstrate just how colorful a tune becomes once ornamentation is added.

TRACK 67

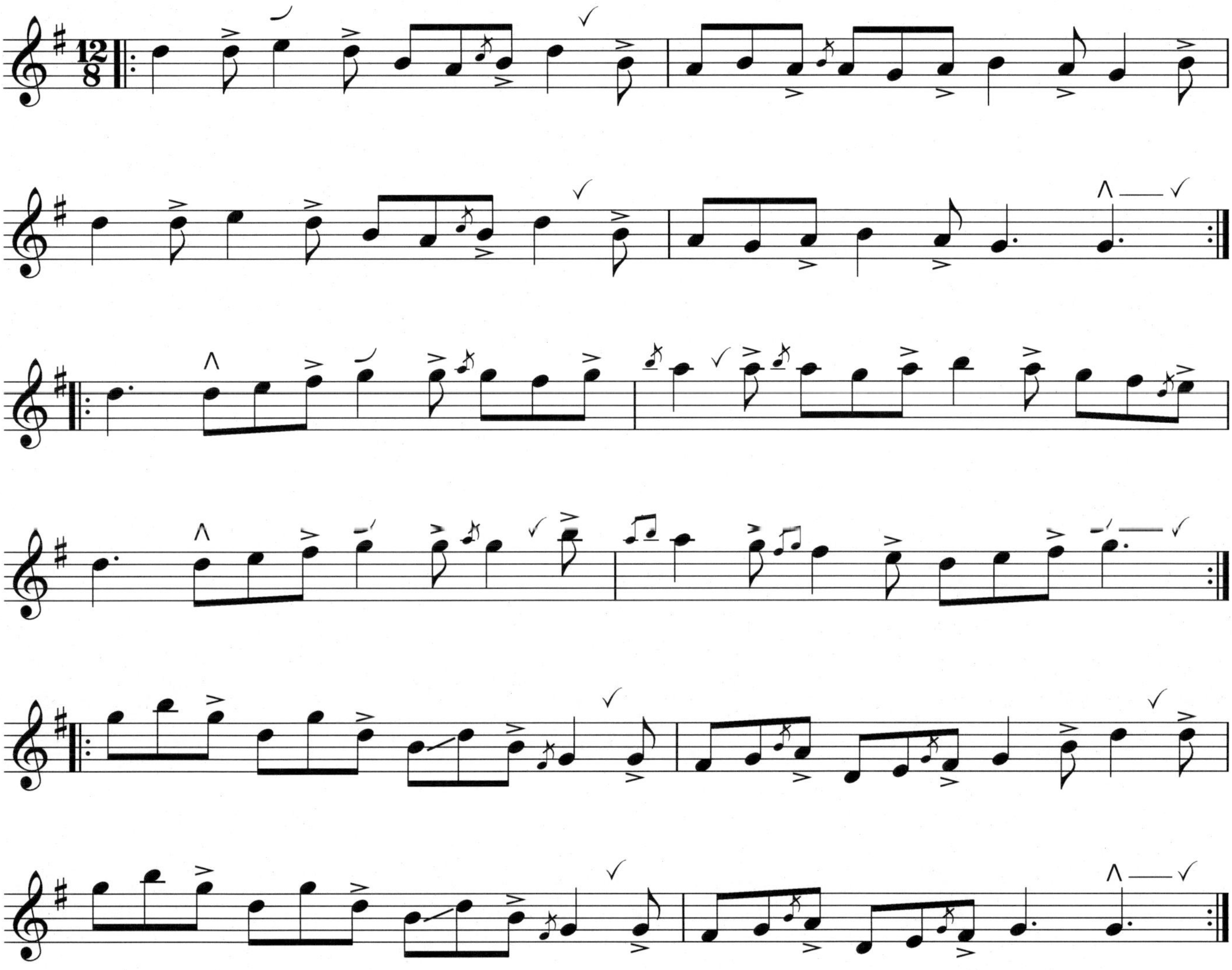

BCD' Triplet: The Pretty Blue Seagull

The Pretty Blue Seagull has BCD' triplets that begin both on strong and weak beats. This is another tune that hasn't been recorded since the first chapter. Compare this version to page 16, track 13 in *Glottals*, and notice all the ornamentation we've added over the course of this book.

TRACK 68

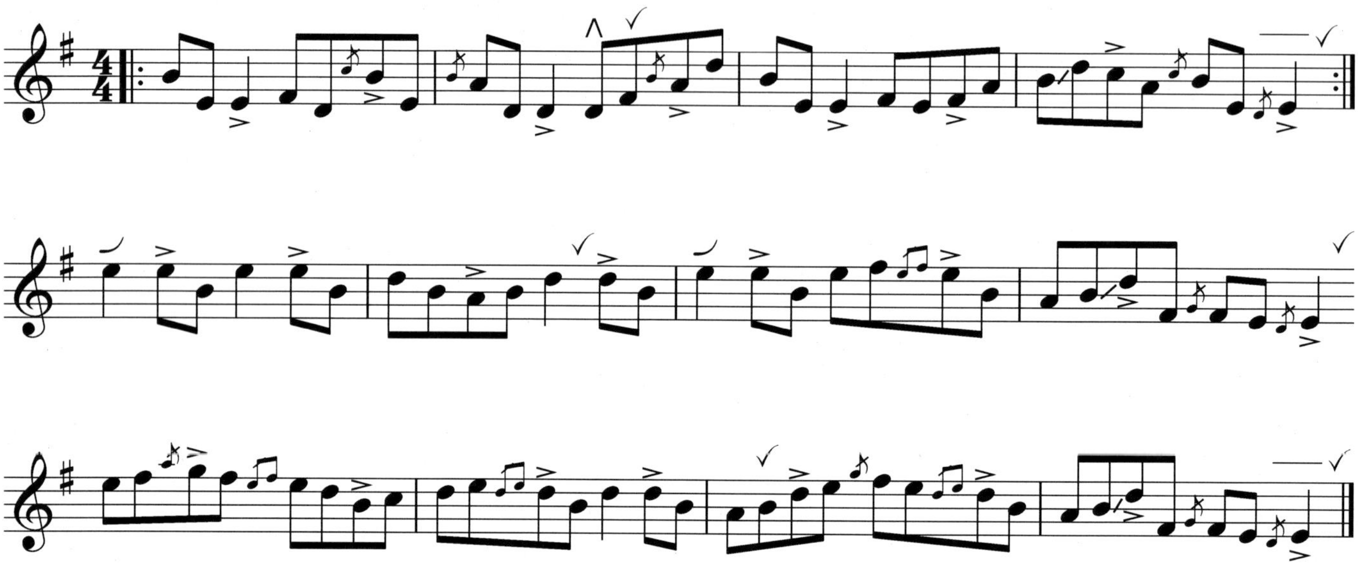

BCD' Triplet: The Congress Reel

The Congress Reel is a wonderful tune for BCD' triplets, particularly when they're combined with glottals. Compare this version to page 17, track 14 in *Glottals*. In contrast to this earlier, simpler version, here the tune bursts to life with colorful ornamentation—and it will become even more vivid once we add *The Advanced Color Palette* in Volume III!

TRACK 69

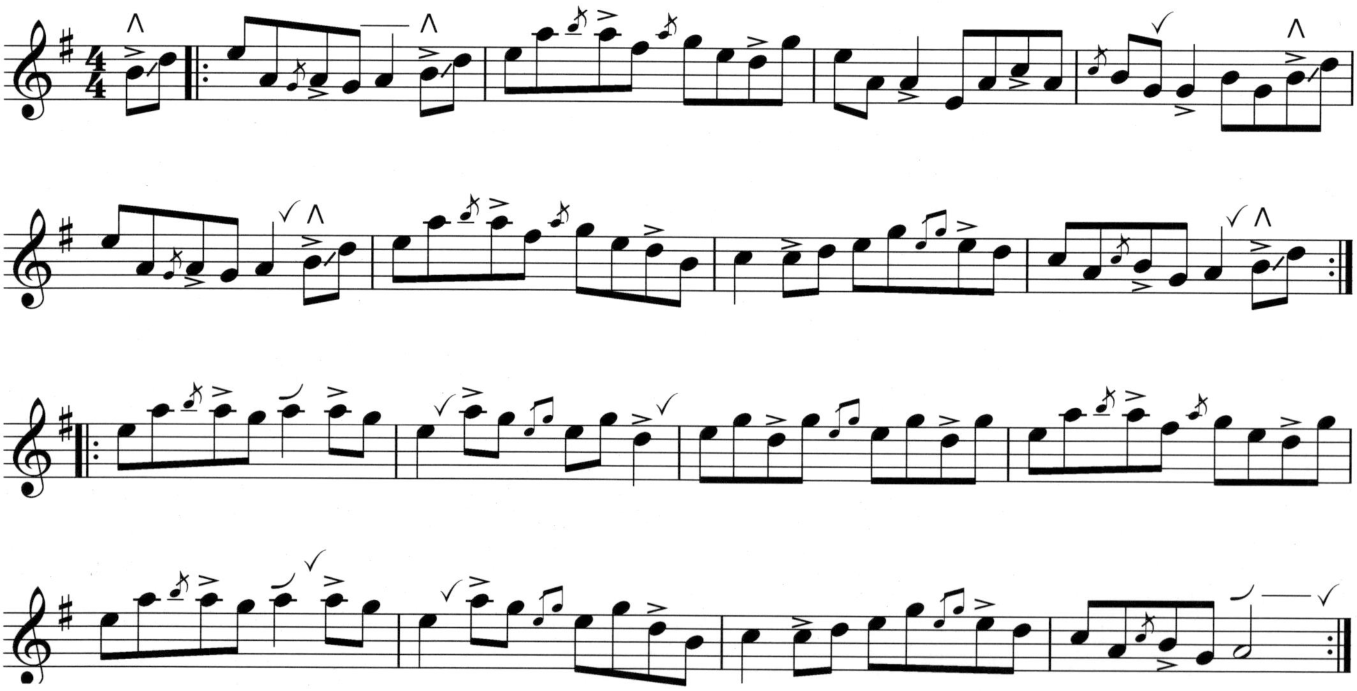

In Closing:
Review and Next Steps

Congratulations on completing Volume II! This book contains a lot of information on single ornaments, many of which can feel challenging to keep straight when you're first starting out. Be sure to review their definitions and uses before moving on, and feel free to refer back to this page whenever you have the need.

Glottal: An effect created in the throat with the glottis, similar to coughing or scoffing.
Finger vibrato: "Fluttering" a finger or fingers against open holes or keys to create a shimmer.
Slide: A scoop or smear up to a primary note from below.
Cut: An upper grace note used to articulate the beginning of a note.
Tap: A lower grace note used to articulate the beginning of a note.
Bounce: Two grace notes played in very quick succession right before the beginning of a note.
BCD' Triplet: A quick effect used to link B to D' ascending motion.

Ornaments that work well on longer notes:
- Finger vibrato
- Slides

Ornaments that work well when ascending:
- Slides
- Cuts
- BCD' triplet *(between B and D' only)*

Ornaments that work well when descending:
- Slides
- Cuts
- Taps
- Bounces

Ornaments for separating notes of the same pitch:
- Glottals
- Cuts
- Taps

Ornaments exclusive to certain pitches:
- Finger vibrato *(all notes except D)*
- Slides *(all notes except D)*
- Cuts *(all notes except C♯, although Boehm flutists can use trill keys)*
- Taps *(all notes except D)*
- Bounces *(all notes except D-C♯, although Boehm flutists can use trill keys)*
- BCD' triplet *(between B and D' only)*

Once you feel comfortable with the material covered in *The Primary Color Palette: Single Ornaments for Irish Flute*, you are ready to continue working through the rest of the Playing Outside the Lines series. The books are sequential and built on information from previous volumes, so it is recommended that you progress through the series in order:

Volume III
The Advanced Color Palette: Combined Ornaments for Irish Flute
Exercises and thorough discussion of rolls, short rolls, advanced rolls, crans, advanced crans, and breathing in on- and offbeat rolls and crans.

Volume IV
Painting Works of Art: Personal Expression within the Irish Flute Tradition
Exercises for melodic modification, discussion of pathways for producing unique versions and variations, and suggestions for tunes moving forward.

As you're working through this series, remember to listen a lot and see if you can begin playing with other musicians. You can also visit www.LeslieAnneHarrison.com for additional resources and lesson information.

Happy fluting!

Acknowledgements

What would we write without the people who have shaped, educated, and guided us? I certainly wouldn't have written this series, that's for sure. Thank you to Dale Harrison, for showing me that the pursuit of knowledge is a lifelong journey, for offering guidance when I was a very young writer, and for continuing to provide support even today with a sharp-eyed, eleventh-hour read through. Thank you to Bob Harrison, for teaching me the importance of critical thought and methodical problem solving in any field of inquiry. To both Bob and Dale, thank you for always believing that music and creative projects are important endeavors. To Kevin Harrison, thank you for demonstrating an enthusiasm for exploration, a great sense of humor, and an unwavering commitment to excellence. To my extended family, thank you for showing me that *smart*, *creative*, and *kind* are admirable and important qualities. Je voudrais aussi dire merci à ma famille française—grosses bises à toutes et à tous!

I've been very lucky to study with many unique and talented musicians. Thank you to Claudia Anderson, Nina Barwell, Robert Dick, Carl Dimow, Rebecca Gilbert, Wendy Herbener Mehne, Susan Milan, and Nicole Rabata for helping me learn and explore the possibilities of the Boehm flute. Thanks especially to Dr. Mehne, who encouraged me to play the Irish flute in the middle of a classical music degree program, and to Carl Dimow, who seemed to always understand what I needed even when I didn't. Thank you to Tony Boffa, Tom Lizotte, and Terry White for their encouragement and enthusiasm for music education, and to Norm Richardson, for making me determined to cross the bridge. Gratitude must also be extended to Allison Allen and Suzanne Van Wye, who showed me that art in any form is a powerful means of expression and a valuable lens through which to see the world, and to Margaret Welch, who first showed me the power and beauty of truly great writing. Thank you to Nicole Rabata and Christopher Layer, for helping me take my first steps into the world of Irish traditional flute playing, and to Jane and Tyler, who brought me to my first sessions in New York City. And to the sessions around the world that have offered me a seat, thank you!

A huge amount of gratitude to everyone at the University of Limerick. Thank you to Sandra Joyce, Niall Keegan, Majella Bartley, Harry Bradley, Kevin Crawford, Tom Doorley, Brian Finnegan, John Kelly, Catherine McEvoy, Kieran Munnelly, Muireann Nic Amhlaoibh, Conal Ó Gráda, and Jean-Michel Veillon for their instruction and guidance. Thank you to my UL classmates, particularly to Leah Bernini Cronin, Liz Davis Maxfield, Frédéric Pouille, and Kay Vickers for their friendship and collaboration.

I feel very lucky to have received encouragement from Carl, Cory, Danny, Fred, Janelle, John, Katie, Maddox, Mary, Michael, Leah, Liz, and Tiana. To Robert Dick, Richard Gee, and Grey Larsen, thank you for providing invaluable advice when I first started thinking about publishing. Thank you to the members of the Kindred Spirits Food and Book Club as well, for their friendship and support. To Carl, Cory, Dale, Leah, Liz, Maddox, and Michael, who braved their way through various chapters and versions of the manuscript, I can't tell you how much I appreciate your time and input. Thank you to Molly Johanson for design, layout, and typesetting; Maddox Pennington for proofreading; Bradford Krieger at Big Nice Studio for recording and mastering; Frédéric Pouille for photography. To Mr. Bay, Joanne, Julie, Sharon, and the entire team at Mel Bay Publications, thank you for turning this book into a reality.

This book would have been impossible without the grace, vision, constructive criticism, and creative spirit of the indefatigable Carl Dimow, teacher, mentor, and friend, who agreed to come on board as my editor for this project. Thank you for the vast amount of time and energy you put into editing this book and thank you for always telling me what you thought. Your feedback was indispensable. Gratitude as well to Grey Larsen, for providing a thorough read through and many helpful references and suggestions. I'm very thankful for your insight.

Most of all, I would like to express thanks to my husband, Fred, who has listened to me talk about all things flute perhaps far too much, but who has contributed to the conversation with creativity, enthusiasm, and interest. Without your kindness, generosity, intellect, sense of humor, and level head under pressure (as well as your photography skills), this book would have been a difficult undertaking indeed. You are an inspiration in all that you do, and I am very lucky to have met you and privileged to know you still. Merci beaucoup pour tout, et je te souhaite bonne chance dans tous tes projets musicaux!

Complete Symbols Key

SYMBOLS KEY:

Volume I: Backbeat and Breathing	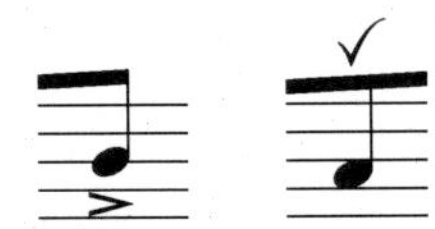 b. beat · breath
Volume II: Single Ornaments	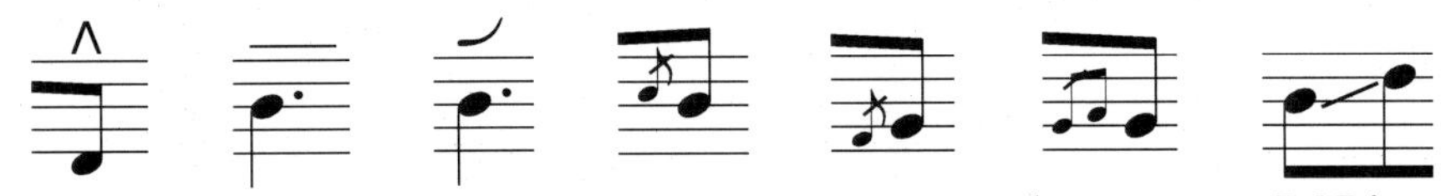 glottal · finger vibrato · slide · cut · tap · bounce · BCD' triplet

Most tune collections and transcriptions have little to no notation to assist in the interpretation of a tune, while Irish traditional method books may use a variety of symbols (see Grey Larsen's *Essential Guide to Irish Flute and Tin* Whistle, Conal Ó Gráda's *An Fheadóg Mhór,* and June McCormack's *Fliúit* and *Fliúit 2.* For our purposes, we will use the above Symbols Key. Many of the ornaments may look familiar to classical players and may have very similar interpretations. This is why these symbols were chosen: they are intended to build upon the knowledge and muscle memory that many players may already have, particularly since this book is intended for Boehm flutists as well as simple system flutists.

It is very important to understand that their execution will sound different than the equivalent classical technique. To this end, be sure to read each chapter carefully, and listen to the accompanying recordings. Also remember that these symbols are simply intended to aid your progress; your goal should be to one day not need them at all.

Fingering Chart

ABC notation uses apostrophes (or sometimes lowercase) to denote the higher octave. This fingering chart therefore starts on low D and moves upwards, with apostrophes marking the change in octave.

Fingering Chart:

	Boehm	Simple System
D	X X X | X X X o o x	X X X | X X X
E	X X X | X X O o o x	X X X | X X O
F♯	X X X | O X O o o x *or* X X X | O O X x o x	X X X | X O O
G	X X X | O O O o o x	X X X | O O O
A	X X O | O O O o o x	X X O | O O O
B	X O O | O O O o o x	X O O | O O O
C	X O O | O O O o o o	O X X | O O O
C♯	O O O | O O O o o o	O O O | O O O
D'	O X X | X X X o o x	O X X | X X X *or* X X X | X X X

E'	X X X | X X O o o x	X X X | X X O
F♯'	X X X | O X O o o x *or* X X X | O O X x o x	X X X | X O O
G'	X X X | O O O o o x	X X X | O O O
A'	X X O | O O O o o x	X X O | O O O
B'	X O O | O O O o o x	X O O | O O O
C'*	X O O | O O O o o o	x O O | O O O
C♯'**	O O O | O O O o o o	O O O | O O O
D''**	O X X | O O O o o x	O X X | O O O

**Note small x for simple system: this means a finger is only half on the hole.*
***Not commonly used, but just in case!*

Accompanying Recordings

1. Glottals: Preliminary Exercise 1 *(Simple System)*
2. Glottals: Preliminary Exercise 4 *(Boehm)*
3. Glottals: Preliminary Exercise 10 *(Simple System)*
4. Glottals: Contextual Exercise 1 *(Simple System)*
5. Glottals: Contextual Exercise 7 *(Boehm)*
6. Glottals: Contextual Exercise 10 *(Simple System)*
7. Glottals: Combined Exercise 1 *(Boehm)*
8. Glottals: Combined Exercise 8 *(Simple System)*
9. Glottals: *Boiled Goat's Milk (Simple System)*
10. Glottals: *Dever the Dancer (Simple System)*
11. Glottals: *The Dingle Regatta (Boehm)*
12. Glottals: *My Love is in America (Simple System)*
13. Glottals: *The Pretty Blue Seagull (Boehm)*
14. Glottals: *The Congress Reel (Simple System)*
15. Finger Vibrato: Preliminary Exercise 1 *(Simple System)*
16. Finger Vibrato: Preliminary Exercise 10 *(Simple System)*
17. Finger Vibrato: Contextual Exercise 1 *(Boehm)*
18. Finger Vibrato: Contextual Exercise 4 *(Simple System)*
19. Finger Vibrato: Combined Exercise 1 *(Boehm)*
20. Finger Vibrato: Combined Exercise 9 *(Simple System)*
21. Finger Vibrato: *Boiled Goat's Milk (Simple System)*
22. Finger Vibrato: *My Love is in America (Simple System)*
23. Slides: Preliminary Exercise 1 *(Simple System)*
24. Slides: Preliminary Exercise 9 *(Simple System)*
25. Slides: Preliminary Exercise 10 *(Simple System)*
26. Slides: Preliminary Exercise 11 *(Simple System)*
27. Slides: Contextual Exercise 8 *(Simple System)*
28. Slides: Contextual Exercise 9 *(Boehm)*
29. Slides: Combined Exercise 2 *(Simple System)*
30. Slides: Combined Exercise 8 *(Boehm)*
31. Slides: *Boiled Goat's Milk (Simple System)*
32. Slides: *My Love is in America (Simple System)*
33. Cuts: Preliminary Exercise 1 *(Simple System)*
34. Cuts: Preliminary Exercise 10 *(Boehm)*
35. Cuts: Contextual Exercise 1 *(Simple System)*
36. Cuts: Contextual Exercise 5 *(Boehm)*
37. Cuts: Combined Exercise 2 *(Simple System)*
38. Cuts: Combined Exercise 5 *(Boehm)*
39. Cuts: *Boiled Goat's Milk (Simple System)*
40. Cuts: *My Love is in America (Simple System)*
41. Taps: Preliminary Exercise 1 *(Simple System)*
42. Taps: Preliminary Exercise 10 *(Boehm)*
43. Taps: Contextual Exercise 1 *(Boehm)*
44. Taps: Contextual Exercise 5 *(Simple System)*
45. Taps: Combined Exercise 8 *(Simple System)*
46. Taps: Combined Exercise 9 *(Boehm)*

47. Taps: Combined Exercise 10 *(Boehm)*
48. Taps: *Boiled Goat's Milk (Simple System)*
49. Taps: *My Love is in America (Simple System)*
50. Bounces: Preliminary Exercise 1 *(Simple System)*
51. Bounces: Preliminary Exercise 8 *(Boehm)*
52. Bounces: Contextual Exercise 7 *(Simple System)*
53. Bounces: Contextual Exercise 10 *(Boehm)*
54. Bounces: Combined Exercise 4 *(Simple System)*
55. Bounces: Combined Exercise 9 *(Simple System)*
56. Bounces: Combined Exercise 10 *(Boehm)*
57. Bounces: *Boiled Goat's Milk (Simple System)*
58. Bounces: *Dever the Dancer (Simple System)*
59. Bounces: *My Love is in America (Simple System)*
60. BCD' Triplet: Preliminary Exercise 1 *(Simple System)*
61. BCD' Triplet: Preliminary Exercise 4 *(Boehm)*
62. BCD' Triplet: Contextual Exercise 3 *(Boehm)*
63. BCD' Triplet: Contextual Exercise 5 *(Simple System)*
64. BCD' Triplet: Combined Exercise 3 *(Boehm)*
65. BCD' Triplet: Combined Exercise 5 *(Simple System)*
66. BCD' Triplet: *Boiled Goat's Milk (Simple System)*
67. BCD' Triplet: *The Dingle Regatta (Boehm)*
68. BCD' Triplet: *The Pretty Blue Seagull (Boehm)*
69. BCD' Triplet: *The Congress Reel (Simple System)*

Suggested Listening

Hopefully you've been enjoying the suggested listening in Volume I. You may recall that most of those suggestions were solo flute, or at least "flute-centric." Listening to solo Irish flute is a great way to familiarize yourself with the style of the instrument. Now I suggest turning your ears towards slightly larger groups. The majority of Volume II's suggested listening are duo recordings, with two instrumentalists playing the melody in unison. This allows you to keep paying attention to the style of the flute while also getting a sense of how other instruments meld with and influence Irish traditional flute playing.

Many of these recordings are flute and fiddle, which is a common and beloved combination in Irish traditional music. There are also some that include button accordion, concertina, or pipes. There have been a number of wonderful albums released in just the last few years, as well as recent releases of older remastered or reissued recordings. Where possible, consider buying recordings directly from the artists themselves. Other resources for finding and buying albums are Custy's Traditional Music Shop, Claddagh Records, or Bandcamp.

Carty, Paddy and Conor Tully. *Traditional Music of Ireland*, 1989, remastered 2009.
Clifford, Billy and Gerry Harrington. *Now She's Purring*, 2018.
Clifford, Billy and Julia Clifford. *Ceol as Sliabh Luachra*, 1982.
Crawford, Kevin and Cillian Vallely. *On Common Ground*, 2009.
Crotty, P.J., Carol Cullinan and James Cullinan. *Happy to Meet*, 2002.
Fitzharris, Tommy and Dónal McCague. *The Bank of Turf*, 2018.
Horan, Peter and Gerry Harrington. *Fortune Favours the Merry*, 2005.
Kelly, Liam and Philip Duffy. *Sets in Stone*, 2015.
Kennedy, Frankie and Mairéad Ní Mhaonaigh. *Ceol Aduaidh*, 1983, remastered 2009.
Kerr, Barry and Laura Kerr. *Castor Bay*, 2018.
Maloney, P.J. and Seán Ryan. *Traditional Music of Ireland, Volume I*, 1959, remastered 2018.
McEvoy, Catherine, Caoimhín Ó Raghallaigh and Mícheál Ó Raghallaigh. *Comb Your Hair and Curl It*, 2010.
McGoldrick, Mike and Dezi Donnelly. *Dog in the Fog*, 2018.
Molloy, Matt and John Carty. *Pathway to the Well*, 2007.
Moloney, Patsy and John Regan. *Over the Bog Road*, 2014.
Moloney, Sean and Kevin Moloney. *Bridging the Gap*, 1997.
Ní Choisdealbha, Neansaí and Tommy Mellett. *An Tower*, 2018.
O'Connor, Francis and Áine O'Connor. *They Didn't Come Home Until Morning*, 2020.
Ó Fearghail, Caoimhín and Paddy Tutty. *Flute & Fiddle*, 2018.
O'Loughlin, Peadar and Maeve Donnelly. *The Thing Itself*, 2004.
O'Riordan, Eamonn and Tony O'Connell. *Rooska Hill*, 2015.
Quigney, Anthony and Aidan McMahon. *A Clare Conscience*, 2002.
Wynne, John and John McEvoy. *Pride of the West*, 2008.

This list is just a starting point; enjoy exploring as many recordings as you can find. Remember that archives are also valuable listening resources, so be sure to check out the Comhaltas Archive and the Irish Traditional Music Archive, both of which are accessible online. These are great places to listen to recordings by musicians who may never have released commercial albums.

Additional Resources

In addition to the works cited in the bibliography, this is a brief list of resources that I've found to be helpful when searching for information, music, flutes, and more. If you are interested in further education and you don't have a teacher, I also teach flute lessons in person or online. Lesson information is available on my website: www.leslieanneharrison.com.

Advocacy

FairPlé
An organization dedicated to achieving gender balance in Irish traditional music, as well as equal opportunity and representation for everyone

Archives and Collections

Comhaltas Traditional Music Archive
A resource for recordings, documents, and photos collected by Comhaltas Ceoltóirí Éireann

Irish Traditional Music Archive
An archive including a digital library with audio, video, books, photos, and manuscripts

The Séamus Connolly Collection of Irish Music
Presented by Boston College, a free digital collection of music collected by fiddler Séamus Connolly

Education

University of Limerick
Offering courses and degrees in the study of Irish traditional music and more

Flutes

The Irish Flute Store
An online store featuring used and new flutes from different makers

Martin Doyle Flutes
Flute Information Section offers FAQs, fingering charts, and information on wood types, care and maintenance, and African Blackwood conservation

Patrick Olwell Flutes
Also features a blog with great information on Irish flutes, including bore size and care and upkeep.

Solen Lesouef Flutes
Offering keyed and keyless flute in several types of wood

Online Communities and Indices

TheSession.org
"A community website dedicated to Irish traditional music"

IrishTune.info
Irish Traditional Music Tune Index: Alan Ng's Tunography

Bibliography

Much of this book is informed by the author's personal studies, as well as her performance and teaching experience. Additional sources include:

Breathnach, Breandán. *Ceol Rince na hÉireann, I.* Dublin, Iona, 1963.

Bunting, Edward. *The Ancient Music of Ireland.* Waltons, 1969. (Edition of three publications from 1796, 1809, and 1840.)

Cohen, Sheryl. *Bel Canto Flute: The Rampal School.* Winzer, 2003.

Comhaltas Traditional Music Archive. Comhaltas Ceoltóirí Éireann, 2000, archive.comhaltas.ie.

Doyle, Martin. *Martin Doyle Flutes.* www.martindoyleflute.com.

Hamilton, S.C. *The Irish Flute Players Handbook*, Coolea, Breac, 1990.

Horne, Jackie C. "Six Decades of Picture Book Illustration: The Art of Barbara Cooney." *Children's Literature in Education*, vol. 32, no. 2, 2001, pp. 91-108.

ITMA. Irish Traditional Music Archive, www.itma.ie.

Larsen, Grey. *The Essential Guide to Irish Flute and Tin Whistle.* Mel Bay, 2003.

McCormack, June. *Fliúit.* June McCormack, 2006.

---. *Fliúit 2.* June McCormack, 2009.

Ng, Alan. *Irishtune.info: Irish Traditional Music Tune Index.* www.irishtune.info.

Ó Gráda, Conal. *An Fheadóg Mhór: Irish Traditional Flute Technique.* Daorla, 2011.

O'Neill, Francis. *The Dance Music of Ireland.* 1907. Dublin, Waltons, 2011.

---. *Music of Ireland.* Edited by Miles Krassen, Oak, 1976.

---. *O'Neill's Music of Ireland.* 1903. Rockchapel, 1979.

Petrie, George. The Petrie Collection of the Ancient Music of Ireland. Edited by David Cooper, Cork University, 2002.

Toff, Nancy. *The Development of the Modern Flute.* 1979. University of Illinois, 1986.

Vallely, Fintan. *The Companion to Irish Traditional Music.* Cork, Cork University, 1999.

---. *The Companion to Irish Traditional Music.* 2nd Edition, Cork, Cork University, 2011.

---. *Timber: The Flute Tutor.* Miltown Malby, Long Note, 1986.

Wye, Trevor. *Practice Book for the Flute: Book 1 Tone.* 1980. London, Novello, 2003.

Index

A

A part, 15
ABC notation, 110
abdomen, **2-3**, 9
accompanying recordings, vii, **112-113**
An Fheadóg Mhór, **2**, 109
articulation, **vii**, 2
    ha, 3
ascending ornaments, 107
    BCD' triplet, 98
    cuts, 49
    slides, 33

B

B part, 15
backbeat, **v**, vii, 2, 3, 9-11, 56-57, 62-65, 76, 88, 98-101
BCD bounce, *see* BCD' triplet
BCD' triplet, 98
    combined exercises, 102
    contextual exercises, 100
    fingering chart, 98
    preliminary exercises, 99
    tunes, 104
Boehm flute, vi
Boehm tip, vi
Boiled Goat's Milk, vii
    BCD' triplet, 104
    bounces, 93
    cuts, 62
    finger vibrato, 28
    glottals, 13
    slides, 44
    taps, 78
bounces, 83
    combined exercises, 89
    contextual exercises, 86
    descending third bounces, **83**, 85
    preliminary exercises, 83
    ring finger bounces, 86, 88
    stepwise bounces, 83
    tunes, 93
breathing, **v**, vii, 10

C

C part, 15
closing, 107
color palette, **v-vi**, 1
combined exercises, vi
    BCD' triplet, 102
    bounces, 89
    cuts, 58
    finger vibrato, 25
    glottals, 9
    slides, 40
    taps, 74
Congress Reel, The, vii
    BCD' triplet, 106
    bounces, 97
    cuts, 66
    finger vibrato, 32
    glottals, 17
    slides, 48
    taps, 82
contextual exercises, vi
    BCD' triplet, 100
    bounces, 86
    cuts, 55
    finger vibrato, 22
    glottals, 6
    slides, 37
    taps, 71
Crawford, Kevin, 2
cuts, 49
    ascending cuts, **49**, 54, 56, 57, 64
    C natural cuts, **51**, 54, 56, 57
    combined exercises, 58
    contextual exercises, 55
    fingering chart, 49-52
    narrow cuts, 49-51
    preliminary exercises, 52
    separating cuts, **49**, 55, 57
    tunes, 62
    wide cuts, 49-52

D

descending ornaments, 107
    bounces, 83
    slides, 33
    taps, 67
Dever the Dancer, vii
    bounces, 94
    cuts, 63

finger vibrato, 29
glottals, 14
slides, 45
taps, 79
diaphragm, *see* abdomen
Dingle Regatta, The, vii
BCD' triplet, 105
bounces, 95
cuts, 64
finger vibrato, 30
glottals, 15
slides, 46
taps, 80
downbeat, 7, 9, 35, 52-53, 62-65, 83, 88, **98-101**

F

F sharp, 101-111
with middle finger, 8-9
with ring finger, 27
finger vibrato, 18
combined exercises, 25
contextual exercises, 22
fingering chart, 18-19
preliminary exercises, 20
tunes, 28
fingering chart, 110-111
BCD' triplet, 98
cuts, 49-52
finger vibrato, 18-19
slides, 34
taps, 67-68
flattement, *see finger vibrato*

G

general tip, vi
glissando, **33**, 36
glottal stop, *see* glottals
glottals, 2
combined exercises, 9
contextual exercises, 6
preliminary exercises, 3
tunes, 13

H

ha attack, 3
half-hole, **19**, 21, 23, 31
hard D, 6
harmonics, 2
hyperextension, 52

I

Irish flute, *see* simple system flute

J

jig, 13

L

left hand, vi
lower grace note, 67
lower neighbor notes, **33**, 37-38, 45

M

My Love is in America, vii
bounces, 96
cuts, 65
finger vibrato, 31
glottals, 16
slides, 47
taps, 81

O

Ó Gráda, Conal, 2
ornaments, v-vi, vii, **1**
BCD' triplet, 98
bounces, 83
cuts, 49
finger vibrato, 18
glottals, 2
slides, 33
taps, 67
overtones, 6-7

P

pats, *see* taps
playing outside the lines, v-vi
pull slides, 33
push slides, 33
preparing the canvas, v
primary color palette, v-vi, **1**
primary note, **33**, 54, 83
preliminary exercises, vi
BCD' triplet, 99
bounces, 83
cuts, 52
finger vibrato, 20
glottals, 3
slides, 35
taps, 68
Pretty Blue Seagull, The, vii
BCD' triplet, 106
bounces, 96

cuts, 65
finger vibrato, 31
glottals, 16
slides, 47
taps, 81

R

reel, 16-17
review, v, **107**
right hand, vi, **20-21**, 33, 71, 83-85, 99
ring finger, **8**, 23, 27, 35, 53, 85-86, 88

S

scoop, 33
separating ornaments, 76, **107**
session, v, vi
simple system flute, vi
simple system tip, vi
single ornaments, 1
sketching the shape, v
slide (tune type), **15**, 46
slides (ornament), 33
combined exercises, 40
contextual exercises, 37
preliminary exercises, 35
pull slides, 33
push slides, 33
tunes, 44
slip jig, 14
slurs, **vii**, 5
strikes, *see* taps
suggested listening, 114
syllables, **2-4**, 9
symbols key, 109
sympathetic motion, 67

T

taps, 67
combined exercises, 74
contextual exercises, 71
descending taps, 72-73
narrow taps, 67-68
preliminary exercises, 68
separating taps, 71
tunes, 78
wide taps, 67-68
throat vibrato, **18**, 20
throating, *see* glottals
tips, *see* taps
tone, 2
tonguing, vii
transition tip, vi
triplet, 98
tune parts, 15
tune type, v, **15**, 33
tunes, **vi**, 13
BCD' triplet, 104
bounces, 93
cuts, 62
finger vibrato, 28
glottals, 13
slides, 44
taps, 78

U

uh syllable, 2
uhha syllable, **11**, 25
upper grace note, 49

W

weak beat, 6-7, 76, 89, **99-101**, 106

About the Author

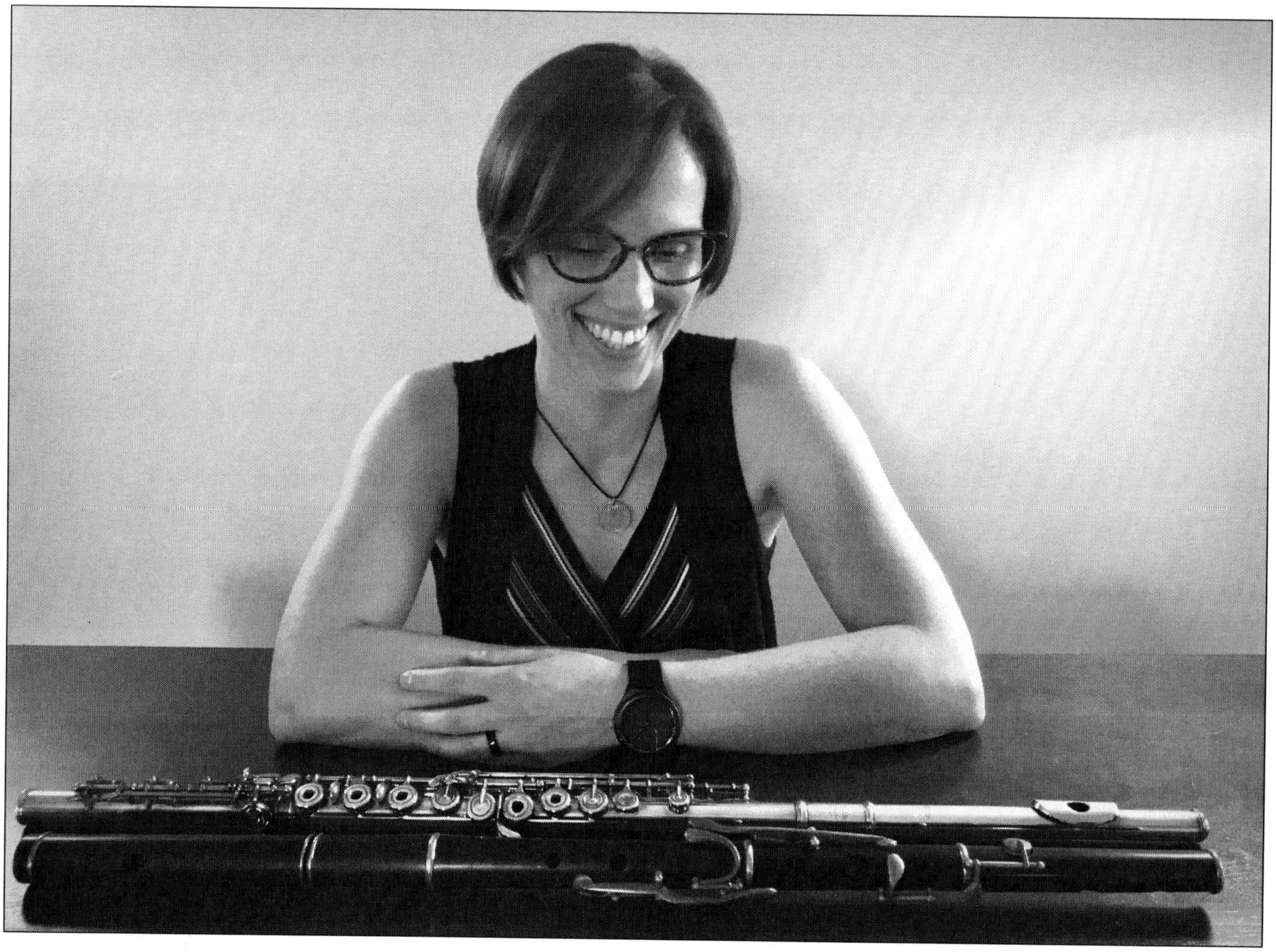

Leslie Anne Harrison is a musician, educator, ethnographer, and writer. She has performed, taught, and conducted research in Europe and the United States and has performed and recorded with Folk Ragoût, New Time Ensemble, and The Public Theater's Shakespeare in the Park. Leslie holds degrees in classical music performance from Ithaca College and New York University, and a degree in Irish traditional music performance from the University of Limerick.

While at Ithaca and NYU, she began playing Irish traditional flute and examining the relationship between classical and Irish traditional flute technique. From there, she moved to Ireland for several years, where she taught music and continued studying Irish traditional flute at the University of Limerick. Leslie has also conducted and presented original research on women in Irish traditional music and is a supporter of equal opportunity in the arts. She lives in New England with her husband.

Visit www.LeslieAnneHarrison.com for further information and current projects.